TREASURES OF TAO

TREASURES OF TAO

FENG SHUI   CHINESE ASTROLOGY   SPIRITUAL QI GONG

David Twicken

Writers Club Press
San Jose New York Lincoln Shanghai

Treasures of Tao
Feng Shui   Chinese Astrology   Spiritual Qi Gong

Writers Club Press
an imprint of iUniverse, Inc.

For information address:
iUniverse, Inc.
5220 S. 16th St., Suite 200
Lincoln, NE 68512
www.iuniverse.com

ISBN: 0-595-21548-3

Printed in the United States of America

Disclaimer

The information in this book is based on the author's knowledge and personal experience. It is presented for educational purposes to assist the reader in expanding their knowledge of Asian philosophy and Arts. Before using any of the techniques in this book consult a licensed physician for advice on whether or not to practice them. The techniques and practices are to be used at the reader's own discretion and liability. The author is not responsible in any manner whatsoever for any physical injury or damage to property that may occur by following instructions in this book.

Acknowledgments

During the past twenty five years I have had the opportunity to meet some unique people that have influenced my life in the area of Taoist Arts and Asian Philosophy, each in their special way have inspired me to learn and share ancient Asian knowledge. I would like to thank and acknowledge Maezumi Roshi, Dr. Huang, Mary Chow, Daniel Lee, Hawkins Cheung, Virginia Bailey, Michael Winn, Gregory Leblanc, Huang Chi Ni, Joseph Yu, Mantak Chia, Peter Leung and Hoc Man Lam.

Author Contact
www.healingqi.com

Contents

Four Pillars of Destiny

Introduction

In an ancient time, men and women lived close to nature and were able to perceive the subtle influences of physical, mental and spiritual aspects of life, in these deep states of awareness they realized three major influences on the destiny of a person: Heaven, Humanity and Earth or the Three Treasures. Heaven's influences are revealed in Astrology and are a blueprint of a life, Human influences include one's actions, deeds and personal cultivation, and Earth influences are the effects of the environment. These three aspects of life are integrated, influencing each other throughout a lifetime. The material in this book includes beginning through advanced levels of these "Taoist Arts", it is the first book of its kind and represents a comprehensive, clear and user-friendly expression of these Treasures of Tao. The following is an introduction to each Taoist Art.

Heaven's Influence–Chinese Astrology

Four Pillars of Destiny, also referred to as Zi Ping, Ba Zi or Five-Element Chinese Astrology, is the predominant astrology practiced in Asia. Four Pillars reveals Heaven's Influence on Destiny and Luck and shows the probable life path, including personality, character, health, marriage, wealth and career and is a map for knowing the optimal time to pursue opportunities. Its highest use is assisting people in creating a happy, healthy and spiritually positive life. Human Influences/Spiritual Qi Gong and Earth Influences/Feng Shui can transform Heaven's Influence.

Earth Influence–Feng Shui

Feng Shui is the ancient art of harmonizing human life with one's environment. This natural art includes perceiving the influences of land forms, time, geographical direction and interior design in a home, office or any living space, Feng Shui offers methods to generate prosperity, positive relationships, good health and personal development. There are many styles and forms of Feng Shui, this book contains proven methods that are easy to understand and apply; professionals around the world practice them. Feng Shui is Earth Luck and can transform the effects of Heaven and Human Influences.

Human Influence–Spiritual Qi Gong

Qi Gong means energy exercises or energy cultivation. It is an ancient practice of cultivating energy or Qi for health, vitality and if one chooses spiritual development. There are hundreds of styles and forms of Qi Gong, on a basic level they are gentle types of breathing and movements that harmonize emotions and generate vitality. Qi Gong can also become Spiritual Qi Gong, which are specific meditations to assist a person in revealing and experiencing their true spiritual nature. The Spiritual Qi Gong method in this book is safe, simple and profound, no previous experience is necessary and people of any ethnic, social or economic background can practice Spiritual Qi Gong, it is a Universal practice. This Human Cultivation transforms Heaven and Earth Influences.

Principles of Asian Philosophy

Qi

The ancients view the universe as filled with energy, an energy that moves through endless flows of transformation. This energy comprises all of life including Stars, Planets, Trees, Mountains, Water, Animals and Human Life and is called Qi, it includes both matter and energy, it is also the force that allows a transformation from energy to matter and matter to energy, for example, Water is a type of Qi and is a perfect example of how Qi transforms. Water can be in the form of ice, ice can transform into Water and Water into steam; Qi is ice, Qi is Water, Qi is steam and Qi is the heat that allows the transformation to occur. Qi is all of life, it takes form to become the densest substances and is also contained in the subtlest of substances. Every part of the universe is a blend of different types of Qi, to understand this blending of Qi is to understand the Treasures of Tao. Knowing the rhythms and expressions of Qi is to be able to predict and transform life.

All tools used in the Asian arts are variations of Qi. This book introduces Yin-Yang, Eight Trigrams, Five-Elements, Stems, Branches and cycles of time, they are different aspects or transformations of Qi, and help calculate the effects of Qi on a person throughout a lifetime.

Yin-Yang

From the beginning of time humanity has searched to understand Heaven, Earth and Human life, whether it be ancient Hindus in India, Aztecs in Mexico, Jews of Israel or the ancient Egyptians. In China a model of understanding nature evolved which would become the roots of Chinese philosophy, Acupuncture, Herbal Medicine, Qi Gong, Nutrition, Martial Arts, Feng Shui and Astrology. This system is Yin-Yang, its theory includes viewing the Universe as one integrated whole, as well as two opposing, but inter-dependent aspects. All aspects of life can be categorized into Yin-Yang, for example, Heaven-Earth, Man-Woman, Hot-Cold, Left-Right, Light-Dark, Front-Back, Hard-Soft, North-South, East-West, Root-Branch, Top-Bottom, Fast-Slow, Waxing-Waning, Timely-Untimely, Empty-Full and Auspicious-Inauspicious. Yin-Yang theory categorizes any situation into two parts, and a key is each part gives life to its opposite, there must be a Left to have Right, a Strong to have Weak, a Front to have Back, they are not two separate entities, but two sides of the same situation, they give life to each other, never separate. Yin-Yang is a model which views a situation into two parts, as well as one inseparable whole, this dynamic is integral to understanding Yin-Yang.

Yin-Yang is a predominant component in Asian Arts, one major application of Yin-Yang theory is Yang represents a growing or expanding phase and Yin a declining phase, all of life flows through this basic model of rising and declining, each expansion leads to a decline, leading to another expansion and decline in an endless cycle. This universal reality is the basis for this book.

Five-Elements

Five-Elements or Wu Xing is the basis or foundation of the Treasures of Tao, they are the ABC's of calculating, evaluating and applying the knowledge of Spiritual Qi Gong, Feng Shui and Four Pillars of Destiny Chinese astrology. The following explains the Five-Elements.

A circle can be viewed as one integrated whole.

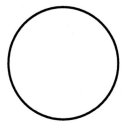

This same circle can be viewed in two aspects, Yin and Yang.

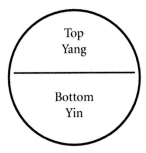

A circle can be viewed with five segments or phases, the Five-Elements/Phases.

Five-Elements/Phases

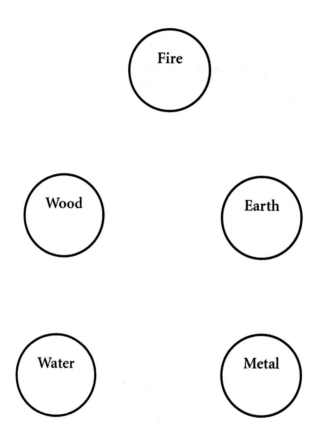

Each circle or phase is assigned an element: Water, Wood, Fire, Earth and Metal and each element maintains a position within the circle, for example, Wood is positioned where the circle begins to move upward and represents growth or Spring; Fire is located where the portion of the circle reaches its peak symbolizing Summer; Earth is positioned where harvesting takes place representing Indian Summer; Metal represents turning inward or contraction representing Autumn and Water is where the circle turns completely inward to regenerate representing Winter. Water also reflects preparation for a new spring, Wood or growth cycle, this cycle continues infinitely and reflects self-generation and the eternal nature of life.

The relative position of each of the Five-Elements or Five Phases in the circle determines its specific relationship with every other element, for example, Water is mother to Wood, grandparent to Fire, grandchild of Earth and child of Metal, each element has those distinct relationships with the four remaining elements. The ability to apply those relationships is a key to learning and applying these Asian Arts, the table below summarizes these relationships.

Five-Element relationships

Element　━▶	Water	Wood	Fire	Earth	Metal
Parent	Metal	Water	Wood	Fire	Earth
Sibling - Same	Water	Wood	Fire	Earth	Metal
Child – Offspring	Wood	Fire	Earth	Metal	Water
Grandchild	Fire	Earth	Metal	Water	Wood
Grandparent Controller	Earth	Metal	Water	Wood	Fire

Interpreting this chart

Water's parent is Metal
Water's sibling is Water
Water's child is Wood
Water's grandchild is Fire
Water's Controller is Earth

From these five relationships we see five key interactions.

1. Each element gives to another element, the parent.
2. Each element controls another element, the grandparent or controller.
3. Each element is controlled by another element, the grandchild.

4. Each element receives from another element, the child.

5. Each element is supported by another element, the same element or sibling.

These relationships are expressed in the actions of giving, receiving, controlling and being controlled, obtaining a natural healthy life depends on finding balance within these five interactions. One action is not better than another, there is only meaning when a situation is compared to a given situation. Some people need nourishment, others control, and still others need to give, what is beneficial is relative to the condition of all elements. These Five-Elements are applied in unique ways in Feng Shui, Four Pillars of Destiny and Spiritual Qi Gong. The following table summarizes these relationships.

Situation	First Action
Weakness	Nourish 1. Add same the Sibling element 2. Add the Parent Element
Too Strong or Excessive	Control 1. Add the Child 2. Add the Grandparent

The following diagrams illustrate how each element is affected by all elements, familiarize yourself with these relationships, they are integral in the application of the Four Pillars, practice selecting which elements are needed in conditions of excessive or deficiency.

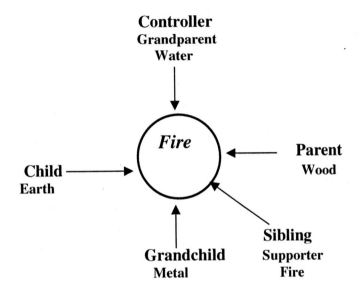

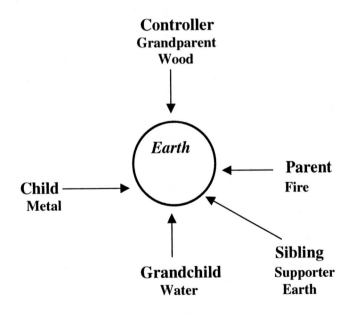

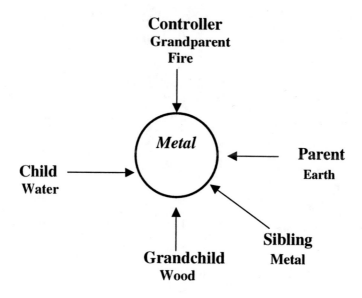

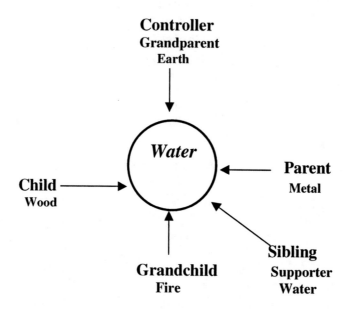

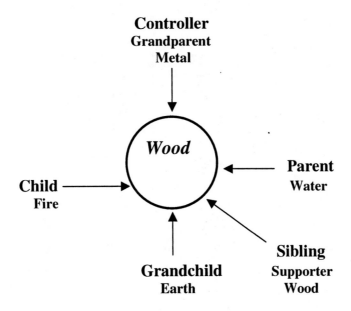

Five-Element corrections

Element	Corrections for Excess	Corrections for Weakness
Water	Wood, Earth	Water, Metal
Wood	Fire, Metal	Wood, Water
Fire	Earth, Water	Fire, Wood
Earth	Metal, Wood	Earth, Fire
Metal	Water, Fire	Metal, Earth

Five-Element Cycles

The Five-Elements interact in a variety of ways or cycles, three major cycles are promotion, controlling and reduction and they are the basis for many applications in these Taoist art. The following diagrams explain each cycle.

Promotion Cycle

The Promotion cycle is the Parent to Child relationship, it is a cycle that nourishes, supplements or strengthens its child element. Its influence can be favorable or unfavorable depending on the condition of the elements. The following diagram illustrates the Promotion cycle.

Promotion Cycle

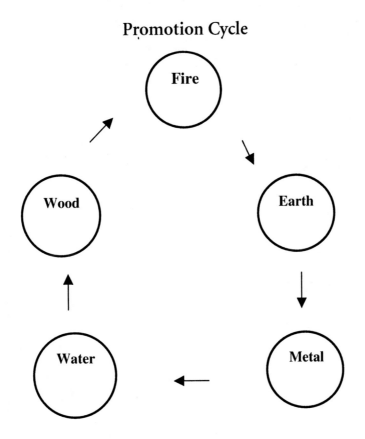

Promotion Cycle

1. Water placed on Wood promotes growth, Water is the mother of Wood.
2. Wood placed in Fire promotes growth, Wood is the mother of Fire.
3. Fire transforms substances into Ashes or Earth, Fire is the Mother of Earth.
4. Metal is found within Earth, Earth is the Mother of Metal.
5. Metal can be liquefied into Water, Metal is the Mother of Water.

Controlling Cycle

The controlling cycle is the grandparent to grandchild relationship or the controlling cycle, its influence can be favorable or unfavorable depending on the conditions of the elements. The following diagram illustrates the controlling cycle.

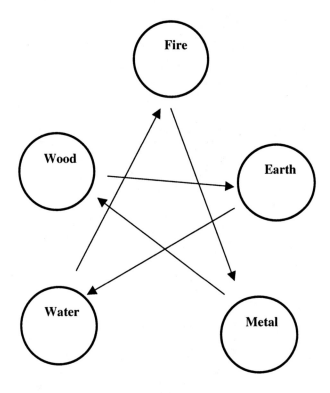

The arrows direct the controlling cycle sequence, the relationship is the controlling cycle.

Controlling Cycle

1. Fire melts Metal or controls Metal, Grandparent relationship.
2. Metal cuts Wood or controls Wood, Grandparent relationship.
3. Wood absorbs nutrients from the Earth and controls Earth, Grandparent relationship.
4. Earth absorbs Water or controls Water, Grandparent relationship.
5. Water puts out Fire or controls Fire, Grandparent relationship.

Reduction Cycle

The Controlling cycle controls, dominates or weakens and when it overacts or is too strong it creates an imbalance, the Reduction cycle is used to harmonize this condition. The Promotion and Reduction cycles are arranged identically, the only difference is the flow of energy, the Promotional cycle flows clockwise and the Reduction cycle flows counter-clockwise.

Reduction Cycle

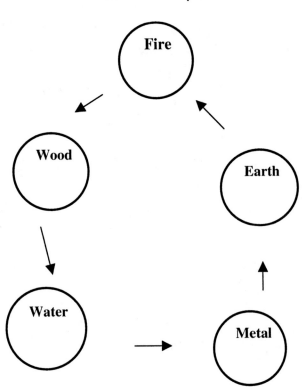

Reduction Cycle

1. Water is the child of Metal, Water takes from Metal reducing its influence.
2. Metal is the child of Earth, Metal takes from Earth reducing its influence.
3. Earth is the child of Fire, Earth takes from Fire reducing its influence.
4. Fire is the child of Wood, Fire takes from Wood reducing its influence.
5. Wood is the child of Water, Wood takes from Water reducing its influence.

The parent wants to give to the child and the child wants to take from the parent, this dynamic results in a decrease or reduction in the potency or magnitude of the parent.

Classical Feng Shui

A Professional Course in Flying Stars Feng Shui

Introduction

Feng Shui is the art and science of living in harmony with one's environment. It consists of principles and methods from Chinese philosophy, metaphysics, divination, science and experimentation. These natural principles are used to evaluate how nature influences health, marriage, emotions, finances, career, wealth, creativity, fertility and happiness. As with most ancient Chinese Arts, Feng Shui's roots can be found in the I Ching/Book of Changes. The I Ching describes how the universe functions, a profound concept in the I Ching is life always changes and to obtain happiness, one needs to learn to live in harmony with change. Flying Stars Feng Shui is about change, it teaches how to evaluate the changing influences of nature and offers ways to optimize favorable and minimize unfavorable influences.

Flying Stars Feng Shui is a natural and dynamic form of Feng Shui and is the most common form practiced by professional Feng Shui consultants throughout Asia, the advanced levels of this system have been a closely guarded secret and seldom clearly explained. Environmental Forms, Interior Design, Time and Direction comprise the major aspects of Flying Stars Feng Shui. Flying Stars is comparable to a Catscan or MRI, these medical devices capture the deepest aspects hidden to the human eye. Flying Stars Feng Shui captures visible and hidden influences affecting living environments, it has the capacity to perceive influences that other systems of Feng Shui are incapable of perceiving, it is a powerful tool for transformation.

The ancient Chinese view of the Universe includes ways human life is influenced by the three treasure: Heaven, Human and Earth or Tien, Ren and Ti, predicting the fortune of a person is based on these three influences. Four Pillars Chinese Astrology reflects Heavenly Influences, which is a blueprint of one's life, Earthly Influences include the effects of Feng Shui and Human Influences are reflected by each person's character, actions, beliefs, cultivation and deeds. Feng Shui provides an opportunity to influence one's life outside Heavenly Influences or Astrology. Each of these three influences can be affected individually, but when jointly optimized a synergy is generated, often creating magical benefits. Heavenly Influences, reflected by one's astrological birth chart is fixed but choices a person makes are dynamic and free. Feng Shui is a choice each person can make to optimize his or her life and overcome the parameters of Heaven's Luck with Earth Luck.

Background

Feng Shui has evolved over thousands of years revealing nature's influences on all aspects of life. This body of knowledge has been passed from generation to generation and is called "Kan Yu" Feng Shui. Feng means Wind and Shui means Water. The classics say: "When Qi rides wind, it is scattered; when it encounters water it is retained". Favorable Feng Shui is when living environments (wind and water) generate favorable results. Unfavorable results are when Wind and Water generate unfavorable influences. Kan means the way of heaven or the influences of "Time" and Yu means the way of Earth, Kan Yu means the study of how Time (Heaven) influences living environments (Earth). Feng Shui began with the Forms School, which evaluates the landscape and evolved to include Qi formulas that evaluate the effects of Time and Space/Direction. Traditional Feng Shui evolved to include Forms, Time and Space.

Modern traditional Feng Shui has four major Branches, the following summarizes these systems.

1. Classical San Yuan has two major styles
   1. Primordial San Yuan (Three Cycles), believed to be developed by Yang, Yun Son, in the Tang Dynasty (618-906 CE). This system uses a compass with the 64 hexagrams of the Yi Jing/I Ching, nine stars and Stems and Branches to determine the most auspicious directions of a building. It was primarily used for Yin Feng Shui or selection and placement of gravesites, emphasizing Land or Forms Feng Shui.
   2. San Yuan Xuan Kong is the next stage of evolution of San Yuan and focuses on Yang Feng Shui or the buildings where people live. This system uses the nine palaces, time, mountain, water, annual and monthly Flying Stars, as well as environmental forms and interior design, Five-Element remedies and cycles of time. It integrates Land Forms and Flying Stars of the building.

2. Classical Xuan Kong

This system uses Flying Stars, nine palaces, special star conditions and emphasizes Construction/Base/Time star and Water Star interactions. Environmental forms are not emphasized. This system was founded by Hsu, Jen Wang, during the Song Dynasty (960-1279). This system was designed for buildings, enhancing Primordial San Yuan to include Forms and Qi in a building. The application and meanings of Stars can differ from San Yuan Feng Shui.

3. San Ho

This style uses a special compass, San Ho Lo Pan, it emphasizes Stems, Branches and nine stars to select the proper site and auspicious facing positions; this system focuses on Mountain Qi (Dragon Veins) and Water Qi (Water Dragons). It is believed Yang, Yun Son, founded this system too.

4. Eight Mansions

This system is a newer development created in the Qing Dynasty, 1644-1911 and the People's Republic of China, 1911-1949. This method applies the Gua of the person and/or building to identify auspicious areas in a building. Eight Mansions is based on the eight trigrams and Ba Gua. Eight Mansions was founded by Jo Kuan, Tao Jen.

In my experience current professionals combine the best of these classical Feng Shui styles, the material in this book presents foundation and integral aspects of these traditional forms of Feng Shui and very applicable for modern day life and living environments.

The origins of Feng Shui are found in an ancient time, the discovery of the eight trigrams by the legendary Fu Xi are its roots and lead to King Wen in the Chou Dynasty, 1122-207 BCE. King Wen had a profound influence on the classic book, I Ching, which is the basis of all Taoist Arts and Feng Shui. These two men are associated with the Early Heaven and Later Heaven Ba Guas, the foundation of Flying Stars Feng Shui. During the Han Dynasty, 206 BCE - 210 CE, the art of Kan Yu was developed. Until 265-420 CE, Feng Shui was primarily used by the Emperor, but during the Chin Dynasty, 265- 420 CE, Feng Shui was available to people throughout China.

Tracing Feng Shui through history reveals the following pioneers of Classical Feng Shui. I propose the following people are those publicly known for these arts, but others not seeking publicity, contributed to the development of this ancient art.

Ching Wu

Han Dynasty (206 BCE–220 CE)
Wu wrote the " Burial Classic" and is a pioneer of Kan Yu Feng Shui. He was influential in the development of the Forms Schools.

Guo Po

Jin Dynasty (265–316)
Guo Po wrote the classic "Treatise of Burial", which contains many of the principles of traditional Feng Shui.

Yang Yun Son

Tang Dynasty (618–907)
Yang was the dominant Feng Shui Master in the Tang and Sung Dynasties. Yang founded the San Yuan (Three Cycles or Periods) and San Ho (Three Combinations) systems of Feng Shui, emphasis was on the energy and influence of Mountains and Land Forms. Yang, known as "Yang helper of the Poor", was best known as revealing Valleys have an influential Qi, exerting as important an influence as Mountains.

Hsu Jen Wang

(Song Dynasty (906–1279)
Hsu transformed the San Yuan School to include Flying Stars and their influence in buildings and is considered the father of Xuan Kong Feng Shui. This style of Feng Shui includes Land, Forms and Flying Stars and is especially applicable for modern society which does not have the same land forms as ancient times.

Jiang Da Hong

Ming Dynasty (1368 - 1644)
Qing Dynasty (1644 - 1911)
Jiang lived in the Ming and Qing Dynasties and is considered the first to write publicly about Xuan Kong/Flying Stars Feng Shui. He wrote in deep metaphor and unless one was trained it would be virtually impossible to understand the text's true meaning. Jiang Da Hong is one of the most famous of all Feng Shui masters.

Zhang Zhung Shan

Qing Dynasty (1644 - 1911)
Zhang lived during the last years of the Qing Dynasty and is credited for producing written texts clarifying Jiang's work.

Shen Ju Reng

Qing Dynasty (1644 - 1911)
Shen is responsible for organizing and clearly explaining Flying Stars Feng Shui, particularly Jiang's and Zhang's work, he is known for revealing information clearly to those that desired to learn, unlike his predecessors who kept this information primarily a secret. A very interesting note is Shen never studied under a teacher, he learned through books. Shen lived during the end of the Qing Dynasty and his son published "Shen's Xuan Kong Feng Shui.

Flying Stars Feng Shui's effectiveness and power resides in its application of time and space. The combination of time and space creates an energy field in a building, direction is constant, while time changes and each new cycle of time brings new energetic influences that effect health, wealth, finances, romance, creativity and performance. In addition to time and direction, environment, forms, interior design, architecture and personal energy are also key aspects of Flying Stars Feng Shui.

A major form of Feng Shui is San Yuan, which means Three Cycles or Three Combinations and is the base of Flying Stars Feng Shui. San Yuan consists of three cycles of 20-Years comprising one great cycle of 60, which has parallels to the Jia-Zi Cycle of 60-

Stems and Branches used in Four Pillars of Destiny/Zi Ping Chinese Astrology; the cycle of 60 is part of a greater cycle of 180.

Cycle	Cycle	Years
Upper	1	1864-1883
	2	1884-1903
	3	1904-1923
Middle	4	1924-1943
	5	1944-1963
	6	1964-1983
Lower	7	1984-2003
	8	2004-2023
	9	2024-2043

The essence of Flying Stars is a particular Qi is prevalent during each 20-Year Cycle, this Qi is the related Period Number or Star Qi, for example, during 2004-2023 the predominant or Timely Qi is number Eight. These twenty year cycles are based on the cycles of planets Jupiter/Wood and Saturn/Earth, approximately every 20-Years these two Planets align causing a major energy shift, playing an integral role in Flying Stars Feng Shui.

Feng Shui's Yin-Yang, Qi and Five-Elements

Yin-Yang is a predominant component in Feng Shui. One major application of Yin-Yang theory is Yang representing a growing or expanding phase and Yin a declining phase, all of life flows through this basic model of rising and declining, each expansion leads to a decline, leading to another expansion and decline, in an endless cycle. In Flying Stars Feng Shui energies or Stars move through phases of favorable (Yang) and unfavorable (Yin) cycles. This process of positive and negative or Yin or Yang is an integral aspect of Feng Shui and one of the most important applications of Yin-Yang theory.

Qi has many meanings including Air, Energy, Life Force, Spirit, Matter and any influence in life.

In Feng Shui there are two major applications:

1. Sheng Qi includes favorable or positive influences of Qi
2. Sha Qi includes unfavorable or negative influences of Qi

In traditional or classical Feng Shui the terms Sha and Sheng Qi are commonly used, a building next store can be a Sha, meaning a negative influence or a lake in front of the house can be Sheng Qi or a positive influence.

Every element of the Universe including stars, planets, lakes, oceans, mountains, people, etc., is made of Qi and has a particular influence in life, evaluating the effects of Qi on the human body is the profession of Acupuncturists, evaluating those influences in living environments is the job of Feng Shui consultants, the tools each uses are slightly different but the principles are the same.

One way to view life is everything is a blend of Qi, if we can learn how to manage Qi we learn how to manage life, Feng Shui is about managing Qi. We first learn to diagnose a Qi condition and then manage it by optimizing opportunities and reducing negative influences. Yin-Yang and Five-Elements are the key diagnostic tools used and are the basis for diagnosis and treatment.

Five-Elements

There are three cycles used in Flying Stars Feng Shui:

1. Promoting–Creation–Nourishing–Parent–Sheng Cycle
2. Controlling–Dominating–Grandparent–Ko Cycle
3. Reduction–Sedation–Child Cycle

The following are general Rules for applying the Five-Elements

1. When two favorable elements in the promotion cycle interact no correction is necessary.

   Examples

   1. Water and Wood
   2. Wood and Fire
   3. Fire and Wood
   4. Earth and Metal
   5. Metal and Earth

2. When elements in the controlling cycle interact the ideal method of correction is the Reduction Cycle.

   Method:

   1. Identify the element that is the controller, add the child element of this controller to reduce its influence.

      Ex. Metal and Wood.

Metal controls Wood and Water is the child of Metal, Water takes energy from Metal directing Metal's energy away from Wood. The proper correction is adding Water. Water is also the parent of Wood and strengthens it.

Example
Water and Fire
Water controls Fire and is its controller. Water produces Wood, therefore, Wood is the Child of Water, add Wood to this combination to break the domination and achieve harmony.

Basically every situation in Flying Stars consist of one of three situations:

1. A Promotion Cycle interaction, for example, Water and Wood or Fire and Earth

2. A Controlling Cycle situation, for example, Fire and Metal or Earth and Water.

3. The Same Element, for example, Water and Water or Fire and Fire.

If two of the same elements interact and they are favorable the following can be applied.

1. Add the same element to reinforce it

2. Add the parent element to strengthen it

If two of the same elements interact and they are unfavorable it is best to do the following.

1. Add the child element, for example, if Fire and two negative Earths exist add Metal, it reduces the influence of negative Earth.

These principles are the key to learning Flying Stars Feng Shui.

Eight Trigrams

The Universe can be viewed in a macro or micro way, evaluating the Universe in a micro way categorizes the Universe into smaller parts, Yin-Yang views the whole in two parts, Five-Elements views the whole in five parts and the Eight Trigrams views the whole in eight parts; each system provides a different and unique method to perceive, understand and manage Universal influences.

The ancient book Yi Jing/I Ching begins with Yin-Yang and expands itself into the Eight Trigrams, the following diagram illustrates this process. Each Trigram has three lines, for Feng Shui purposes the top line represents the sky, middle line a building and the bottom line the landscape.

_____   Sky or Stars
_____   Building
_____   Landscape

A Trigram reflects the concept of integration whereby each line influences the other two lines, evaluating all lines is required to obtain a complete understanding of a situation, for example, Sky/Stars, Building and Landscape must all be evaluated. Each Trigram is a code that has a variety of related information, which is the foundation information for Flying Stars Feng Shui.

────   — —

Yang   **Yin**

────   — —
────   — —
────   — —

— —   ────
— —   ────
— —   ────

— —   ────
— —   ────
— —   ────

────   — —
— —   ────
— —   ────

Eight Trigram Relationships

Trigram	Name	Number	Element	Color	Location	Family	Disease
— — ——— — —	Kan	1	Water	Blue Black	North	Second Son	Kidneys, Ears, Blood
— — — — — —	Kun	2	Earth	Yellow Beige	South West	Mother, Elderly Women	Stomach, Spleen, Abdomen, Digestion
— — — — ———	Zhen	3	Wood Thunder	Green	East	Eldest Son	Feet, Lungs, Throat
——— ——— — —	Xun	4	Wood Wind	Green	South East	Eldest Daughter	Buttocks, Thighs, Colds
		5	Earth		Center		Spleen, Stomach, Digestion, All kinds of illness
— — ——— ———	Dui	7	Metal Lake	White Gold	West	Youngest Daughter	Pulmonary Disease, Headaches
——— ——— ———	Qian	6	Metal Heaven	White Gold	North West	Father, Elderly Male	Head, Lungs, Mouth
——— — — — —	Gen	8	Earth Mountain	Yellow Beige	North East	Youngest Male	Hands, Fingers, Back
——— — — ———	Li	9	Fire	Red Purple	South	Second Daughter	Heart, Eyes

Ba Gua

The origin of Feng Shui begins in ancient time (estimated 3000 B.C.) with the legendary Fu Xi, who saw a mystical animal with special markings on its back revealing a specific pattern, these markings came to be known as "He Tu" or the Early Heaven Ba Gua arrangement of the Eight Trigrams. He Tu means "River Map".

Fu Xi's Ba Gua
Early Heaven Arrangement
Xian Tian Ba Gua

Lake	Heaven	Wind

Fire		Water

Thunder	Earth	Mountain

- Heaven is above and Earth below
- Thunder is the eldest son and Wind the eldest daughter.
- Mountain is the youngest son and Lake is the youngest daughter
- Water is the middle son and Fire the youngest daughter
- This arrangement represents the transformation from Yang to Yin in a clockwise flow

Wen Wang, the founder of the Zhou Dynasty revealed a variation of the Ba Gua called the "Later Heaven Arrangement". This arrangement is based on the Five-Elements, eight geographical directions and eventually the Luo Shu Nine Stars, this arrangement is more commonly used in Feng Shui.

Wen Wang Ba Gua
Later Heaven Arrangement
Hou Tian Ba Gua

Wind	Fire	Earth

Thunder		Lake

Mountain	Water	Heaven

   The relationship between the Early Heaven and Later Heaven Arrangements reveal why "Usable Stars" are usable and is the basis for special prosperity formulas explained in the book.

   Below are the Eight Trigrams arranged in the Nine Palaces in Early Heaven, Later Heaven and combined patterns, all three applications are used in Flying Stars Feng Shui.

Early Heaven Ba Gua

Dui 7	Qian 6	Xun 4
Li 9		Kan 1
Zhen 3	Kun 2	Gen 8

Later Heaven Arrangement

Xun 4	Li 9	Kun 2
Zhen 3		Dui 7
Gen 8	Kan 1	Qian 6

Early and Later Heaven
Arrangements Combined

7 **Dui** **4** **Xun**	**6** **Qian** **9** **Li**	**4** **Xun** **2** **Kun**
9 **Li** **3** **Xun**		**1** **Kan** **7** **Dui**
3 **Zhen** **8** **Gen**	**2** **Kun** **1** **Kan**	**8** **Gen** **6** **Qian**

Lo Pan–Compass

A Lo-Pan is a Chinese Feng Shui compass, it is a basic compass with a variety of Feng Shui information including Eight Trigrams, Five-Elements, eight cardinal geographical locations, Heavenly Stems and Earthly Branches. Stems and Branches are explained in Chinese Astrology. A compass has 360–degrees and eight major directions which contain 45-degrees, they are referred to as the eight cardinal directions. Each cardinal direction is segmented into three, 15–degree sections, 3-sections multiplied by eight cardinal directions produces 24–sections. Each section is called a Mountain and there are 24 Mountains on a standard Flying Stars Feng Shui compass. The following table lists each of the eight cardinal directions and their 45–degree areas or palace.

North West 292.5 – 337.5	North 337.5 – 22.5	North East 22.5 – 67.5
North West 1 292.5 – 307.5	North 1 337.5-352.5	North East 1 22.5 – 37.5
North West 2 307.5 – 322.5	North 2 352.5- 7.5	North East 2 37.5 – 52.5
North West 3 322.5 – 337.5	North 3 7.5 – 22.5	North East 3 52.5 – 67.5
West 247.5 – 292.5	Center	East 67.5 – 112.5
West 1 247.5 – 262.5		East 1 67.5 – 82.5
West 2 262.5 – 277.5		East 2 82.5 – 97.5
West 3 277.5 – 292.5		East 3 97.5 – 112.5
South West 202.5 – 247.5	South 157.5 – 202.5	South East 112.5 – 157.5
South West 1 202.5 – 217.5	South 1 157.5 – 172.5	South East 1 12.5 – 127.5
South West 2 217.5 – 232.5	South 2 172.5 – 187.5	South East 2 127.5 – 142.5
South West 3 232.5 – 247.5	South 3 187.5 – 202.5	South East 3 142.5 – 157.5

Lo Pan Positions

Lo-Pan Position	Lo-Pan Position
North 1 337.5-352.5	South 1 157.5-172.5
North 2 352.5-7.5	South 2 172.5-187.5
North 3 7.5-22.5	South 3 187.5-202.5
North East 1 22.5-37.5	South West 1 202.5-217.5
North East 2 37.5-52.5	South West 2 217.5-232.5
North East 3 52.5-67.5	South West 3 232.5-247.5
East 1 67.5-82.5	West 1 247.5-262.5
East 2 82.5-97.5	West 2 262.5-277.5
East 3 97.5-112.5	West 3 277.5-292.5
South East 1 112.5-127.5	North West 1 292.5-307.5
South East 2 127.5-142.5	North West 2 307.5-322.5
South East 3 142.5-157.5	North West 3 322.5-337.5

The following tables list key information for a standard Flying Stars Feng Shui Compass.

Lo Pan

Chinese Feng Shui Compass for 24 Mountains

Direction	Direction Trigram	Stem, Branch or Trigram	Compass Degrees
North 1	Kan 1	Ren – Yang Water	337.5-352.5
North 2	Kan 2	Zi – Rat	352.5-7.5
North 3	Kan 3	Gui – Yin Water	7.5-22.5
North East 1	Gen 1	Chou – Ox	22.5-37.5
North East 2	Gen 2	Ken – Mountain	37.5-52.5
North East 3	Gen 3	Yin – Tiger	52.5-67.5
East 1	Zhen 1	Jia - Yang Wood	67.5-82.5
East 2	Zhen 2	Mao – Rabbit	82.5-97.5
East 3	Zhen 3	Yi – Yin Wood	97.5-112.5
South East 1	Xun 1	Zhen – Dragon	112.5-127.5
South East 2	Xun 2	Xun – Wood	127.5-142.5
South East 3	Xun 3	Si – Snake	142.5-157.5
South 1	Li 1	Bing – Yang Fire	157.5-172.5
South 2	Li 2	Wu – Horse	172.5-187.5
South 3	Li 3	Ding – Yin Fire	187.5-202.5
South West 1	Kun 1	Wei – Sheep	202.5-217.5
South West 2	Kun 2	Kun - Earth	217.5-232.5
South West 3	Kun 3	Shen – Monkey	232.5-247.5
West 1	Dui 1	Geng - Yang Metal	247.5-262.5
West 2	Dui 2	You – Cock	262.5-277.5
West 3	Dui 3	Xin – Yin Metal	277.5-292.5
North West 1	Qian 1	Xu – Dog	292.5-307.5
North West 2	Qian 2	Qian – Metal	307.5-322.5
North West 3	Qian 3	Hai – Pig	322.5-337.5

Lo Pan

Chinese Feng Shui Compass for 24 Mountains

Direction	Direction Trigram	Stem, Branch or Trigram	Compass Degrees	Direction	Direction Trigram	Stem, Branch or Trigram	Compass Degrees
North 1	Kan 1	Ren: Yang Water	337.5-352.5	South 1	Li 1	Bing: Yang Fire	157.5-172.5
North 2	Kan 2	Zi: Rat	352.5-7.5	South 2	Li 2	Wu: Horse	172.5-187.5
North 3	Kan 3	Gui: Yin Water	7.5-22.5	South 3	Li 3	Ding: Yin Fire	187.5-202.5
North East 1	Gen 1	Chou: Ox	22.5-37.5	South West 1	Kun 1	Wei: Sheep	202.5-217.5
North East 2	Gen 2	Ken: Mountain	37.5-52.5	South West 2	Kun 2	Gen: Earth	217.5-232.5
North East 3	Gen 3	Yin: Tiger	52.5-67.5	South West 3	Kun 3	Shen: Monkey	232.5-247.5
East 1	Zhen 1	Jia: Yang Wood	67.5-82.5	West 1	Dui 1	Geng: Yang Metal	247.5-262.5
East 2	Zhen 2	Mao: Rabbit	82.5-97.5	West 2	Dui 2	You: Cock	262.5-277.5
East 3	Zhen 3	Yi: Yin Wood	97.5-112.5	West 3	Dui 3	Xin: Yin Metal	277.5-292.5
South East 1	Xun 1	Zhen: Dragon	112.5-127.5	North West 1	Qian 1	Xu: Dog	292.5-307.5
South East 2	Xun 2	Xun: Wood	127.5-142.5	North West 2	Qian 2	Qian: Metal	307.5-322.5
South East 3	Xun 3	Si: Snake	142.5-157.5	North West 3	Qian 3	Hai: Pig	322.5-337.5

Each mountain is 15 degrees

Facing and Sitting Positions

Mountain and Water positions are determined with a compass and are opposite each other; a Mountain position is referred to as the Sitting position and a Water position is the Facing position. Mountain/Sitting and Water/Facing terms are used interchangeably throughout this book, these two positions determine a building's orientation. In most cases the front door will be the Water position and its opposite is the Mountain position. A Lo Pan compass reveals the relationship between each Mountain and Water position. When a Mountain or Water position is determined its opposite position is automatically known, this relationship is referred to as Mountain/Water directions or Facing/ Sitting directions.

The initial objective in Feng Shui is determining a building's orientation, which means finding its structure or alignment; the following are guidelines for determining Facing and Sitting directions.

1. The front door direction is often the facing direction, in some cases it will be another direction. Stand with your back to the front door, the direction straight ahead is the facing direction and the direction to the back is the sitting direction.

Often a street or road in front of the structure is the Facing or Water direction, this is called the *Yang Direction* of a building. The facing direction is often positioned near the building entrance, windows near the entry, front door or where the most sunlight is located. Combine this knowledge of building orientation and street location to accurately determine the Facing orientation.

2. Place a compass in your hands and keep it flat or parallel to the ground, some compasses will automatically align the arrow in the middle to North-South, others have a movable dial which needs to be turned until the arrow in the middle is aligned to North-South. The front of the compass will have a mark, usually an arrow on the outside of the compass, the arrow will point at a degree on the dial, this degree is the

45

Water or Facing direction and its exact opposite degree is the Mountain or Sitting direction. Some compasses have one end of the dial red and the other white, red is usually north, you should confirm whether this is correct for your compass.

3. Metal can alter a compass's accuracy. It is important to remove metal or jewelry and stand away from major metal or electric structures, for example, telephone lines, metal stairways or automobiles.

4. It is suggested to take three or more readings in different locations along the same axis or facing the same direction, this should eliminate potential influences that may alter a compass reading, if the reading is consistent in numerous positions the compass has not been influenced.

5. Remember each 24-Mountains or sections consist of 15–degrees of distance, if the compass reading falls within this range the reading is accurate, the dial does not have to be the exact degree reading each time it only needs to fall within the 15–degree range.

Flying Stars

There are nine special influences in Flying Stars Feng Shui and they are referred to as Stars. Each Star is not really a physical Star, it represents energetic qualities or influences of nature. A number, trigram, color and other basic attributes represent each star and some change with cycles of time. The following table lists each star.

Nine Stars

	Star	Basic Nature
1	White Star	Favorable
2	Black Star	Unfavorable
3	Green Star	Unfavorable
4	Dark Green Star	Unfavorable
5	Yellow Star	Unfavorable
6	White Star	Favorable
7	Red Star	Unfavorable
8	White Star	Favorable
9	Purple Star	Favorable

The basic quality of Stars 1, 6, 8, and 9 are favorable. Stars 2, 3, 4, 5, and 7 are unfavorable. Star 5 is the most unfavorable, followed by Star 2.

The basic nature of each Star is the condition of the Star when it is in a neutral condition as determined by "Timeliness". The concept of time and condition of a Star will be explained fully in the next two chapters. When the time factor is incorporated into the quality of Stars there are more fortunate Stars than unfortunate Stars. Timeliness is of primary importance when determining the quality of Stars. The following tables list the Nine Stars and an explanation of their color and name, one table lists Stars in numerical order and the other follows the pattern of the four seasons. The colors of the Stars are named after the seasons.

Nine Stars

Numerical order

Star Number	Explanation of Star colors	Star Name	Gua
1 White	In the North winter is full of White snow.	Tan Lang Angel of Sheng Qi	Kan
2 Black	Earth is in the South West and represents late Summer where Fire burns creating ash.	Ju Men Monarch of Sickness	Kun
3 Green	Wood is located in the East and presents Spring where Green vegetation grows.	Lu Cun Phantom of Misfortune	Zhen
4 Green	South East represents Wood, it is late Spring and Green vegetation prospers.	Wen Qu Emperor of deception	Xun
5 Yellow	This represents the center and takes the color of Earth.	Lien Zhen Devil of Ferocity	Center
6 White	Metal in the North West represents late Fall and the beginning of frost and Snow.	Wu Qu Angel of Gallantry	Qian
7 Red	Metal in the West represents Autumn when leaves turn Red.	Po Jun Spirit of Solemnity	Dui
8 White	The North East represents the end of winter and the Earth is covered with White snow.	Zuo Fu Angel of Wealth and Happiness	Gen
9 Red	The South represents Fire and it is very hot creating Red-Purple colors.	You Bi Angel of Vigor	Li

Nine Stars

Seasonal flow

Star Number	Explanation of Star colors	Star Name	Related Trigram
3 Green	Wood is located in the East and presents Spring where Green vegetation grows.	Lu Cun	Zhen
4 Green	South East represents Wood, it is late Spring and Green vegetation prospers.	Wen Qu	Xun
9 Red	The South represents Fire and it is very hot creating Red-Purple colors.	You Bi	Li
2 Black	Earth is in the South West and represents late Summer where Fire burns creating ash.	Ju Men	Kun
7 Red	Metal in the West represents Autumn when leaves turn Red.	Po Jun	Dui
6 White	Metal in the North West represents late Fall and the beginning of frost and Snow.	Wu Qu	Qian
1 White	In the North winter is full of White snow.	Tan Lang	Kan
8 White	The North East represents the end of winter and the Earth is covered with White snow.	Zuo Fu	Ken
5 Yellow	This represents the center and takes the color of Earth.	Lien Zhen	Center

Nine Star Timeliness

Stars are a type of energy or Qi and reflect influences that affect one's life, this Qi moves through cycles of birth, growth and decline and exert favorable and unfavorable influences, the cause of these different influences is "Timeliness". When Qi or a Star is Timely, the favorable aspects manifest, when a Qi or Star is Untimely, unfavorable aspects may manifest. The Timely Water Star is called "Water Dragon Spirit" or "Shui Li Long Shen" and the Timely Mountain Star is called "Mountain Dragon Spirit" or "Shan Li Long Shen".

The Chinese calendar is the foundation for Asian Arts, Feng Shui uses two major cycles, the first is a 20-Year Cycle and the second is an Annual cycle. Each twenty years a new cycle begins and is referred to as the Construction Year, Earth, Base or Time Star. Numbers or Stars are assigned to each 20-Year Cycle and during those time frames its related Star is the "Predominant or Timely Star". The table below lists each cycle with its corresponding number or Star.

Stars and their related 20-Year Cycle

Number	20-Year Cycle
1	1864-1883
2	1884-1903
3	1904-1923
4	1924-1943
5	1944-1963
6	1964-1983
7	1984-2003
8	2004-2023
9	2024-2043

Timeliness includes stages and there are three main stages:

1. The first is Timely or Wang. It is the current 20-Year Cycle
2. The Second is Future Timely or Sheng. It is the future 20-Year Cycle
3. The third is Distant Future Timely or Sheng. It is the future 40-60 Year cycle.

For example, 1984-2003 is cycle Seven, the Seven Star is most Timely and most favorable during the 1984–2003 Cycle, star Eight is Future Timely or the time frame which is next and it is favorable as the energy is close and its influence is strong. Star Nine is in the distant future and is favorable because its energy will follow soon. Six Star, the distant past Star reverts to its basic nature but the energy is weak and does not exert a strong influence. All other Stars revert to their Untimely qualities except two stars that are "Safe and Usable", which is explained later in the book. The following tables show the Timeliness of each Star for Cycle Seven, 1984-2003 and Cycle Eight, 2004-2023.

Timeliness during Cycle Seven
(1984-2003)

Star	Timeliness
1	Untimely (Safe and Usable)
2	Untimely
3	Untimely
4	Untimely (Safe and Usable)
5	Distant Untimely
6	Close Distant Untimely Reverts to Basic Nature
7	Timely
8	Future Timely
9	Distant Future Timely

Timeliness during Cycle Eight
(2004-2023)

Star	Timeliness
1	**Distant Future Timely**
2	**Untimely**
3	**Untimely** (Safe and Usable)
4	**Untimely**
5	**Untimely**
6	**Untimely** (Safe and Usable)
7	**Close Distant Untimely** **Reverts to Basic Nature**
8	**Timely**
9	**Future Timely**

Nine Stars in Timely or Untimely Cycles

	Star	Timely	Untimely	Disease
1	White Star Water	Wealth, money, fame, spirituality, wisdom, philosophy	Divorce, death, isolation, miscarriage, impotency, sexual problems, mental instability.	Kidneys, Ears, Blood
2	Black Star Earth	Fertility, leadership, high productivity	Sickness, potential miscarriage, digestive difficulties, loneliness.	Stomach, Spleen, Abdomen, Digestion
3	Green Star Wood	Wealth, prosperity, growth, youth, leadership	Gossip, arguments, lawsuits, slander, robbers, disability.	Feet, Lungs, Convulsions, Hysteria
4	Dark Green Star Wood	Academic success, intelligence, creativity, artistic skills, fame, good fortune	Divorce, family pressure, affairs, infidelity, manipulation.	Buttock, Thigh, Colds, Flu
5	Yellow Star Earth	Sudden wealth, prosperity, fame	Disease, pain, sickness, potential disaster, most negative energy, lack knowledge, laziness.	Spleen, Stomach, digestion, all kinds of illness.
6	White Star Metal	Wealth, leadership, success, ambition, kindness, success in technology & science	Isolation, loneliness, sadness, blockages in all areas of life.	Pulmonary disease, Headaches
7	Red Star Metal	Wealth, fertility, great verbal skills and languages, divination	Robbery, bleeding, arguing, fire, bickering, isolation, promiscuous, legal problems, STD's	Head, Lungs
8	White Star Earth	Fame, wealth, spirituality, success for young people and family unity	Children may have injuries, loneliness, boredom, and reversal of fortune.	Hands, Fingers, Back
9	Purple Star Fire	Achievement, success, growth	Eye disease, fires, mental disturbance, miscarriage, and employment difficulties.	Heart, Eyes

Mountain and Water Stars

Calculating a Flying Stars Feng Shui Chart

In Flying Stars Feng Shui life is categorized into two major aspects:

1. Health, relationships and fertility are represented by Mountain/Sitting Stars
2. Finances, wealth and career are represented by Water/Facing Stars

These aspects of life are main focuses of Flying Stars Feng Shui

This Chapter explains the technique to calculate a Flying Stars Feng Shui chart. The Appendix includes all Flying Stars Feng Shui charts, refer to these charts to confirm your calculations. The following example explains the procedure. The first step is determining the 20-Year Construction Cycle number and is also referred to as the Time Star, for example, a house built in 1999 is in Cycle Seven.

Step 1

The Time Star is placed in the center palace of the Ba Gua.
Example: House built in 1999 is Cycle Seven

SE	S	SW
NE	7	W
NE	N	NW

The 20-Year Construction Cycle Star in this case is Seven, Time Star is always placed in the center and is floated in an ascending sequence, Seven, the Time Star will "Fly" or float in ascending order through the Ba Gua, the Time Star always floats in ascending order. The following table illustrates the "Floating" pattern of the Stars.

Pattern for floating Construction Cycle Star

South East	South	South West
Place **Ninth** Star Here	Place **Fifth** Star Here	Place **Seventh** Star Here
East	Begin Here	West
Place **Eight** Star Here	Place **First** Star Here	Place **Third** Star Here
North East	North	North West
Place **Fourth** Star Here	Place **Sixth** Star Here	Place **Second** Star Here

Another method to float Time Stars is to place them in the following order: Center, North West, West, North East, South, North, South West, East, South East.

Step 2

Place Seven in the center or A, place Eight in section B, Nine in section C and follow the pattern below. This is the standard floating pattern for all 20-year Construction Cycle numbers, for example, if the Construction Year was 2008, the Construction Cycle would be Eight, Eight would be placed in the center, Nine in the North West, One in the West and continue until Seven is placed in the South East.

South East $\frac{6}{I}$	South $\frac{2}{E}$	South West $\frac{4}{G}$
East $\frac{5}{H}$	$\frac{7}{A}$	West $\frac{9}{C}$
North East $\frac{1}{D}$	North $\frac{3}{F}$	North West $\frac{8}{B}$

The floating of the Construction Cycle Star is completed and the next step is to determine the Mountain and Water Stars for each palace. *The Construction Cycle Star or Time Star always floats in ascending order but Mountain and Water Stars float in ascending or descending order.*

The following is a method to calculate the floating sequence for Mountain and Water Stars:

1. The following formula determines whether a Star floats in ascending or descending order.

   A. Odd numbers are Yang, they are 1,3,7 and 9
      Five is a special case and is explained in step 8
      Yang numbers float in an ascending sequence

Even numbers are Yin, they are 2,4,6 and 8
Even numbers float in descending sequence

B. *An even number has a Yin, Yang, Yang sequence*
   An odd number has a Yang, Yin, Yin sequence

2. Determine the Mountain or sitting position, for example, if a structure is sitting in North 1 or 338 degrees the sitting position is North which contains number 3, place number 3, the sitting section Star in the left hand position within the center of the Ba Gua. The left side is always the sitting or Mountain Star.

Facing
157.5–172.5
S

	Facing Section 2	
6		**4**
E	**3 2**	**W**
5	7	**9**
	Sitting Section	
1	3	**8**

N
Sitting
337.5–352.5

3. The Water position is always opposite the Mountain position, in this case the South section contains number 2, place number 2 in the right position in the center of the Ba Gua. The right position is always the facing or Water Star.

4. Determine the polarity of the Mountain and Water Stars in the center of the Ba Gua, Mountain Stars are on the left side and Water Stars are on the right side. *Odd numbers are Yang and even numbers are Yin.*

5. Determine the polarity of the Mountain Star, in this case Yang for number 3, see below, place Yang in the first position of the Sitting palace, place Yin in the second position and Yin in the third position. Always begin by placing Yin or Yang in the first position then follow the formula format for the second and third positions. There are only three positions, for example, North 1, North 2 or North 3.

Lo Pan Positions

Lo Pan Position			Lo Pan Position		
North 1	337.5-352.5	Yang	South 1	157.5-172.5	Yin
North 2	352.5-7.5	Yin	South 2	172.5-187.5	Yang
North 3	7.5-22.5	Yin	South 3	187.5-202.5	Yang
North East 1	22.5-37.5		South West 1	202.5-217.5	
North East 2	37.5-52.5		South West 2	217.5-232.5	
North East 3	52.5-67.5		South West 3	232.5-247.5	
East 1	67.5-82.5		West 1	247.5-262.5	
East 2	82.5-97.5		West 2	262.5-277.5	
East 3	97.5-112.5		West 3	277.5-292.5	
South East 1	112.5-127.5		North West 1	292.5-307.5	
South East 2	127.5-142.5		North West 2	307.5-322.5	
South East 3	142.5-157.5		North West 3	322.5-337.5	

6. Identify the Mountain or sitting position, in this case North 1, locate the polarity of North 1 from the polarity formula, in this case Yang in North 1, the Mountain Star floats in ascending order because Yang always ascends, see below.

Facing
157.5–172.5

	Facing Section **South** **7** 2	
2 6		**9** 4
West **1** 5	**3** 2 7	**East** **5** 9
6 1	**North** **8** 3 Sitting Section	**4** 8

Sitting
337.5–352.5

7. Determine the polarity of the Water or Facing Star in the center of the Ba Gua, in this case it is 2 which is Yin, place the **Yin, Yang, Yang** formula in the South palace which is the Water or Facing geographical palace, South 1 is Yin see step 5. Water Star floats in descending order because the facing direction is in South 1 or 157.5-172.5 degrees and is Yin, Yin descends. See below.

Facing
157.5–172.5

2 3 6	**South** 7 7 2 **Facing Section**	9 5 4
East		**West**
1 4 5	3 2 7	5 9 9
6 8 1	**North** 8 6 3 **Sitting Section**	4 1 8

Sitting
337.5–352.5

8. *Special Case.* If the Mountain or Water Star in the center palace is Five use the 20-Year Construction Cycle number or Time Star located in the center palace to determine the polarity of Star Five. This is used because there are Eight Trigrams and Star Five does not have a related Trigram, it has no polarity and must take the polarity of another Star, the Time Star. In our case, Seven is the 20-Year Construction Cycle, because Seven is odd Star Five takes the polarity of Star Seven, which is odd. The formula used is Yang, Yin, Yin.

The following chart identifies Sitting and Facing positions and their related Nine Stars, these positions are the same for all Feng Shui charts. The Stars or numbers will change but the Sitting and Facing positions remain the same.

Facing
157.5–172.5

Sitting Facing 2 3 6	**South** 7 7 2 **Facing Section**	Sitting Facing 9 5 4
East Sitting Facing 1 4 5	**Center** Sitting Facing 3 2 7	**West** Sitting Facing 5 9 9
Sitting Facing 6 8 1	**North** 8 6 3 **Sitting Section**	Sitting Facing 4 1 8

Sitting
337.5–352.5

Summary

Constructing a Flying Stars Feng Shui Chart:

1. Determine the construction year or completion time of the structure and locate the 20-Year Construction Cycle Number.

2. Place the Construction Year Cycle number in the center of the Ba Gua and float the number in ascending order.

3. After floating the 20-Year construction number star determine the Sitting and Facing positions using a compass or Lo Pan. The sitting or Mountain Star is located in the sitting palace, place this sitting number Star in the Left hand or Mountain position in the center palace, and place the Facing Star, located in the facing palace in the Water position in the center palace.

4. Identify the polarity of the Mountain Star in the left/sitting/mountain position, place the Feng Shui chart formula in the sitting locations, locate the exact degree of the sitting position and take note of its gender, Yin or Yang, which will be position 1, 2 or 3 in each palace. Float the Mountain Star in ascending order if the position is Yang or descending order if Yin. Repeat the process for the Water Star.

Special Cases

1. If a compass or Lo Pan reading is right on a line of transition from one Mountain to another Mountain, set up two charts and determine which is accurate by presenting an evaluation to the residents. The feedback will identify the correct chart. There are alternative methods, for example, replacement stars, in the appendix are tables listing the method to calculate the replacement stars. If you use replacement stars refer to its chart in the appendix, not the traditional ones discussed.

2. *Evil Lines* are lines located at the beginning and ending of the eight cardinal directions and there are numerous applications of these evil lines. Most practitioners believe if a building's facing and sitting direction falls on these lines there will be very unfavorable consequences in all aspects of life. Most believe the lines extend 1.5 degrees to each side of the line, generally avoid these buildings.

Evil Lines	Locations
22.5	North 3/North East 1
67.5	North East 3/East 1
112.5	East 3/South East 1
157.5	South East 3/South 1
202.5	South 3/South West 1
247.5	South West 3/West 1
292.5	West 3/North West 1
337.5	North West 3/ North 1

Five-Element Remedies

Five-Element relationships are one method for correcting Flying Stars Feng Shui situations. Each palace contains a Mountain-Sitting Star, Water-Facing Star and Time Star and each Star represents one of the Five-Elements, interactions between Stars will be in either a production or controlling cycle relationship. From a purely Five-Element relationship and on a basic level if the cycle is productive no correction is necessary. If the cycle is controlling the following method is applied to obtain balance.

1. Identify the controlling element and locate it in the Reduction cycle, from a clockwise perspective identify the element that is adjacent to it, refer to the arrows in the Five-Element Reduction Cycle chart, the element which has an arrow going into the controlling element is the element which reduces it. Another way to view this is the reducing element is the child element of the controlling element, for example, where Water controls Fire, Water is the controlling element, Wood is the child element of Water and Wood is the reducing element.

The table below lists recommended Five-Element remedies

Element	Color	Remedies and Shapes
Water	Black, Blue	Aquarium, fountains swimming pool Curvy or Wavy shapes
Wood	Green	Plants, flowers, bamboo flute, plant with only water and no soil Beam or rod shapes
Fire	Red, Purple, Pink, Orange	Red candles, lamp with red lamp shades, red objects, red light Triangle shapes
Earth	Yellow, Beige, Brown, Tan	Soil, rocks, crystals, ceramics, porcelain Square shapes
Metal	White, Gold, Silver, Shiny	Grandfather clock, metal chimes, coins, metal objects Sphere shapes

Nine Stars

Individual and Combinations

Facing, Sitting and Construction Star combinations exist in each of the nine places and these stars can have meanings that are unique and different than their individual meanings. In this chapter "Timely" qualities of Stars are presented, including individual and Star combinations. Utilize these combinations in conjunction with the individual meanings of Mountain and Water Stars.

Stars represent potential, there is a possibility they will manifest but they require forms to activate them causing the Qi to come alive and actually manifest in one's life. When the proper Five-Element remedies and forms are applied to Star combinations the negative aspects are harmonized and the favorable influences are expressed. It is critical to realize that forms and five element remedies can activate both favorable and unfavorable influences of Stars.

The ancients explain Feng Shui in the following way:

Advanced level Feng Shui consultants watch the Stars, Time, Space and Forms; this is Xuan Kong and Flying Stars Feng Shui.

The following tables present the meanings of Stars for cycle 7, 1984-2003 and cycle 8, 2004-2023.

Meanings of Stars for Cycle 7

1984-2003

	Star	Meaning	Disease
1	White Star Water	Wealth, money, fame, spirituality, wisdom, philosophy Weak Influence	Kidneys, Ears, Blood
2	Black Star Earth	Sickness, potential miscarriage, digestive difficulties, loneliness Strong Influence	Stomach, Spleen, Abdomen, Digestion
3	Green Star Wood	Gossip, arguments, lawsuits, slander, robbers, disability Strong Influence	Feet, Lungs, Convulsions, Hysteria
4	Dark Green Star Wood	Academic success, intelligence, creativity, artistic skills, fame, good fortune Weak Influence	Buttock, Thigh, Colds, Flu
5	Yellow Star Earth	Disease, pain, sickness, potential disaster, most negative energy, lack knowledge, laziness Strong Influence	Spleen, Stomach, digestion, all kinds of illness.
6	White Star Metal	Wealth, leadership, success, ambition, success in technology & science Weak Influence	Pulmonary disease, Headaches
7	Red Star Metal	Wealth, fertility, great verbal skills and languages, divination Very Strong Influence	Head, Lungs
8	White Star Earth	Fame, wealth, spirituality, success for young people and family unity Strong Influence	Hands, Fingers, Back
9	Purple Star Fire	Achievement, success, growth Strong Influence	Heart, Eyes

Meanings of Stars for Cycle 8

2004-2023

	Star	Meaning	Disease
1	White Star Water	Wealth, money, fame, spirituality, wisdom, philosophy **Strong Influence**	Kidneys, Ears, Blood
2	Black Star Earth	Sickness, potential miscarriage, digestive difficulties, loneliness **Strong Influence**	Stomach, Spleen, Abdomen, Digestion
3	Green Star Wood	Wealth, prosperity, growth, youth, leadership **Weak Influence**	Feet, Lungs, Convulsions, Hysteria
4	Dark Green Star Wood	Divorce, family pressure, affairs, infidelity, manipulation **Strong Influence**	Buttock, Thigh, Colds, Flu
5	Yellow Star Earth	Disease, pain, sickness, potential disaster, most negative energy, lack knowledge, laziness **Strong influence**	Spleen, Stomach, digestion, all kinds of illness.
6	White Star Metal	Wealth, leadership, success, ambition, success in technology & science **Weak Influence**	Pulmonary disease, Headaches
7	Red Star Metal	Robbery, bleeding, arguing, fire, bickering, isolation, promiscuous, legal problems, STD's **Strong Influence**	Head, Lungs
8	White Star Earth	Fame, wealth, spirituality, success for young people and family unity **Very Strong Influence**	Hands, Fingers, Back
9	Purple Star Fire	Achievement, success, growth **Strong Influence**	Heart, Eyes

Nine Star Combinations

The following Star combinations include qualities that are different than their individual meanings. Sometimes two stars interacting create a synergy that cannot be explained from standard meanings, when evaluating Stars the following must be considered:

1. Stars are potential Qi which can be activated by forms and Five-Element remedies, when they are activated we must factor in Timeliness to obtain their meaning and this includes two major aspects:

   1. Original Star nature:

      Favorable: 1,6,8,9

      Unfavorable: 2,4,3,5,7

   2. Timeliness of Stars

      1. Most Timely (In Cycle 7, it is Star 7)
      2. Future Timely (Star 8 for Cycle 7)
      3. Distant Timely (Star 9 for Cycle 7)
      4. Close Distant (Star 6)
      5. Untimely (1,3, 4, 5,)
      6. Additionally, there are "Usable Stars", which can be Untimely by definition but are safe and usable. (For Cycle 7 they are Stars 1 & 4)

2. Stars can be categorized as Guest or Host

   - When considering Wealth the Facing or Water Star is the Host and the Mountain or Sitting Star is the Guest. The Time, Annual and Monthly Stars are also Guest Stars.

- When considering Health, Relationships or Fertility the Sitting or Mountain Star is the Host and the Water or Facing Star is the Guest. The Time, Annual and Monthly Stars are also Guest Stars.

3. Consider the Original Five-Element energy in each palace and how it affects the Host and Guests Stars, does it support, reduce or control the Stars?

4. Forms surrounding the structure have a profound effect on Stars, they can trigger them in unfavorable or favorable ways.

5. Forms inside the structure (interior design) have a profound effect on Stars, they can trigger them in unfavorable or favorable ways.

6. For more information refer to each trigram and their correspondences.

7. All aspects must be considered to get a complete and accurate picture of Flying Stars Feng Shui influences.

8. Stars can be evaluated in a rigid or broad way, a rigid way is a Mountain Star only relates to People and Water Stars to Wealth, a broader way is there is overlap between them.

9. Stars contain potential Qi and they need to be activated to manifest and create an influence, exterior or interior forms activate Stars. Without forms to activate Stars they do not exert an influence on the stars.

10. When correct forms are present, whether they exist already or are created they trigger Stars to exert their unique influences. In addition to forms, Five-Element remedies can be introduced inside a building, which can diminish or eliminate unfavorable aspects of Stars.

11. Forms, both exterior and interior, can activate Facing-Sitting or Water-Mountain Stars. Annual, Monthly, Sitting, Facing and Time Stars in each palace can combine creating "Star Combinations", they are an integral part of Flying Stars Feng Shui

The following are the 81 Star combinations; please refer to these combinations as well as their individual meanings to capture a comprehensive understanding of Flying Stars Feng Shui.

Star Combination	Meanings
1,1	Romance, Affairs, Alcoholism, Legal Problems, Scholastic Achievement
1,2	Spousal/Relationship difficulties, female domination, gynecological problems, potential automobile accidents
1,3	Gossip, arguments, lawsuits, loss of money, tempers are activated, success when traveling
1,4	Romance for women, intelligence, use a small amount of non-moving water as a remedy
1,5	Womb and genital problems, food and fluid poisoning
1,6	Good for middle son and their good fortune, scholastic achievement, intelligent children
1,7	Romance
1,8	Trouble with business partners
1,9	Venereal disease, changes jobs/careers, heart disease
2,1	Gynecological disorders, abortion, diminished sex drive, infertility, spousal relationship difficulties-the women may be too controlling
2,2	Miscarriage
2,3	Bullfighting Combination, gossip, arguments, lawsuits, digestive and abdominal problems, especially older females, serious situations, family troubles, avoid using this area of a building or room
2,4	Unfavorable sexual encounters for young females, mother/daughter in-law problems, others cause emotional stress
2,5	Most Serious situation, health (particularly abdominal), cancer, miscarriages, financial disaster, illness, accidents, take no action, avoid this area, pay close attention to annual and monthly stars which may activate this Star combination Add: Metal, especially moving metal that makes sound, grandfather clocks, etc. Do not use wind chimes here. Use a substantial amount of metal weight.
2,6	Pain, Sickness (especially abdominal), blockages
2,7	If 9 Star enters a possible Fire
2,8	Good for real estate, possible monk/ nun or loner, good financial prospects
2,9	Romance/ peach blossom for women, potential eye problems

3,1	Theft, loss of money, possible violence
3,2	Possible auto accident, females get sick easy, mother-son difficulties, avoid this area of a building or room
3,3	Possible theft, cold disposition
3,4	Mental-Emotional Difficulties, males attract females, difficulties for elderly females, theft
3,5	Difficulties with money, unfavorable for young males, auto accidents, infectious diseases, loss when gambling
3,6	Difficulties for young adults, leg problems, car accidents, headaches, accidents with sharp objects
3,7	Robbery, betrayal
3,8	Difficulties with young children, possible miscarriage, homosexuality
3,9	Birth of intelligent baby, robbery, possible fire accident
4,1	Romance for females, possible affairs, academic and literary success
4,2	Unfavorable sexual affairs for women, mother-daughter in-law problems, unfavorable for elderly females, others cause stress
4,3	Good for arts, unfavorable affairs, males attract females
4,4	Attract the opposite sex, travel
4,5	Skin disease, pain, infectious disease, gambling, breast cancer
4,6	Possible miscarriage, colds, flu, relationship breakups, loss of wife
4,7	Possible miscarriage, divorce, injury with sharp objects, pregnant women, favorable love affairs, turmoil between women
4,8	Back problems, good for real estate
4,9	Male child is a genius, caution about fire accidents, female homosexuality
5,1	Bladder problems, reproductive difficulties, ear diseases, pain, blockage, food poisoning
5,2	Most serious condition, widow, widower, pain, illness, stay away from this space, keep it inactive, pay close attention to annual and monthly stars which may activate this area
5,3	Illness (especially of the eldest son), unfavorable for youths, bankruptcy, loss of money, deception
5,4	Skin disease, flu, viruses, loss of money due to gambling
5,5	Serious situation, illness, blockages, accidents
5,6	Head problems, lung diseases, impotence

5,6	Head problems, lung diseases, impotence
5,7	Mouth related problems, food poisoning, sexual diseases
5,8	Paralysis, emotional disorders
5,9	Poison, eye difficulties, ulcer, caution when gambling or investing, caution about fire accidents
6,1	Peach blossom, favorable for writing and the middle son, cunning, good for career growth
6,2	Blockages especially in career and money, abdominal diseases, gynecological problems
6,3	Unfavorable for young people, lower limb problems, auto accidents, headache
6,4	Relationship difficulties, loneliness, broken hearts
6,5	Natural disasters, lung disease, serous disease, men stress over career
6,6	Difficulties with family members
6,7	"Double Metal Clash", Males fight with each other, robbery
6,8	Possible loneliness, emotional disorders
6,9	"Fire Burns Heaven Gate", bickering with the elderly, toothache, high blood pressure, trouble with sons, do not have kitchen stove here, lung disease, head of family has many problems
7,1	Romance, possible affairs, good for travel
7,2	Infertility, females argue
7,3	Robbery, loss of money
7,4	Romance, good for travel
7,5	Arguing, deception, STD's, emotional disorders, unfavorable sexual behavior
7,6	Skin disease, jealousy, arguing
7,7	Robbery, possible unfavorable affairs for men
7,8	Romance, success in competition, sudden money
7,9	Possible fire and heart disease, flirting, irritable disposition
8,1	Arguments among partners
8,2	Potential miscarriage, nun/monk types, loss of money
8,3	Difficult for young kids (under 12)
8,4	Difficult for young kids, difficulty having kids and getting married, martial stress

8,5	Paralysis, serious illness
8,6	Easily emotional upset
8,7	Good for young females and males in relationships until 2004.
8,8	Great for real estate
8,9	Joyful activities including marriage
9,1	Venereal disease, peach blossom, change jobs, heart and eye problems, miscarriage, academic success
9,2	Unfavorable for children, gynecological problems, fertility difficulties
9,3	Possible fire accidents and robberies
9,4	Caution for fire accidents, unfavorable sexual relations
9,5	Negative for gambling and investments, possible eye problems, rigid personality
9,6	"Fire Burns Heaven Gate", do not have kitchen stove here, arguments with the elderly, avoid fire mountain in the forms near this palace, lung disease, head of family has lots of stress Remedy: Add Earth
9,7	Fertility, possible fires
9,8	Good for joyful activities and marriage
9,9	Good for activities that have the nature of change: fashion, toys, etc.

Flying Stars Charts

There are many Flying Stars methods for harmonizing a living environment. Some of these methods are integrated, others are stand alone and not dependent on the integrated methods. We can view a building and its surrounding environment as an energy field and this field can be harmonized or influenced with different methods to get the same results. The following describes one prevalent and potent method within Flying Stars Feng Shui.

Individual stars and their combinations are one aspect of Flying Stars Feng Shui, another integral aspect of Feng Shui is the configuration or arrangement of the Flying Stars in a chart, they reveal a deep and influential aspect of Feng Shui. The following four types or styles of Flying Stars Feng Shui charts are primary charts and one of them will be in every regular Flying Stars Chart.

1. Favorable for Health and Wealth or *Wang Shan Wang Shui*
2. Unfavorable for Health and Wealth, a Reversed or *Shang Shan Xia Shui*
3. Favorable for Wealth, Unfavorable for Health, A Double Facing or *Xing Dao Xiang*
4. Favorable for Health, Unfavorable for Wealth, a Double Sitting or *Xing Dao Zuo*

Most Feng Shui practitioners agree the special qualities for these structures exist during the 20-year construction period, when the 20-Year Construction Cycle is over the special qualities listed no longer exist and other methods to optimize the building are needed. Some believe the chart qualities last longer, it seems to me the safest method is to follow the principle they no longer exist, because the Stars in the Facing and Sitting Palaces are no longer Timely. When the 20-Year Construction cycle is over, new forms will be required to activate the new Timely Stars and the palaces they in, this principle particularly applies to the following charts:

1. Wang Shan Wang Shui-Favorable for Health and Wealth
2. Shang Shan Xia Shui-Unfavorable for Health and Wealth

4. Xing Dao Xiang-Double Facing

5. Xing Da Zuo-Double Sitting

6. Sum to Ten

7. Fu Mu San Gua–Parent String

8. Lin Chu San Pan Kua-Pearl String

The three most important palaces are the Facing, Center and Sitting Palaces, their influence permeates the entire building, it is most auspicious to have the Timely or Wang Stars in the Facing and Sitting Palaces.

A building is only favorable when the proper corrections in each palace and proper Forms are present (this will be discussed here and in the chapter on forms). If the chart is unfavorable, make the suggested remedies for its type of chart, then correct each palace and forms if necessary. ***It is very important to realize there are certain types of charts and methods, including special "Water Placement Formulas," that override these Flying Stars formations.***

The method for identifying each of these four types of charts is based on the location of the 20-Year Construction Cycle Stars. Each chart will have three Stars for each of the Nine Stars, for example, three ones, three twos, three threes or three fours for a normal chart, this does not include replacement star charts. This is because we float the Construction, Sitting and Facing Stars through each palace, generating a complete cycle of nine stars. *The three Time or Construction Year Stars will always be located in some variation in the Center, Facing and Sitting Palaces.* The order or flow of those Stars determines a specific type of Flying Stars Feng Shui chart and the distribution of the Time Stars is a code, which reveals some of the most powerful influences of the Flying Stars.

The ideal form correction should be placed outside the building in the surrounding area. One can view forms as a potent source of Qi, far stronger than small five element remedies.

The following are examples for each of the four types of structures, some charts need form corrections that consist of the proper placement of Water and Mountain. *Water corrections include oceans, lakes, streams, fountains, ponds, swimming pools, flat lands, streets and hallways and Mountain corrections include Mountains, Hills, Buildings, Earth based sculptures, rocks and soil.*

1. Favorable for Health and Wealth
   Wang Shan Wang Shui
   Prosperous Sitting and Facing

Facing Direction

	North	
	Facing Palace	
	Sitting Facing **7**	
West		**East**
	7	
	Sitting Facing **7**	
	Sitting Palace **South**	

Sitting Direction

In this situation the Sitting and Facing Stars are in their proper position. The 20- Year Construction Cycle Star is Seven, this is referred to as the Time Star. When a Time Star is in the Facing position in the Facing Palace another *Time Star* will be located in the Sitting position in the Sitting palace, this relationship always exists. This reflects the proper distribution and influence of Time Stars, it means the underlying influence is good for Health and Wealth. A Wang Shang Wang Shui structure increases the magnitude of favorable Stars and decreases the magnitude of unfavorable Stars.

The proper Form for this structure is Water to be located in front of the Facing Palace to activate the Facing Star and Mountain or Earth behind the Sitting palace to activate the Sitting Star, both should be located outside the physical building.

The following are examples of Wang Shan Wang Shui structures.

1. Cycle Seven, Sitting West 3
2. Cycle Eight, Sitting North East 1
3. Cycle Eight, Sitting South West 1

2. Unfavorable for Health and Wealth

 Reversed Chart

 Shang Shan Xia Shui

Facing Direction

	North **Facing Palace** *Sitting* Facing **7**	
West		**East**
	7	
	Sitting Facing **7** **Sitting Palace** **South**	

Sitting Direction

In this situation the Facing and Sitting Stars are in reversed order. The 20-Year Construction Cycle Star is Seven and is referred to as the Time Star, when a Time Star is in the Sitting position in the Facing Palace another Time Star will be located in the Facing position in the Sitting palace, this reflects a reversed distribution and influence of the Time Star. It means the underlying influence is unfavorable for Health and Wealth. A Shang Shan Xia Shui structure decreases the magnitude of favorable Stars and increases the magnitude of unfavorable Stars.

The correction for this chart is to place a Mountain or Earth element in front of the Facing part of the Structure to activate the Mountain Star and Water behind the Mountain position of the structure to activate the Water Star, this reverses the energy to bring it back into balance. If corrections already exist in the environment no additional remedies are necessary.

The following are examples of Unfavorable for Health and Wealth or Shang Shan Xia Shui structures.

1. Cycle Two, North East 3
2. Cycle Seven, Sitting South East 2
3. Cycle Eight, Sitting North East 3
4. Cycle Eight, Sitting South West 2

3. Double Facing

   Xing Dao Xiang

   Double Stars meet at Facing

Facing Direction

	North Facing Palace Sitting Facing _7_ _7_	
West	7	East
	Sitting Facing Sitting Palace South	

Sitting Direction

In this situation both Time Stars are in the Sitting and Facing positions in the Facing Palace and are not properly placed, all Time Stars are in the Facing or Water palace and are favorable for Wealth. A Time Star is not in the Sitting or Mountain palace revealing this chart is unfavorable for Health.

The proper placement for a Double Facing chart is to place Mountain or Earth in front of the Facing direction to activate the Mountain star and Water in the front as well to activate the Water Star. These two form placements activate both stars in the facing palace.

The following are examples of Double Facing Structures

1. Cycle One, Sitting North 2
2. Cycle Two, Sitting East 1
3. Cycle Eight, Sitting North 3
4. Cycle Eight, Sitting East 2

4. Double Sitting

   Xing Dao Zuo

   Double Stars meet at Sitting

Facing Direction

	North Facing Palace Sitting Facing	
West	 7	East
	Sitting *Facing* 7 7 Sitting Palace South	

Sitting Direction

In this situation two of the Time Stars or 20-Year Construction Cycle Stars are placed in the Sitting or Mountain palace revealing this chart is unbalanced. A Time Star is positioned in the Mountain palace and is favorable for Health. There are no Time Stars in the Facing palace revealing this chart is unfavorable for Wealth.

The correction for a Double Sitting chart is to place Water behind the Sitting Palace of the structure to activate the Water star and Earth in this area as well to activate the Mountain star.

The following are examples of Double Sitting structures

1. Cycle One, Sitting North 1
2. Cycle Seven, Sitting South West 1
3. Cycle Eight, Sitting North 1
4. Cycle Eight, Sitting East 1

Early and Later Heaven Ba Gua

Usable Flying Stars

For each 20-Year Cycle the Time Star has two associated Stars that are usable and safe, even if they are Untimely by definition. The table below lists each cycle with its Timely and Usable Stars.

Safe and Usable Stars

Number	20-Year Cycle	Timely Star	Usable Stars
1	1864-1883	1	Stars 2, 7
2	1884-1903	2	Stars 1, 4
3	1904-1923	3	Stars 8, 9
4	1924-1943	4	Stars 2, 7
5	1944-1963	5	Stars 2, 8
6	1964-1983	6	Stars 8, 9
7	1984-2003	7	Stars 1, 4
8	2004-2023	8	Stars 3, 6
9	2024-2043	9	Stars 3, 6

Theory and Application

This application is based on the relationship between Early Heaven and Later Heaven arrangements of the Ba Gua, the following diagrams illustrate those relationships.

Early Heaven Ba Gua

South East Dui 7	South Qian 6	South West Xun 4
East Li 9	Center Earth	West Kan 1
North East Zhen 3	North Kun 2	North West Gen 8

Later Heaven BaGua

South East 4	South 9	South West 2
East 3	5	West 7
North East **8**	North 1	North West 6

1. During 1984–2003 or cycle 7, Timely star 7 is located in the West in the Later Heaven Ba Gua, locate the trigram-number in the West in the Early Heaven Ba Gua, it is Kan or 1.

2. For cycle 7 locate star seven in the Early Heaven Ba Gua, it is in the South East, locate the trigram in the South East in the Later Heaven Ba Gua, it is 4 or Xun.

3. Kan-1 and Xun-4 are the two usable stars for cycle 7; they are the associated stars for cycle seven in the Early and Later Heaven Ba Guas.

The following table combines the Early Heaven and Later Heaven Ba Gua, this combines usable stars for each Palace and their associated time frame.

Early and Later Heaven
Ba Gua combined

South East Dui 7 Xun 4	South Qian 6 Li 9	South West Xun 4 Gen 2
East Li 9 Zhen 3	Center Earth	West Kan 1 Dui 7
North East Zhen 3 Ken 8	North Gen 2 Kan 1	North West Ken 8 Qian 6

- The Early Heaven arrangement is located in the top row and the Later Heaven trigrams are located in the lower row.

Primary Fortunate Palaces

Direct and Indirect Palaces
Zheng Shen Palaces

During each 20-Year Cycle certain directions are more fortunate than others, the chart below is the Later Heaven arrangement of the Ba Ga, the years 1984-2003 is Cycle Seven, Star Seven resides in the West palace and its opposite East palace create a powerful matrix for prosperity.

North West 6	North 1	North East 8
West *7* *Direct Spirit*	5	East *3* *Indirect Spirit*
South West 2	South 9	South East 4

The ideal is to have a Mountain/Earth behind the Direct Spirit Palace and Water in front of the Indirect Spirit creating an auspicious Water and Mountain influence. Water is inauspicious in the West Palace for cycle seven.

The following table lists the Direct and Indirect palaces table for each cycle and their proper forms.

Direct and Indirect Palaces

Number	20-Year Cycle	Direct Spirit Palace	Indirect Spirit Palace
1	1864-1883	North Mountain	South Water
2	1884-1903	South West Mountain	North East Water
3	1904-1923	East Mountain	West Water
4	1924-1943	South East Mountain	North West Water
5	1944-1963	1st 10 years South West Mountain 2nd 10 years North East Mountain	1st 10 Years North East Water 2nd 10 Years South West Water
6	1964-1983	North West Mountain	South East Water
7	1984-2003	West Mountain	East Water
8	2004-2023	North East Mountain	South West Water
9	2024-2043	South Mountain	North Water

This Flying Star Feng Shui method is applicable in all nine cycles.

Second Direct Spirit Palace

Zhui Shen Palace

A Second Fortunate Palace exists for each 20-Year Cycle. A business placing Water in this palace generates new customers, residences and businesses adding Water may generate sudden or unexpected wealth. Water should be placed outside the building and can be placed in the building if Water is in harmony with the Mountain and Water Stars in the palace.

This method is based on the trigram relationship of the Later Haven Ba Gua.

Wen Wang's Trigrams
Later Heaven Ba Gua

	South Fire 4, 9	
East Wood 3, 8	Center Earth	West Metal 2, 7
	North Water 1, 6	

Examples 1 and 2 explain the formula.

Example 1

For the year 1935 the 20-Year Construction Cycle is Four, in Fu Xi's Trigrams four is paired with nine and the location of nine in the Later Heaven Ba Gua is the South palace, see below. South is the Secondary Fortunate Palace for Cycle Four.

Example 2

For the years 1984-2003 the cycle is Seven, it is paired with two in Fu Xi's Trigams and the palace containing two in the Later Heaven Ba Gua is South West. South West is the Secondary Fortunate Palace for Cycle Seven, see the following Ba Gua.

Later Heaven Ba Gua

North West	North	North East
6	1	8
West		East
7	5	3
South West	South	South East
2	9	4

Second Spirit Palace Table

Number	20-Year Cycle	Second Direct Spirit Palace
1	1864-1883	North West
2	1884-1903	West
3	1904-1923	North East
4	1924-1943	South
5	1944-1963	1st Ten Years: South East 2nd Ten Years: North West
6	1964-1983	North
7	1984-2003	South West
8	2004-2023	East
9	2024-2043	South East

This Flying Star Feng Shui method is applicable in all nine cycles.

Sum to 10 Chart

There are special Flying Stars Feng Shui charts that are very favorable based solely on the Nine Star distribution in each palace, one type is when the total value of the Time Star in each palace is added to either the Water or Mountain Star and equals ten. The following examples illustrate this condition.

Example
1904-1923
Sitting or Mountain position: South 2

8 7 2	3 3 7 **sitting**	1 5 9
9 6 1	7 8 3	5 1 5
4 2 6	2 4 8 **Facing**	6 9 4

Each palace has a combination of two Stars that equal ten, one Star must be the Time Star and the other can be the Mountain or Water Star. The particular Star that sums to 10 is the Star and its related area of life that is fortunate, for example, in the South East the Mountain Star combines with the Time Star promoting health and fertility. In the South both Stars combine with the time Star, health and wealth are fortunate for those that reside or spend time in this palace.

This chart promotes the smooth flow of energy through every palace in the building creating auspicious health, relationships and fertility, proper forms must be present for this chart to be activated. The following lists proper forms:

1. *The proper forms must be located near Timely Stars, Water near the Timely Water Star and Mountain near the Timely Mountain Star.*

2. *The building must be a complete square or rectangle, missing portions are not allowed for this special chart to be activated.*

3. *For this Qi field to be fully activated Water or Mountain should be located near the palace with this combination, for example, if the sum is the Water Star, Water should be located near the Timely Water Star.*

Examples: Cycle 6, Sitting West 1
Cycle 8, Sitting South West 1

Parent String

"Fu Mu San Gua"
1,4,7   2,5,8   3,6,9   Structures

One special Flying Stars Feng Shui chart includes the following Star combinations in each palace, 1,4,7 or 2,5,8 or 3,6,9. Every palace must have one of these combinations, they generate great fortune and luck. The influence of this is so strong these charts override unfortunate charts and bring very good fortune.

Example: Construction Year 1965
Sitting or Mountain position: North East 1

SE	S	SW
8 2 5	4 7 1	3 9 3 **Facing Palace**
6 1 4	9 3 6	2 5 8
3 6 9 **Sitting Palace**	5 8 2	1 4 7
NE	**N**	**NW**

This is a very favorable chart even though this is reversed or unfavorable for Health and Wealth. This 1,4,7 and 2,5,8 and 3,6,9 style house transforms the reverse chart into great luck and fortune. For this chart, make the normal corrections for a reversed structure to activate great prosperity.

Pearl String

"Lin Chu San Pan Kua"

This special and potentially prosperous Flying Stars Feng Shui chart is when Stars flow in a sequential order in each Palace, for example, each palace flows in the following patterns:

1,2,3 4,5,6 7,8,9 in any order

The way this special star distribution is activated is to have Water in front and Mountain in the back of the building, it generates enormous prosperity which lasts during the 20-Year Cycle it was built, for example, a building built in Cycle 7 will have this potential good fortune for 1984-2003, but will not exist after 2003.

This Qi distribution can flow from the Mountain, Time and Water stars generating enormous Wealth and can also flow from the Water, Time and Mountain stars generating favorable Health and Relationships.

Fan Fu Yin

Inverse and Hidden Siren

This classic Flying Stars chart is when the center palace contains a Five Star in the Mountain or Water Star position in the center palace.

- The "Inverse Siren" or "Fan Yin" is when the Five star Flies or Floats downward/descending or in a yin pattern.

- The "Hidden Siren" or Fu Yin is when the Five Star Flies or Floats upward/ascending or in a yang pattern.

If proper forms are present these structures are neutralized, if not these buildings generate Health, Relationship or Wealth problems. Creating proper forms for the four styles of buildings, for example, Favorable for People and Wealth, Unfavorable for People and Wealth, Favorable for People and Unfavorable for Wealth and Favorable for Wealth and Unfavorable for People provides the proper remedy to harmonize this condition.

Locked Flying Stars Charts

A Locked or Prison Flying Stars Chart is when the Timely or current cycle Star is in the center palace in the Mountain or Water position. Locked buildings influence People or Wealth, when they are not remedied, very unfavorable luck will affect the occupants. The following explains this structure.

Locked Chart

	North **Facing Palace** **Sitting** **Facing**	
West	**Sitting** **Facing** **<u>7</u>** **<u>7</u>**	**East**
	Sitting **Facing** **Sitting Palace** **South**	

In this case the current period or Timely Star is located in the center palace in the Sitting position, therefore this structure is Locked in the Mountain position and the influence is unfavorable for Health and People during Cycle 1984-2003, unless it is harmonized.

For the years 2004-2023, Eight is the Timely Star and during Cycle Eight, Seven is Distant Untimely, if a Seven Star is in the Mountain or Facing position in the center palace it would not be in Locked, only an Eight can be locked during 2004–2023, in other words *only a Timely Star can be Locked.*

If the Seven Star is located in the facing position in the center palace the Facing, Water or Wealth aspect of life will be Locked for Cycle 7, 1984-2003.

A Locked structure will be unfavorable for either Health/Fertility/People, Relationships or Wealth unless the proper remedy is implemented.

Locked Corrections

A Locked or Prison structure is when the Dominant or Most Timely Star is located in the Sitting or Facing position in the center Palace, the goal is to release this timely star so it can favorably influence the building. One could say this pattern is part of the energetic DNA or blueprint of a structure, even if each of the key palaces contain favorable stars they will not manifest unless the Lock is released.

Prison can influence People or Wealth but not both. Using traditional Flying Stars charts it is impossible to have two of the same Stars in the Water and Mountain positions in the **Center** palace. The benefit of knowing how to calculate a chart by hand reveals the mechanics of this process. During the years 1984-2003 if the Seven Star is located in the facing position in the center palace the Facing, Water or Wealth aspect of life is unfavorably affected, in essence it means every Facing Star in each palace is unfavorably influenced, the same is true for Mountain Stars.

The following includes three remedies for Locked structures

First Remedy

1. Identify whether the Facing or Sitting position is in Prison. If the Facing position is in Prison locate Star Five in the Facing position in one of the Eight palaces, every chart will have one palace containing a Five Star in the Mountain and Water positions. The only way they will be in the same palace is if the structure is a Double Facing or Double Sitting Chart. *If the physical area from the center palace to the palace containing Facing Star Five is open with no obstructions, Star Seven or the Locked Star can Fly and be released. In this situation no corrections are necessary. Physical obstructions include walls, partitions or doors that separate the area from the center palace to the Five Star, this obstacle traps the imprisoned Seven Star.*

Perform the same evaluation if the Mountain Star is in Prison.

Some Feng Shui Masters place Water in the Palace containing the Five Star, others believe the Water may activate the Unfavorable Five Star. My preference is not to take a chance and not use this method.

Second Remedy

If a building is located close to and in view of a body of water the prison is automatically released, for example, an ocean, lake, etc. Residents need to be able to see water from the building.

Third Remedy

Change Heaven's Heart

When evaluating a Flying Stars Feng Shui chart the center has profound influences, the classics refer to the center as "Heaven's Heart", and it influences the entire chart/building. The chart begins with the Star relating to the 20-Year Construction Cycle, which is called the Time, Construction, Earth or Base Star.

Heaven's Heart has four major purposes:

1. The center is used to float the 20-Year Construction Number, which is the first step in constructing a Flying Stars Feng Shui chart.
2. The center is used to determine the type of Flying Stars structure
3. The center contains information to determine a Prison or Locked structure
4. The center Stars indicate an underlying influence on the total structure

Heaven's Heart

One Flying Stars Feng Shui strategy to change the Qi of a building is to change Heaven's Heart. The following are a few methods to change Heaven's Heart:

1. If a structure's roof and ceiling is removed and then rebuilt, the time the new ceiling-roof is enclosed becomes the new 20-Year Construction Cycle. For example, a house built in 1925 is Cycle Four, if the total roof and ceiling is removed and replaced in 2009 it becomes a Construction Cycle Eight Structure, Eight will be placed in the center palace and floated not Four. Removing the ceiling means that if it were to rain it would come inside

the house and get the floor and furniture wet or sunlight would shine inside the house. The roof should be opened at least 24 hours, some believe it should be removed for 7 days. It does not mean merely removing shingles or the top of the roof, to be exact the time the ceiling-roof is enclosed is considered the time used for the Construction Cycle. Ideally, the front door is removed for the same time as the roof.

Changing the Twenty Year Construction Cycle by removing the roof has two major applications, the first application is when remodeling takes place and a roof is replaced a new chart must be calculated, evaluated and remedied. Additionally, when a building is in a good cycle and is entering a negative cycle or is currently in a negative cycle, opening up a house creates a new Twenty Year Cycle and a new chart. By calculating the new chart before remodeling, it can be determined whether the new chart is favorable. If it is favorable it is a strategic decision to remodel and create an auspicious environment.

If the structure is completed close to the beginning or end of a twenty-year cycle the exact date must be determined. If the date cannot be determined and it is close to the transition time calculate two charts and present the client with information about each chart and determine which is correct, this method is very effective.

2. Performing renovations include removing part of the roof, removing and placing a new front door (the one actually used) and/or adding extensions, this can include a sky roof greater than 1/3 the size of the original building.

The following are examples of Locked structures.

1. Cycle Six, Sitting North West 2 during years 1984-2003, Star Seven is Locked

2. Cycle Seven, Sitting South East 1 during 2004-2023, Star Eight is Locked

3. Cycle Six, Sitting East 1 during 2004-2023, Star Eight is Locked

Special Case

If the Five Star is "Locked" the following remedies are recommended.

1. Change Heaven's Heart

2. Activate Palaces containing the Future and Distant Future Timely Stars in the building.

3. If a large body of water is in site the lock is released.

Feng Shui and Forms

Forms or environmental factors have a profound influence in Flying Stars Feng Shui and in this section two major aspects are presented.

The following is a popular Chinese saying that has applications in Feng Shui, Traditional Chinese Medicine and Taoist internal alchemy.

The Green Dragon resides to the left, White Tiger to the right, Red Phoenix flies in front while the Black Turtle sits to the back.

These metaphorical animals are often connected to the four cardinal directions, for example, Black Turtle sits in the North or behind a structure, Red Phoenix flies in the South or in front of a structure, White Tiger is to the right or in the West and Green Dragon is to the left or in the East. In reality these animals reflect types of support created by the environment. In Flying Stars Feng Shui support is most important not direction, connecting animals and direction was created based on an ideal site and specific environmental factors located in China. Regardless of the geographical orientation the position, either rear, front, left or right represents the actual application. The following table lists each animal and their respective qualities.

Animal	Direction	Example	Qualities
Black Turtle	North or Rear	Mountain, Hills, Neighboring Buildings	Support, Protection
Green Dragon	East or Left	Neighboring Buildings	Support, Protection
White Tiger	West or Right	Neighboring Buildings	Support, Protection
Red Phoenix	South or Front	Water, Lake, Sea, Pool, Fountain, Roads, Flat Lands	Prosperity

Mountains or their virtual expression buildings provide protection from winds or negative influences from other buildings, roads, trees, telephone poles or other environmental factors providing stability and security. Water or its virtual counterpart streets or roads represent wealth and prosperity. *The proper location of each "Animal" provides support, protection and good fortune.* These animals must be evaluated in conjunction with Flying Stars structures, Forms and Interior Design to obtain a complete understanding of Feng Shui. The following section explains Flying Stars structures and their forms.

Flying Stars Feng Shui Forms

The key elements of Flying Stars Feng Shui are Time, Space, Interior Design and Forms. Forms include environmental factors. In Flying Stars Feng Shui a key factor is the location of Mountains and Water, which can be real or virtual, good fortune occurs when a Form surrounding a structure is auspicious, misfortune is when inauspicious forms surround a structure.

The Combination of Form and Flying Stars Feng Shui Stars create favorable and unfavorable influences, good fortune occurs during the following conditions:

- The Timely Facing Star is located in the facing position in the Facing Palace, Water is located in front of the Facing Palace to activate this auspicious star.

- The Timely Sitting Star is located in the sitting position in the Sitting Palace, Mountain is located behind the Mountain Palace to activate this auspicious star.

- Timely Star sees Water in all cycles, it activates the Timely Stars.

- Timely Mountain Star sees Mountain in all cycles, it activates the Mountain Star.

If a Form is reversed it can alter a favorable structure or correct an unfavorable one. For example, a Wang Shan Wang Sui structure is when the Facing Palace contains the Facing Star in the facing position and the Mountain Palace contains the Mountain Star in the sitting position, if this structure has a Form with a Mountain in front of the Facing palace and Water behind the Sitting palace, it will alter the good fortune of the Wang Shang Wang Shui structure and create misfortune. New Forms must be created to reverse the energy to create good fortune. The table below lists Water and Earth remedies in two ways, the first is real examples and the second is virtual examples. Real Water or Mountain is most powerful, virtual Water and Mountain are effective but not as powerful as the real form.

Water-Mountain Forms

Element	Real	Virtual
Water	River, Lake, Fountains, Aquarium	Road, Flat Land, Hallways, Lower Ground, *Activity*
	Moving Water is best	
Mountain	Mountains, Hills, High Ground	Buildings, Walls, *Inactivity*

If Water or Mountain cannot be placed outside a structure place these items inside it, for example, residents of an apartment or condominium may not be able to place Mountain or Water outside the structure, place it at the edge of the wall of the Sitting and Facing positions within the structure. Evaluate the influence of Mountain or Water on the Stars in the Palace and place these forms only if they are in harmony with the stars. Proper forms are critical in Flying Stars Feng Shui and activate both Timely and Untimely Stars, if an Untimely Mountain Star is located in the Mountain Palace and there is a Mountain behind the Palace it will activate or trigger this Untimely Star.

Forms activate both Timely and Untimely Water and Mountain Stars. The harmony between Forms and Flying Stars Feng Shui is called "He Ju" and means "Forms activating the auspicious Qi of the Stars". Some use the term "Dragon Method" to refer to the style and influence of Mountains, when they say "Mountain Dragon is satisfied it means the Mountain Form properly activates Stars.

Water needs to be managed carefully because it represents activity and stimulates Qi. Water can create favorable and unfavorable activities; for example, Water can activate an untimely water star. Ideally the Timely Facing Star should be supported by Water Forms, including actual Water, lower ground and open areas like a street, flat land, valley or a hallway. Ideally Mountain Forms, including a Mountain, Hill or high land should support the Timely Mountain Star.

Flying Stars Feng Shui and Interior Forms

Interior design in Flying Stars Feng Shui follows the basic principles of Water and Mountain form remedies. Interior Design Water forms include corridors, hallways, doors and passageways and should be located with Timely Facing Stars as they activate them. Interior Design Mountain forms include Walls, Rooms, Partitions, Stairs (walls) and large static objects and should be located with Timely Mountain Stars to activate them.

- Timely Facing Stars should have Water Interior design forms to activate them
- Timely Mountain Stars should have Mountain Interior design forms to activate them
- Avoid activating Untimely Water and Mountain Stars with Interior Forms

Annual Flying Stars

In addition to Mountain and Water Stars, Annual Flying Stars have a strong influence in Feng Shui. These Stars are easy to calculate because they always float in ascending sequence. The following is a formula to determine Annual Flying Stars.

1. Select a year, for example, 1998

2. Sum all digits in the year. $1 + 9 + 9 + 8 = 27$ Total is 27

3. Sum the total again if it is greater than 9

    $2 + 7 = 9$

4. Subtract the total in step 3 from 11

    $11-9=2$

5. Two is the Annual Flying Stars for Year 1998

The table below lists Annual Flying Stars for years 2000-2010

Annual Flying Stars

Star	Year
9	2000
8	2001
7	2002
6	2003
5	2004
4	2005
3	2006
2	2007
1	2008
9	2009
8	2010
7	2011

Floating Annual Flying Stars

Annual Stars are floated in ascending order, the annual Star is placed in the center palace and floats in the same sequence as the 20-Year Construction Cycle Star. The order is Center, North West, West, North East, South, North, South West, East and South East; see the following example.

Year 2002
Annual Flying Stars is 7.

SE	S	SW
6	2	4
5	7	9
1	3	8
NE	N	NW

For Feng Shui purposes the New Year begins on February 4 or February5, if you need to know the exact day feel free to contact the author.

Annual Flying Stars effect Water, Mountain and Time Stars. As with all Stars determine their Timeliness and evaluate the meanings they have individually and in combination with the Time, Mountain and Water Stars in each palace and if the Annual Star is unfavorable use Five-Elements as a remedy. It is vital to review all forms, including exterior and interior and their influence on timely and untimely stars.

The table below lists the Annual Flying Stars for Cycles 1-9

Annual Flying Stars

Year CYCLE	CENTER	NW	W	NE	S	N	SW	E	SE
1	1	2	3	4	5	6	7	8	9
2	2	3	4	5	6	7	8	9	1
3	3	4	5	6	7	8	9	1	2
4	4	5	6	7	8	9	1	2	3
5	5	6	7	8	9	1	2	3	4
6	6	7	8	9	1	2	3	4	5
7	7	8	9	1	2	3	4	5	6
8	8	9	1	2	3	4	5	6	7
9	9	1	2	3	4	5	6	7	8

Locate the Construction Year Cycle in the first column then place the Annual Stars located in the horizontal row in the related geographical palaces, for example, during Cycle 8 place 8 in the center, 9 in North West, 1 in West, 2 in North East, 3 in South, 4 in North, 5 in South West, 6 in East and 7 in the South East.

Monthly Flying Stars

Water, Mountain and Construction/Time Stars are the most influential Stars followed by Annual and Monthly Flying Stars, these last two stars can trigger both favorable and unfavorable activities and must be evaluated to obtain a complete understanding of a living environment as they are often a hidden cause of unfavorable and favorable activities. The Annual and Monthly Stars can combine with each other and Mountain, Water or Time Stars.

Method:

Locate the Chinese Animal for the Year in question in the top row of the table below and identify the month in question, the Star in the box that intersects the Year Animal and Month is the Month Star.

Monthly Flying Stars

Month	Year of Rat, Rabbit, Horse, Cock	Year of Ox, Dragon, Sheep, Dog	Year of Tiger, Snake, Monkey, Pig
February 5	8	5	2
March 6	7	4	1
April 5	6	3	9
May 6	5	2	8
June 6	4	1	7
July 7	3	9	6
August 8	2	8	5
September 8	1	7	4
October 8	9	6	3
November 7	8	5	2
December 7	7	4	1
January 6	6	3	9

Grand Duke

Tai Sui

The planet Jupiter is referred to as the "Grand Duke" and circles the Sun every twelve years creating an energetic influence that permeates the planet Earth. Each year this energy encompasses a 15-degree area on a compass and exerts a potentially unfavorable influence. Basically one should not face this direction or perform renovations or remodeling in this area, this area should remain inactive. These locations cover 15-degrees of the Lo Pan Compass and relates directly to the Chinese annual zodiac animal. The following Table lists locations for the Grand Duke.

Year	Grand Duke Tai Sui	Lo Pan Position
2001	Snake Yang Fire	142.5-157.5 degrees
2002	Horse Yin Fire	172.5-187.5 degrees
2003	Sheep Yin Earth	202.5-217.5 degrees
2004	Monkey Yang Metal	232.5-247.5 degrees
2005	Cock Yin Metal	262.5-277.5 degrees
2006	Dog Yang Earth	292.5-307.5 degrees
2007	Pig Yang Water	315-345 degrees
2008	Rat Yin Water	352.5-7.5 degrees
2009	Ox Yin Water	22.5-37.5 degrees

Applications:

1. Many practitioners believe this is a critical aspect of Feng Shui and must be managed properly. Traditional recommendations include not facing this direction or disturbing this area, for instance, renovations, reconstruction, etc. during the year.

2. Some believe the influence of the Grand Duke is based on Chinese Astrology or the Four Pillars, if the Year Animal/Branch is favorable to your astrology chart then that area can be favorable to you or the Grand Duke's negative influence will be decreased. If the Year Animal/Branch is unfavorable to your Four Pillars/Astrology Chart it will be unfavorable.

3. The element of the Grand Duke for the year, for example, Fire for year 2002/ Horse will have an influence on the Flying Stars in the related palace of the Grand Duke. If Fire is unfavorable to Stars in its related palace it will exacerbate the star(s).

4. Convention is to avoid facing and disturbing this area

Three Killings

Sarm Sart

Year	Element Frame	Location of Three Killings
Rat, Monkey, Dragon	Water	South
Rabbit, Sheep. Pig	Wood	West
Cock, Ox, Snake	Metal	East
Horse, Dog, Tiger	Fire	North

These are the trinity or element frame relationships found in Four Pillars Astrology, the location of the Three Killings is the element that opposes the Grand Duke Year Element.

Application

- You can face this direction but avoid renovations or repairs in this area for it will bring misfortune.
- You may face this area but do not have it to your back

Evil Lines

These lines are located at the beginning and ending of the eight cardinal directions, there are numerous applications of these evil lines. Most practitioners believe if a building's facing and sitting direction falls on these lines there will be very unfavorable consequences in all aspects of life and most believe the lines extend 1.5 degrees to each side of the line, generally avoid these homes.

Evil Lines	Locations
22.5	North 3/North East 1
67.5	North East 3/East 1
112.5	East 3/South East 1
157.5	South East 3/South 1
202.5	South 3/South West 1
247.5	South West 3/West 1
292.5	West 3/North West 1
337.5	North West 3/ North 1

Macrocosm and Microcosm

One of the first steps in Flying Stars Feng Shui is to create a Flying Stars chart, which is then placed over the entire building, this is the macrocosm. If a room in a building has unfavorable stars, we can identify the most favorable areas inside the room by using the microcosm aspect of Flying Stars Feng Shui. The method is to use the Flying Star Stars Feng Shui chart for the building and place it in the room, we view the room as a miniature Qi field of the building. Once the chart is placed on the room, locate the areas in the room which have favorable energy and try to position the door, bed, desk and other areas where you spend time in these favorable energy areas. This is optimizing an unfavorable position.

Steps for practicing Flying Stars Feng Shui

Determine the Orientation of the building or its Facing and Sitting locations

Identify which of the four types of charts the structure represents and if the cycle is Timely (is the current period the 20-Year Construction period as well)

Check to see if the building is Locked

Evaluate Exterior Forms

Identify and evaluate the Sitting and Facing palaces and the Forms next to them

Identify Timely Stars and exterior and interior Forms next to them

Identify Special Chart Structures and select ones that are applicable with the building

Identify favorable Stars in the structure and use proper Forms and Five-Element remedies

Identify special Star combinations and use Forms and Five-Elements as a remedy

Identify unfavorable Stars and use forms and Five-Element as remedies

Evaluate the Time Star's influence on Mountain and Water Stars

Evaluate Annual and Monthly Stars and their influences

Review the Environment and its Forms and their non Flying Stars Feng Shui influences

Review Interior Design and their Forms and their influences

If a building is out of its 20-Year Construction Cycle, make forms corrections for the type of building, but focus on other Flying Star methods to promote prosperity and auspicious relationships and health. For example, focus on the primary and secondary palaces and supporting Timely Stars with proper forms.

The Facing, Sitting and Center Palace are the most influential on the entire building and need should have priority when evaluating and applying remedies.

Water and Mountains in the environment and interior are vibrant energy sources. They are powerful in any form of Feng Shui and particularly potent in Flying Stars Feng Shui. These forms are most potent as activators of Flying Stars, generally more potent than five element remedies added in palaces to harmonize two flying stars,

The Facing, Center and Sitting Palaces are most important, they influence the entire building. When the 20-Year Construction period is over, new forms must be utilized to activate the new Timely Stars, also the Forms that activated the Timely Stars in the preceding period must now be removed because the Stars are now Untimely and the Forms will activate their Untimely qualities. For example, during cycle 7, 1984-2003, Star Seven is Timely and forms are necessary to activate it, but during cycle 8, the 8 Star is Timely and it needs forms to activate it. The palace containing the now Untimely Seven requires the forms it contains to be removed or it will activate its Untimely qualities.

Remember the Front Door, Bedroom, Office and areas where one spends time is most important in Feng Shui. Always harmonize the Untimely Five Star, whether it is in the original chart or in annual or monthly cycles.

The placement of Water is a critical aspect of Feng Shui, great care is necessary and special care and knowledge is required for all Water placements. When in doubt, do not use Water and consult a professional trained in the art of Water Dragon Placement Formulas.

The following is a suggested method for harmonizing a Flying Stars Feng Shui condition:

1. Proper Exterior Forms of Water and Mountain are most potent
2. Interior Forms of Water and Mountain
3. Interior Five Element Shapes
4. Five Element remedies

The influence of steps 1-4 on the Flying Stars Feng Shui must be evaluated, the key is to perceive the integrated nature of these influences.

Feng Shui Examples

Example 1

Date of consultation: February 2, 2000
House constructed in 1980: Cycle Six
Mountain-Sitting position: North West Three
Water-Facing Position: South East Three

Facing

SE 8 4 5 Living Room	S 3 9 1 Living Room	SW 1 2 3 Living Room
E 9 3 4 Kitchen	<u>7</u> 5 <u>6</u> Living Room	W 5 7 8 Bedroom
NE 4 8 9 Entrance	N 2 1 2 Bathroom	NW <u>6 6</u> 7 Hallway

Sitting

- This structure is "locked" for Health and Fertility from 1984-2003. Locked is reflected by the Seven Star located in the sitting position in the center palace. Select the best remedy for a locked condition.

- This is a Double Sitting Structure, it is favorable for Health and Fertility and unfavorable for Wealth, this is reflected by the two Six Stars in the North West palace. This chart is most vibrant during cycle 6, years 1964-1983, during cycle 7 the qualities of this Double Sitting special chart no longer exist.

- Because the house was built in the previous 20-Year Cycle, the Double Sitting opportunity is not in its most vibrant period, consider forms to the Primary Fortune Palace. Water in the East and Mountain in the West environment is proper in cycle 7.

- The Entrance is 4, 8. Four Star is Wood and Controls Eight Star Earth. Eight Star is Timely and good for fame and fortune, Four Star is usable. Fame, fortune and career is dominated and repressed according to the Five-Elements, this combination may create emotional difficulties, isolation and obstacles for children. Add Fire to break the domination allowing fame, fortune and prosperity to manifest, while eliminating unfavorable influences resulting from Wood controlling Earth. The Timely Eight Star can be activated with water interior forms in this palace or a Water form outside the palace next to this palace.

- The bedroom is 5,7. Seven is the Timely Star and is excellent for Wealth. This combination may create mouth problems and food poisoning if no Five-Element remedy is introduced, the negative Five Star must be reduced and not activated. Add Metal in the bedroom, additionally, the unfavorable Earth Star is the parent of Timely Metal 7 Star and strengthens this favorable Star.

It is critical not to activate the unfavorable Five Star with interior or exterior forms.

It is most auspicious to have a Water form, either in the environment or interior in this palace during the Timely years of 1984-2003 to activate the Seven Star.

- South East is 8, 4. See the *entrance evaluation* above for the meaning of each Star and the 4, 8 combination. Add Fire to break the domination of Four Wood Star on Eight Earth Star, Eight Star is Timely and Four Star is usable.

  A Mountain form is auspicious for the Timely Eight Star.

  This is the facing palace, along with the sitting and center palaces, they are the most influential on the entire building. The proper forms and placement are critical to optimize this Flying Stars Feng Shui Chart.

- In the South, Three Wood Star is Untimely and generates gossip, arguments and lawsuits and Nine Fire Star is Future Timely and favorable. This combination generates wealth and fame, Add Fire to reduce the unfavorable Three Wood Star and its negative influences.

  Water forms activate the Future Distant Timely Nine Star.

- In the South West, unfavorable Two Earth Star controls the usable One Water Star, Water relates to the Kidneys and this 1,2 Star combination can cause health and fertility problems, especially Kidney, Blood and Ear problems as well as spousal difficulty, female domination and abdominal pain. Add Metal to break the domination and reduce the unfavorable Two Earth Star and strengthen Water 1 Star.

  It is critical not to activate the unfavorable Two Star.

Example 2

Date of consultation: June 1, 1997
Year of Construction: 1987
Water - Facing Direction: South East One
Mountain - Sitting Direction: North West One

The following is the standard chart presentation for this apartment

SE 9 <u>7</u> 6	S 4 2 2 Living Room	SW 1 9 4 Living Room
E 1 8 5 Kitchen	8 6 <u>7</u> Living Room	W 6 4 9 Bedroom
NE 5 3 1 Entrance	N 3 1 3 Bathroom	NW <u>7</u> 5 8 Hallway

Sitting

The following chart is the actual floor plan

Sitting Direction

West	North West	North
6 4 9 Bedroom	<u>7</u> 5 8 Hallway	3 1 3 Bathroom
South West 2 9 4 Living Room	8 6 <u>7</u> Dinning Room	North East 5 3 1 Kitchen
South 4 2 2 Living Room	South East 9 <u>7</u> 6 Office Hallway	East 1 8 5 Entrance

Facing Direction

- This is a Wang Shang Wang Sui structure and can be most favorable for Health and Wealth. This apartment has a street in front of the facing direction, which is virtual Water and a building behind the structure representing virtual Mountain, the Forms compliment this structure promoting favorable health, relationships and wealth.

- The entrance has Timely Earth Star Eight and controls Water Star One creating Kidney, Blood and Ear problems, as well as fertility and health difficulties. This combination creates Wealth and difficulties with partners, the remedy is to add Metal as it reduces Earth, breaking the control and strengthening Water. Earth Star Eight, being Timely is very fortunate for Fame, Name and Fortune.

A Water form in this area is most auspicious for cycle 7 and 8 to activate this Timely Star.

- The bedroom contains Metal Star Six and Wood Star Four, both are safe and usable; Star Six controls Star Four creating difficulties with wealth, as well as health problems that include the thigh and buttock, additionally, there is the tendency to catch colds and the flu. The combination creates the possibility for a miscarriage. The correction is to add Water to this palace, it will reduce Metal, breaking the control and strengthening the Wood Star.
- The office contains Timely Star Metal Seven in the Water position and is very fortunate for Wealth, Fire Star Nine is Distant Timely and fortunate, this combination creates the possibility for a fire accident and flirtation. Fire controls Metal and Earth must be added to break the domination and support Metal or wealth will be unfortunate. The good fortune of Seven Star may not manifest until Earth is placed in this palace.

It is most auspicious to have a Water form in the exterior and/or interior forms.

- Metal should be placed in the North West to reduce Star Five, the best remedy is some type of metal that makes a sound.

- Water can be placed in the South West area, outside the structure to activate the Second Fortune palace, generating wealth.
- The center palace contains Star Eight in the Mountain position, this apartment will go into Prison in the year 2004, and a complete evaluation and proper remedies must be made at that time.

Four Pillars of Destiny

A Professional Course in Zi Ping Chinese Astrology

Introduction

Chinese Astrology in one of the most fascinating Branches of the Taoist Arts, it is an ancient art and metaphysical science revealing a blueprint of one's life, it reflects Heaven's Influence. There are many styles of Chinese Astrology, most popular is Four Pillars of Destiny. Li Xu Zhong popularized Four Pillars in the Tang Dynasty and emphasized the Year Branch/Chinese Zodiac Animal as the centerpiece of this style of Chinese Astrology. In the Song Dynasty Xu Zi Ping radically changed the applications of the Four Pillars. One major change was a shift from the year branch to the day stem representing a person, this method is practiced today and is referred as Zi Ping or Four Pillars of Destiny and is a highly accurate divination system for predicting fortune, luck, personality, health, romance, marriage, wealth and family relations.

The common usage of Chinese Astrology in the western community has been evaluating attributes of the Chinese Zodiac animals, this limited analysis captures the birth year aspect of a person's life but does not include the Hour, Day, Month or future cycles of time. In Zi Ping astrology, all cycles of time are evaluated to obtain a complete picture of a person and his or her life path. Calculating a birth chart or "Four Pillars" is the initial step in performing a Four Pillars of Destiny analysis, this information is obtained from the ancient 10,000-Year Chinese Calendar, which includes the influence of each Hour, Day, Month and Year. Because the complete Chinese calendar has been largely inaccessible in the West, the deepest aspects of Chinese Astrology have rarely been revealed. A "Chinese Astrology Calendar" consists of four major parts: Stems, Branches, Months and Years, because this information can be difficult to obtain and understand I have developed an English translation of the Chinese Calendar, "Chinese Astrology Calendar Made Easy ©". This calendar is user-friendly, allowing easy access to the deepest levels of Zi Ping Astrology, in a short period of time you will be able to construct a Four Pillars birth chart in less than 60 seconds, creating the key to unlock the door to the professional level of Chinese Astrology.

Energy Cycles

Stems and Branches

Four Pillars of Destiny is a marvelous illustration of our relationship to nature and is a systematic method of calculating its influences. Applications of Yin-Yang, Five-Elements and cycles of time provide the vehicle for calculating a birth chart that reflects the natal or constitutional condition. This birth chart is based on the influences of time, particularly Hours, Days, Months and Years. Cycles of time are also categorized into the Five-Elements: Water, Wood, Fire, Earth and Metal and each element contains a Yin and Yang aspect, for example, the 10-Heavenly Branches are Yang Wood, Yin Wood, Yang Fire, Yin Fire, Yang Earth, Yin Earth, Yang Metal, Yin Metal, Yang Water, Yin Water and the 12-Earthly Branches include the Five-Elements with their Yin-Yang quality totaling 10-Branches, they also have an additional Earth branch which contains a Yin and Yang aspect producing 12-Branches. Earth is a transformer of one element or season into another, this is why there are two extra Earth elements, one Yin and one Yang, (this will be explained in the next few pages). The 12-Branches are Yang Wood, Yin Wood, Yang Earth, Yang Fire, Yin Fire, Yin Earth, Yang Metal, Yin Metal, Yang Earth, Yin Water Yang Water, Yin Earth; Branches are also referred to by their Chinese Zodiac Animal name. The following two tables list the 10-Heavenly Stems and 12-Earthly Branches.

Heavenly Stems

Tian Yuan

Stem	Element	Image
Jia	Yang Wood	Growing
Yi	Yin Wood	Growth extending beyond the peak
Bing	Yang Fire	Intense
Ding	Yin Fire	Fire extends beyond the peak
Wu	Yang Earth	Qi transforms
Ji	Yin Earth	Qi transforms
Geng	Yang Metal	Sharp
Xin	Yin Metal	Refined/useful
Ren	Yang Water	Strong and flowing
Gui	Yin Water	Moisture

Yang Stems are strong

Yin Stems are slender

Earthly Branches

Di Yuan

Branch	Animal	Outside Element	Main and Hidden Elements-Internal Method
Zi	Rat	Yang Water	**Yin Water** Gui
Chou	Ox	Yin Earth	**Yin Earth**, Yin Water, Yin Metal Ji Gui Xin
Yin	Tiger	Yang Wood	**Yang Wood**, Yang Fire, Yang Earth Jia Bing Wu
Mao	Rabbit	Yin Wood	**Yin Wood** Yi
Chen	Dragon	Yang Earth	**Yang Earth**, Yin Wood, Win Water Wu Yi Gui
Si	Snake	Yin Fire	**Yang Fire**, Yang Earth, Yang Metal Bing Wu Geng
Wu	Horse	Yang Fire	**Yin Fire**, Yin Earth Ding Ji
Wei	Sheep	Yin Earth	**Yin Earth**, Yin Fire, Yin Wood Ji Ding Yi
Shen	Monkey	Yang Metal	**Yang Metal**, Yang Earth, Yang Water Geng Ren Wu
You	Cock	Yin Metal	**Yin Metal** Xin
Xu	Dog	Yang Earth	**Yang Earth**, Yin Metal, Yin Fire Wu Xin Ding
Hai	Pig	Yin Water	**Yang Water**, Yang Wood Ren Jia

Stems represent Qi existing in Heaven and Branches represent Qi in Earth.

Stems and Branches represent an energy flow with each Hour, Day, Month and Year comprising one combination of a Stem and Branch or a binomial. Binomials are organized in a cycle of 60, which includes every combination of Stems and Branches. Six cycles of 10-Stems and five cycles of 12-Branches equals one cycle of sixty; Hours, Days, Months and Years contain those Stem and Branch energy combinations. The following table is the 60-Binomial Cycle, notice binomial one includes Yang Wood, number two has Yin Wood and the Five-Elements continue until Binomial 10. Yang Wood reappears again at 11, 21, 31, 41 and 51. The 10-Stems continue for six cycles, completing a cycle of 60. The Branch Rat begins at number 1 and the 12-Animals or Branches continue until they repeat again with the Rat, at 13, 25, 37 and 49.

Stem and Branch Cycle of 60

For Hours, Days, Months and Years

Number	1	2	3	4	5	6
Stem Branch	Yang Wood Rat	Yin Wood Ox	Yang Fire Tiger	Yin Fire Rabbit	Yang Earth Dragon	Yin Earth Snake
Number	7	8	9	10	11	12
Stem Branch	Yang Metal Horse	Yin Metal Sheep	Yang Water Monkey	Yin Water Cock	Yang Wood Dog	Yin Wood Pig
Number	13	14	15	16	17	18
Stem Branch	Yang Fire Rat	Yin Fire Ox	Yang Earth Tiger	Yin Earth Rabbit	Yang Metal Dragon	Yin Metal Snake
Number	19	20	21	22	23	24
Stem Branch	Yang Water Horse	Yin Water Sheep	Yang Wood Monkey	Yin Wood Cock	Yang Fire Dog	Yin Fire Pig
Number	25	26	27	28	29	30
Stem Branch	Yang Earth Rat	Yin Earth Ox	Yang Metal Tiger	Yin Metal Rabbit	Yang Water Dragon	Yin Water Snake
Number	31	32	33	34	35	36
Stem Branch	Yang Wood Horse	Yin Wood Sheep	Yang Fire Monkey	Yin Fire Cock	Yang Earth Dog	Yin Earth Pig
Number	37	38	39	40	41	42
Stem Branch	Yang Metal Rat	Yin Metal Ox	Yang Water Tiger	Yin Water Rabbit	Yang Wood Dragon	Yin Wood Snake
Number	43	44	45	46	47	48
Stem Branch	Yang Fire Horse	Yin Fire Sheep	Yang Earth Monkey	Yin Earth Cock	Yang Metal Dog	Yin Metal Pig
Number	49	50	51	52	53	54
Stem Branch	Yang Water Rat	Yin Water Ox	Yang Wood Tiger	Yin Wood Rabbit	Yang Fire Dragon	Yin Fire Snake
Number	55	56	57	58	59	60
Stem Branch	Yang Earth Horse	Yin Earth Sheep	Yang Metal Monkey	Yin Metal Cock	Yang Water Dog	Yin Water Pig

Branch	Pig	Rat	Ox	Tiger	Rabbit	Dragon	Snake	Horse	Sheep	Monkey	Cock	Dog
Main Element	Yang Water	Yin Water	Yin Earth	Yang Wood	Yin Wood	Yang Earth	Yang Fire	Yin Fire	Yin Earth	Yang Metal	Yin Metal	Yang Earth

The box above reflects the main element for each of the Branches or animals, they reflect the inner-method for determining Branch-Animal polarity.

Heavenly Stems are in the top row and represent Heavenly or Yang influences, they are always named as a Five-Element, for example, Yang Wood, Yin Wood, Yang Fire or Yin Fire. The lower row contains Earthly Branches or Chinese Zodiac Animals and they can be named as a Five-Element or as an Animal. I recommend using the Animal name because it helps differentiate Branches from Stems, and Branches from Branches, especially since there are four Earthly Branches. Either system can be utilized. The 60-Binomials include every possible energy combination for each Hour, Day, Month and Year has a Binomial.

The diagram below shows the Four Pillars chart and is the foundation for a Four Pillars analysis. Stems and Branches are found in the Chinese Calendar and placed in the Hour, Day, Month and Year Pillars or Palaces.

Four Pillars

Hour	Day	Month	Year
Stem	Stem	Stem	Stem
Branch Animal	Branch Animal	Branch Animal	Branch Animal

Earthly Branches
Chinese Zodiac Animals

The diagram below illustrates the 12-Terrestrial or Earthly Branches and their corresponding main element, Chinese zodiac Animal, geographical location and position, this diagram assists in understanding many of the interactions of two or more Branches. Branches or Animals in the same geographical area have an affinity for each other, they share the same element and therefore support or reinforce each other, additionally a Trinity/Harmonic or Element Frame relationship exists between each fourth Animal, for example, Cock, Ox and Snake are four places apart from each other and therefore are compatible, see the diagram below. This dynamic is very important and is explained in the chapter on Branch combinations. The cardinal or middle positions also have a special relationship with their opposite cardinal position, the Cock/Rabbit and Rat/Horse oppose each other creating a spark, causing excitement, pressure or stress. Branches exert favorable or unfavorable influences on other Stems and Branches.

	South **Red** Snake Horse Sheep - Fire + Fire - Earth 6 7 8 **Summer**	
East **Green** Dragon + Earth 5 Rabbit - Wood 4 Tiger + Wood 3 **Spring**		**West** **Gold-Silver** Monkey + Metal 9 Cock - Metal 10 Dog + Earth 11 **Fall**
	North **Black-Blue** Ox Rat Pig - Earth + Water - Water 2 1 12 **Winter**	

Branch–Animal Relationships

The following table lists the major relationships of Branches including their corresponding name, main element, season, time of day and direction. Located under the main element is the Chinese name for the Branch. This information is foundation knowledge in Zi Ping Astrology.

Branch Correspondences

Branch English Pin Yin	Main Element *	Season	Time of Day	Direction
Pig Hai	Yang Water	Winter	9pm-11pm	North
Rat Zi	Yin Water	Winter	11pm-1am	North
Ox Chou	Yin Earth	Winter	1am-3am	North
Tiger Yin	Yang Wood	Spring	3am-5am	East
Rabbit Mao	Yin Wood	Spring	5am-7am	East
Dragon Chen	Yang Earth	Spring	7am-9am	East
Snake Si	Yang Fire	Summer	9am-11am	South
Horse Wu	Yin Fire	Summer	11am-1pm	South
Sheep Wei	Yin Earth	Summer	1pm-3pm	South
Monkey Shen	Yang Metal	Fall	3pm-5pm	West
Cock Yu	Yin Metal	Fall	5pm-7pm	West
Dog Xu	Yang Earth	Fall	7pm-9pm	West

* Reflects the Internal Method.

Branch Gender

Determining Branch gender or polarity is identifying whether a Branch is Yin or Yang and is an integral aspect in Zi Ping Chinese Astrology. There are two major methods of determining the gender of each Animal, the first is the Outer method and the Second is the Internal Method. The Outer Method assists when calculating 10-Year Luck Cycle, all other calculations use the Internal Method.

The gender is the same for eight Branches whether the Internal or Outer Method is applied, the following four Branches change their gender: Pig, Rat, Snake and Horse. The table below lists the Branches that change gender or polarity.

Branch-Animal	Internal Method	Outer Method
Pig	Yang Water	Yin Water
Rat	Yin Water	Yang Water
Snake	Yang Fire	Yin Fire
Horse	Yin Fire	Yang Fire

Outer Method

In the diagram below the main element depicts the Outer method for calculating the Yin-Yang aspect of each Animal or Branch, the concept of numbers and Yin-Yang explains this method. For example, the Rat is 1, Ox-2, Tiger-3, Rabbit-4, Dragon-5, Snake-6, Horse-7, Sheep-8, Monkey-9, Cock-10, Dog-11 and Pig 12. Odd numbers are Yang and even numbers are Yin.

The Outer Method is used to calculate 10-Year Life Cycles, the + sign means Yang and the–sign means Yin, if a person was born in a Cock year they are *Yin* Metal (Cock). If the person is a woman she is a *Yin Female*, if a man a *Yin male*.

Outer Method

	South Red Snake Horse Sheep - Fire + Fire - Earth 6 7 8 **Summer**	
East Green Dragon + Earth 5 Rabbit - Wood 4 Tiger + Wood 3 **Spring**		**West** Gold-Silver Monkey + Metal 9 Cock - Metal 10 Dog + Earth 11 **Fall**
	North Black-Blue Ox Rat Pig - Earth + Water - Water 2 1 12 **Winter**	

Internal Method

In most applications of Four Pillars the internal method is used. Each of the Branches, except the four Earths (Ox, Dragon, Sheep and Dog) are Yin-Yang pairs and transformers from one season to another and are not considered "pure" aspects of their cardinal position, they are mixtures of numerous elements and unifying forces, for each geographical location there is a pair of "pure" Branches, the first animal is Yang and the second is Yin. Odd numbers are Yang and even numbers are Yin, for example, North contains Pig-Rat, East contains Tiger-Rabbit, South contains Snake-Horse and West contains Monkey-Cock, Pig, Tiger, Snake and Monkey are Yang and the Rat, Rabbit, Horse and Cock are Yin; this formula is used in all calculations *except* the Yin-Yang gender of the Birth Year when calculating 10-Year Life Cycles, *the polarity of the birth year Branch in the Four Pillars is based on the Inner method, as are all Branches.*

Internal Method

	South **Red** Snake Horse Sheep + Fire - Fire - Earth 5 6 **Summer**	
East **Green** Dragon + Earth Rabbit - Wood 4 Tiger + Wood 3 **Spring**		**West** **Gold-Silver** Monkey + Metal 7 Cock - Metal 8 Dog + Earth **Fall**
	North **Black-Blue** Ox Rat Pig - Earth - Water + Water 2 1 **Winter**	

Hidden Elements

Nine of the 12-Branches or Animals contain "Hidden Elements" or "Ren Yuan", they are Qi contained inside a Branch. The Hidden Elements influence each person and must be thoroughly evaluated. The following table shows the Hidden Elements contained in each Animal or Branch and the bottom of each page in the "Chinese Calendar Made Easy" contains a box showing the Main and Hidden elements for each Animal. These elements represent the Internal Method and are used for all calculations *except* the polarity of the Year Branch of birth used to calculate 10-Year Life Cycles.

Branches and Hidden Elements

Ren Yuan

Animal	Pin Yin	Main Element	Direction	Hidden Element	Element Frame
Pig	Hai	Yang Water	North	Yang Wood	Wood Frame
Rat	Zi	Yin Water	North		Water Frame
Ox	Chou	Yin Earth	North	Yin Water, Yin Metal	Metal Frame
Tiger	Yin	Yang Wood	East	Yang Fire, Yang Earth	Fire Frame
Rabbit	Mao	Yin Wood	East		Wood Frame
Dragon	Chen	Yang Earth	East	Yin Wood, Yin Water	Water Frame
Snake	Si	Yang Fire	South	Yang Earth, Yang Metal	Metal Frame
Horse	Wu	Yin Fire	South	Yin Earth	Fire Frame
Sheep	Wei	Yin Earth	South	Yin Fire, Yin Wood	Wood Frame
Monkey	Sheen	Yang Metal	West	Yang Earth, Yang Water	Water Frame
Cock	You	Yin Metal	West		Metal Frame
Dog	Xu	Yang Earth	West	Yin Metal, Yin Fire	Fire Frame

Branches and their Hidden Elements

	Snake Yang Fire Yang Earth, Yang Metal	**Horse** Yin Fire Yin Earth	**Sheep** Yin Earth Yin Fire, Yin Wood	
Dragon Yang Earth Yin Wood, Yin Water				**Monkey** Yang Metal Yang Water, Yang Earth
Rabbit Yin Wood				**Cock** Yin Metal
Tiger Yang Wood Yang Fire, Yang Earth				**Dog** Yang Earth Yin Metal, Yin Fire
	Ox Yin Earth Yin Water, Yin Metal	**Rat** Yin Water	**Pig** Yang Water Yang Wood	

The Main element is the first element listed and the hidden element is the second and/or third element.

The Element Frames

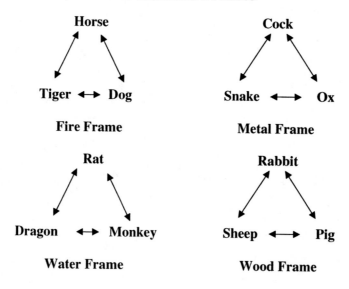

Branch–Animal Relationships

The 12-Branches contain a variety of information, for example, zodiac animal name, corresponding main element, season, time of day and direction. This information is used to calculate specific elemental influences that affect a person and will be explained in detail throughout the book. Please note Ox, Dragon, Sheep and Dog, the four earths have a wet and dry quality, this is very important when determining the influence of these Branches.

Animal	Main Element *	Season	Time of Day	Direction
Pig Hai	Yang Water	Winter	9pm-11pm	North
Rat Zi	Yin Water	Winter	11pm-1am	North
Ox Chou	Yin Earth **This is winter and is called "Wet Earth"**	Winter	1am-3am	North
Tiger Yin	Yang Wood	Spring	3am-5am	East
Rabbit Mao	Yin Wood	Spring	5am-7am	East
Dragon Chen	Yang Earth **This is Winter-Spring and is called "Wet Earth"**	Spring	7am-9am	East
Snake Si	Yang Fire	Summer	9am-11am	South
Horse Wu	Yin Fire	Summer	11am-1pm	South
Sheep Wei	Yin Earth **This is Summer and is called "Dry Earth"**	Summer	1pm-3pm	South
Monkey Shen	Yang Metal	Fall	3pm-5pm	West
Cock You	Yin Metal	Fall	5pm-7pm	West
Dog Xu	Yang Earth **This is Summer and is called "Dry Earth"**	Fall	7pm-9pm	West

* Reflects the Internal Method

Chinese Calendar

The Chinese Calendar is also called the Natural Energy Calendar or the 10,000-Year Calendar. According to legend it began 2698 B.C., the first day of the first year of the reign of Huang Di, the Yellow Emperor. This calendar provides the foundation for the Four Pillars. Legend also states a brilliant man, Da Nao invented a method of counting using a cycle of 60, 10-Stems and 12-Branches, ten cycles of Stems and five cycles of Branches create the 60-Binomial Cycle or Jia-Zi. The Chinese Calendar Made Easy ©, located in the appendix, incorporates all the necessary elements to calculate an authentic Four Pillars chart, it is used to find the Stem and Branch for any Hour, Day, Month or Year.

The following are six integral components necessary to find the correct birth information and Four Pillars.

Chinese Age

When counting in Chinese Astrology the age of a person at birth is one year old, when 12 years old in the western calendar the person is 13 years old in Four Pillars, always add one to the western birth age. This is important for forecasting the timing of events. Cycles associated with age begin on the birthday, not the beginning of the New Year.

Daylight Savings Time

Daylight savings time must be adjusted to determine an accurate Four Pillars chart. If daylight savings time was in effect subtract one hour from the time of birth.

Place of Birth

Use the time of birth in the city in which you were born, do not convert to China time or any other time zone.

Solar Calendar

The Chinese Calendar Made Easy © is based upon the Solar calendar, not the Lunar calendar.

Day

A new day begins after midnight. The Zi or Rat hour pillar is based on 11:00pm-1:00am, a new day does not begin after 11:00pm, only after midnight.

Hour

The Hour of birth is based on the standard double Chinese hours, for example, the Zi hour includes any time from 11:00pm-1:00am.

The Chinese Calendar contains 24-seasonal sections, which are segmented by 30-day periods, the first section is the first day of the Chinese Month and the second is the middle of the month or the 15th day. The first day of the month is called "Jie" and the second section is called "Qi", these sections can be viewed as the beginning and peak periods of a 30-day cycle. The solar year begins on "Li Chun" or the "Beginning of Spring" and is February 4 or 5, it is when the sun enters 15-degrees Aquarius. It is also the beginning of the month of the Tiger "Yin Yue" and the Big Dipper points to the East at this point.

The following is a table outlining these 24-Seasonal Points and shows each Chinese Zodiac Animal and their related monthly correspondences.

Chinese Seasonal Calendar

Date	Jie	Qi	Branch	Direction
Feb 4	Li Chun Beginning of Spring		Tiger Yin	East
Feb 19		Yu Shui Rain Water		
March 6	Jing Zhu Insects Awaken		Rabbit Mao	East
March 21		Chun Fen Spring Equinox		
April 5	Qing Ming Clear and Bright		Dragon Chen	East
April 20		Gu Yu Clear and Bright		
May 6	Li Xai Beginning of Summer		Snake Si	South
May 21		Xiao Man Small Surplus		
June 6	Mang Zhong Planting of Crops		Horse Wu	South
June 21		Xia Shu Summer Solstice		
July 7	Xiao Shu Lesser Heat		Sheep Wei	South
July 23		Da Shu Greater Heat		

August 7	Li Qiu Beginning of Autumn		Monkey Shen	West
August 23		Chu Shu Storage Heat		
September 7	Bai Lu White Dew		Cock Yu	West
September 23		Qiu Fen Autumn Equinox		
October 8	Han Lu Cold Dew		Dog Shu	West
October 23		Shuang Jiang Frost Falls		
November 7	Li Dong Beginning of Winter		Pig Hai	North
November 22		Xiao Han Lesser Snow		
December 7	Da Xue Greater Snow		Rat Zi	North
December 22		Dong Zhi Winter Solstice		
January 5	Xiao Han Lesser Cold		Ox Chou	North
January 20		Da Han Greater Cold		

The following example illustrates how to use the "Chinese Calendar Made Easy ©".
1931

| Column 1 | Column 2 | | Column 3 | | Columns 4 | 5 | 6 |
| | Month | | Year | | | | |
Find Your Day Here	Stem	Branch	Stem	Branch	Day	Day	Time
January 6 – February 5	Yin Earth	Ox	Yang Metal	Horse	Jan	52	14:56
February 5 - March 7	Yang Metal	Tiger	Yin Metal	Sheep	Feb	23	2: 41
March 7 - April 6	Yin Metal	Rabbit	Yin Metal	Sheep	March	51	21: 03
April 6 - May 7	Yang Water	Dragon	Yin Metal	Sheep	April	22	2: 21
May 7 – June 7	Yin Water	Snake	Yin Metal	Sheep	May	52	20: 10
June 7 - July 8	Yang Wood	Horse	Yin Metal	Sheep	June	23	: 42
July 8 - August 8	Yin Wood	Sheep	Yin Metal	Sheep	July	53	11: 06
August 8 - September 9	Yang Fire	Monkey	Yin Metal	Sheep	Aug	24	20: 45
September 9 – October 9	Yin Fire	Cock	Yin Metal	Sheep	Sept	55	23: 18
October 9 - November 8	Yang Earth	Dog	Yin Metal	Sheep	Oct	25	14: 27
November 8 - December 8	Yin Earth	Pig	Yin Metal	Sheep	Nov	56	17: 10
December 8 – January 6	Yang Metal	Rat	Yin Metal	Sheep	Dec	26	9: 41

Branch	Pig	Rat	Ox	Tiger	Rabbit	Dragon	Snake	Horse	Sheep	Monkey	Cock	Dog
Main Element	Yang Water	Yin Water	Yin Earth	Yang Wood	Yin Wood	Yang Earth	Yang Fire	Yin Fire	Yin Earth	Yang Metal	Yin Metal	Yang Earth
Hidden Elements	Yang Wood		Yin Water	Yang Fire		Yin Wood	Yang Earth	Yin Earth	Yin Fire	Yang Earth		Yin Metal
			Yin Metal	Yang Earth		Yin Water	Yang Metal		Yin Wood	Yang Water		Yin Fire

- Column 1 contains solar days, locate the day in question here
- Column 2 is the Stem and Branch for the Month in question and is the Month Binomial
- Column 3 is the Year Stem and Branch and is the Year Binomial
- Column 4 and 5 are labeled "Day, these columns are used to find the Day Binomial, column four lists the twelve months, locate the month in question in column 4 and then move to column 5, *column 5 has a special number which is used to assist in finding the Day Binomial.* Add the day in question to this number creating a binomial number, locate this Binomial number in following table of the 60-Stem and Branch binomials.

Stem and Branch Cycle of 60

For Hours, Days, Months and Years

Number	1	2	3	4	5	6
Stem Branch	Yang Wood Rat	Yin Wood Ox	Yang Fire Tiger	Yin Fire Rabbit	Yang Earth Dragon	Yin Earth Snake
Number	7	8	9	10	11	12
Stem Branch	Yang Metal Horse	Yin Metal Sheep	Yang Water Monkey	Yin Water Cock	Yang Wood Dog	Yin Wood Pig
Number	13	14	15	16	17	18
Stem Branch	Yang Fire Rat	Yin Fire Ox	Yang Earth Tiger	Yin Earth Rabbit	Yang Metal Dragon	Yin Metal Snake
Number	19	20	21	22	23	24
Stem Branch	Yang Water Horse	Yin Water Sheep	Yang Wood Monkey	Yin Wood Cock	Yang Fire Dog	Yin Fire Pig
Number	25	26	27	28	29	30
Stem Branch	Yang Earth Rat	Yin Earth Ox	Yang Metal Tiger	Yin Metal Rabbit	Yang Water Dragon	Yin Water Snake
Number	31	32	33	34	35	36
Stem Branch	Yang Wood Horse	Yin Wood Sheep	Yang Fire Monkey	Yin Fire Cock	Yang Earth Dog	Yin Earth Pig
Number	37	38	39	40	41	42
Stem Branch	Yang Metal Rat	Yin Metal Ox	Yang Water Tiger	Yin Water Rabbit	Yang Wood Dragon	Yin Wood Snake
Number	43	44	45	46	47	48
Stem Branch	Yang Fire Horse	Yin Fire Sheep	Yang Earth Monkey	Yin Earth Cock	Yang Metal Dog	Yin Metal Pig
Number	49	50	51	52	53	54
Stem Branch	Yang Water Rat	Yin Water Ox	Yang Wood Tiger	Yin Wood Rabbit	Yang Fire Dragon	Yin Fire Snake
Number	55	56	57	58	59	60
Stem Branch	Yang Earth Horse	Yin Earth Sheep	Yang Metal Monkey	Yin Metal Cock	Yang Water Dog	Yin Water Pig

Branch	Pig	Rat	Ox	Tiger	Rabbit	Dragon	Snake	Horse	Sheep	Monkey	Cock	Dog
Main Element	Yang Water	Yin Water	Yin Earth	Yang Wood	Yin Wood	Yang Earth	Yang Fire	Yin Fire	Yin Earth	Yang Metal	Yin Metal	Yang Earth

* This table above reflects the inner-method.

Example 1 for determining the Day Stem

February 10, 1931

Refer to column 4 and locate February, move to column 5, which contains the special number 23, add 23 to 10 (February 10), which totals 33. "33" is the Binomial for your Day Stem and Branch. Find number 33 in the Stem and Branch cycle of 60 table.

The Day Binomial is Yang Fire/ Monkey

	Hour	Day	Month	Year
Stem		Yang Fire		
Branch		Monkey		

Example 2

September 20, 1931

The Special Day number is 55, add 20 (September 20) to 55 totaling 75. Subtract 60 from 75 to obtain binomial 15 or Yang Earth/Tiger.

* *

The binomial chart has 60 segments, if the total of the day in question and Special Day number for the month is greater than 60 subtract 60 from the total, in this case subtract 60 from 75 obtaining 15, locate 15 in the Stem and Branch Table.

The binomial must be 1-60, if the combination is greater than 60 subtract 60 from the total, the remainder is the binomial.

* *

	Hour	Day	Month	Year
Stem		Yang Earth		
Branch		Tiger		

- Column 6 is the Month Divider time, if your day is on the first day of the solar month this is the exact time the month changes and this is used for the Month Stem and Branch only.

The Four Pillars

Four Pillars consist of Stems and Branches of the Hour, Day, Month and Year of birth, they comprise the constitutional birth chart. The "Chinese Calendar Made Easy ©" contains the information to construct the Four Pillars. The following example illustrates how to calculate the Four Pillars, use the information below or refer to year 1999 in the Appendix.

A Male born January 28, 1999 at 5:30 am

1999

Find your Day Here	Stem	Branch	Stem	Branch	Day	Day	Time
January 6 – February 4	Yin Wood	Ox	Yang Earth	Tiger	Jan	49	3 : 00
February 4 - March 6	Yang Fire	Tiger	Yin Earth	Rabbit	Feb	20	14 : 42
March 6 - April 5	Yin Fire	Rabbit	Yin Earth	Rabbit	March	48	8 : 52
April 5 - May 6	Yang Earth	Dragon	Yin Earth	Rabbit	April	19	13 : 55
May 6 – June 6	Yin Earth	Snake	Yin Earth	Rabbit	May	49	7 : 29
June 6 - July 7	Yang Metal	Horse	Yin Earth	Rabbit	June	20	11 : 51
July 7 - August 8	Yin Metal	Sheep	Yin Earth	Rabbit	July	50	22 : 14
August 8 - September 8	Yang Water	Monkey	Yin Earth	Rabbit	Aug	21	7 : 57
September 8 – October 9	Yin Water	Cock	Yin Earth	Rabbit	Sept	52	10 : 41
October 9 - November 7	Yang Wood	Dog	Yin Earth	Rabbit	Oct	22	2 : 05
November 7 - December 7	Yin Wood	Pig	Yin Earth	Rabbit	Nov	53	5 : 01
December 7 – January 6	Yang Fire	Rat	Yin Earth	Rabbit	Dec	23	21 : 14

1. Locate the solar day in column 1

   Move directly to the right and take note of the Month Stem and Branch, in this example Column 2 or Yin Wood/Ox. Place this Binomial in the Four Pillar chart below.

	Hour	**Day**	**Month**	**Year**
Stem			Yin Wood	
Branch			Ox	

157

2. Move directly to the right and write down the Year Stem and Branch from Column 3: Yang Earth/Tiger, see Four Pillars below.

	Hour	Day	Month	Year
Stem			Yin Wood	Yang Earth
Branch			Ox	Tiger

3. Move to the right and locate the month in question, January (column 4) and continue to the right to the Day number, take note of the number in the Day Column, Column 5.

Add the day of birth of any day to this number, 49 plus 28 (January 28) = 77

77-60 = *17*,

17 is the Day Stem and Branch Binomial

As a reminder the number in this column assists in finding the Binomial for the Day of birth, there are 60 Binomials or combinations and if the total of the Birthday and the Column Day exceed 60, subtract 60 from the total. In this example the total is 77, subtract 60 resulting in Binomial 17.

In the Stem and Branch Cycle of 60-chart find Binomial 17, this is the Day Stem and Branch Binomial and is Yang Metal/Dragon. Place this binomial in the Four Pillars.

	Hour	Day	Month	Year
Stem		Yang Metal	Yin Wood	Yang Earth
Branch		Dragon	Ox	Tiger

4. Refer to the Hour Stem and Branch Chart below and locate the *Day Stem* in the top row, look directly below it to the Stem and Branch that corresponds to the time of birth.

The Day Stem is Yang Metal and at 5:30 am the binomial is Yin Earth, Rabbit. This is the Hour Stem and Branch. See below.

Hour Stem and Branch

Hour Stem and Branch Chart

Day Stem →	Yang Wood Yin Earth	Yang Metal Yin Wood	Yang Fire Yin Metal	Yang Water Yin Fire	Yang Earth Yin Water
11 pm-1 am	Yang Wood Rat	Yang Fire Rat	Yang Earth Rat	Yang Metal Rat	Yang Water Rat
1 am-3 am	Yin Wood Ox	Yin Fire Ox	Yin Earth Ox	Yin Metal Ox	Yin Water Ox
3 am-5 am	Yang Fire Tiger	Yang Earth Tiger	Yang Metal Tiger	Yang Water Tiger	Yang Wood Tiger
5 am-7 am	Yin Fire Rabbit	Yin Earth Rabbit	Yin Metal Rabbit	Yin Water Rabbit	Yin Wood Rabbit
7 am-9 am	Yang Earth Dragon	Yang Metal Dragon	Yang Water Dragon	Yang Wood Dragon	Yang Fire Dragon
9 am-11 am	Yin Earth Snake	Yin Metal Snake	Yin Water Snake	Yin Wood Snake	Yin Fire Snake
11 am-1 pm	Yang Metal Horse	Yang Water Horse	Yang Wood Horse	Yang Fire Horse	Yang Earth Horse
1 pm-3 pm	Yin Metal Sheep	Yin Water Sheep	Yin Wood Sheep	Yin Fire Sheep	Yin Earth Sheep
3 pm-5 pm	Yang Water Monkey	Yang Wood Monkey	Yang Fire Monkey	Yang Earth Monkey	Yang Metal Monkey
5 pm-7 pm	Yin Water Cock	Yin Wood Cock	Yin Fire Cock	Yin Earth Cock	Yin Metal Cock
7 pm- 9 pm	Yang Wood Dog	Yang Fire Dog	Yang Earth Dog	Yang Metal Dog	Yang Water Dog
9 pm-11 pm	Yin Wood Pig	Yin Fire Pig	Yin Earth Pig	Yin Metal Pig	Yin Water Pig

Four Pillars

	Hour	Day	Month	Year
Stem	Yin Earth	Yang Metal	Yin Wood	Yang Earth
Branch	Rabbit	Dragon	Ox	Tiger

Example

Find the Four Pillars for the following person and confirm your calculations. The following is a step-by-step process for calculating the Four Pillars.

Male born on June 30, 1957 at 6:30 am daylight savings time, adjust the time one hour backwards

1. Locate the Year in question in the Chinese Calendar Made Easy ©

2. Locate the day in question in column 1

3. Column 2 is the Month Stem and Branch

4. Column 3 is the Year Stem and Branch

5. Locate the month in question in Column 4 and then locate the Day number in column 5. Add the day in question to this number to obtain the Day Binomial. Refer to the Stem and Branch Cycle of 60 and locate the Binomial that is the Day Stem and Branch. Refer to the Hour Stem and Branch chart and find the Stem in he top row and move down until the time of birth, this is the Hour Stem and Branch.

1957

	Month		Year		
Find your Day Here	**Stem**	**Branch**	**Stem**	**Branch**	**Day**
January 5 – February 4	Yin Metal	Ox	Yang Fire	Monkey	4
February 4 - March 6	Yang Water	Tiger	Yin Fire	Cock	40
March 6 - April 5	Yin Water	Rabbit	Yin Fire	Cock	8
April 5 - May 6	Yang Wood	Dragon	Yin Fire	Cock	39
May 6 - June 6	Yin Wood	Snake	Yin Fire	Cock	9
June 6 - July 7	Yang Fire	Horse	Yin Fire	Cock	40
July 7 - August 8	Yin Fire	Sheep	Yin Fire	Cock	10
August 8 - September 8	Yang Earth	Monkey	Yin Fire	Cock	41
September 8 - October 8	Yin Earth	Cock	Yin Fire	Cock	12
October 8 - November 8	Yang Metal	Dog	Yin Fire	Cock	42
November 8 - December 7	Yin Metal	Pig	Yin Fire	Cock	13
December 7 - January 6	Yang Water	Rat	Yin Fire	Cock	43

Four Pillars

	Hour	Day	Month	Year
Stem	Yin Wood	Yin Water	Yang Fire	Yin Fire
Branch	Rabbit	Cock	Horse	Cock
Elements	Yin Wood	Yin Metal	Yin Fire Yin Earth	Yin Metal

Ten Year Luck Cycles

Ten Year Luck Cycles are Stem and Branch influences during 10-Year periods throughout one's lifetime and these cycles combine with the Four Pillars to create post-natal influences. When favorable cycles occur life is favorably influenced, conversely when unfavorable elements enter a new cycle life is unfavorably influenced. Ten-Year Luck Cycles represent nature's variable or dynamic influences.

Ten Year Luck Cycles are more influential than Day, Month or Yearly cycles. Evaluating conditions of the Four Pillars and influences of 10-Year Luck Cycles provide a complete picture of how nature influences a person's life; the diagram below illustrates this phenomenon.

Four Pillars   **10-Year Luck Cycles**

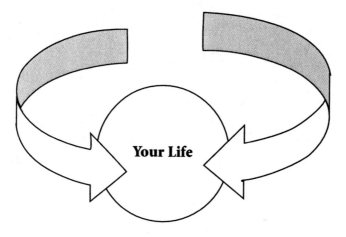

The combination of the Four Pillars and 10-Year Life Cycles reflect the changing aspect of nature and unites pre-natal and post-natal influences.

Calculating 10-Year Luck Cycles

1. Determine if the person is Male or Female

2. Identify the polarity of the Year of birth Branch and note whether the main Element is Yin or Yang, use the Outer Method. The following table lists the Elements for this calculation:

Branch polarity for calculating 10-Year Life Cycles

Branch	*Main Element
Pig	Yin Water
Rat	Yang Water
Ox	Yin Earth
Tiger	Yang Wood
Rabbit	Yin Wood
Dragon	Yang Earth
Snake	Yin Fire
Horse	Yang Fire
Sheep	Yin Earth
Monkey	Yang Metal
Cock	Yin Metal
Dog	Yang Earth

* The polarity is based on the Outer-Method.

3. The following rules are based on the birth year branch

Yin Females: Pig, Ox, Rabbit, Snake, Sheep and Cock count (move) forward in time

Yang Females: Rat, Tiger, Dragon, Horse, Monkey and Dog count (move) backward in time

Yang Males: Rat, Tiger, Dragon, Horse, Monkey and Dog count (move) forward in time

Yin Males: Pig, Ox, Rabbit, Snake, Sheep and Cock count (move) backward in time

4. Locate the birthday in column 1 of the Chinese Calendar Made Easy ©

- If the person is a Yin Female or Yang Male, move forward and count the number of days from the *Birthday* to the end of the solar month (column 1), this is moving forward in time. Use the birthday as the first day counted and the last solar day as a marker. *Do not count the last day.* When counting forward the last day is never counted.

5. If the person is a Yang Female or Yin Male move backward and count the number of days *from the birthday* to the first day of the solar month (column 1), this is backward in time. Use the birthday as the first day counted and *do count* the first day of the solar month. When counting backwards the first day of the month is always counted.

Example
March 15, 1940
1940 is Dragon/Yang Earth
The month dividers are March 6 - April 5

If this person is Female she is a Yang Dragon-Earth, Yang Females count backwards from March 15 to March 6, this is 10 days. We do count March 15, the Birthday and March 6 the first day in the solar month.

If this person is Male he is a Yang Dragon, Yang Males count forward from March 15 to April 5. Count the birthday but not April 5, this is 21 days.

***To assist in counting days refer to the "Counting Days to 10-Life Year Cycles". The first month is 31 days, 2nd is 30 days, 3rd is 30 days, 4th is 31 days, 5th is 30 and 6th is 28 days. Circle the birthday and the beginning or ending day of the month. Count from the day in question to the beginning or ending day. Be very attentive about the number of days in the month; for example, are there 28, 29, 30 or 31 days in the month.

Counting 10-Year Luck Cycles

1	2	3	4	5	6	7	8	9	10	11	12	13	14	15	16	17	18	19	20
21	22	23	24	25	26	27	28	29	30	31	1	2	3	4	5	6	7	8	9
10	11	12	13	14	15	16	17	18	19	20	21	22	23	24	25	26	27	28	29
30	1	2	3	4	5	6	7	8	9	10	11	12	13	14	15	16	17	18	19
20	21	22	23	24	25	26	27	28	29	30	1	2	3	4	5	6	7	8	9
10	11	12	13	14	15	16	17	18	19	20	21	22	23	24	25	26	27	28	29
30	31	1	2	3	4	5	6	7	8	9	10	11	12	13	14	15	16	17	18
19	20	21	22	23	24	25	26	27	28	29	30	1	2	3	4	5	6	7	8
9	10	11	12	13	14	15	16	17	18	19	20	21	22	23	24	25	26	27	28

7. Divide the total number of days counted by 3

Ex. 10 days divided by 3 = 3, with a remainder of 1. *3 is the number used.*

Remainder guidelines

There can be remainders of 0, 1 or 2 and the guidelines are:

1) If the remainder is 0 use the original number

2) If the remainder is 1 use the original number

3) If the remainder is 2 round up one number, for example, if the number is 11, divide 11 by 3 to obtain 3 with a remainder of 2, round up to 4.

   4 becomes the number utilized.

The following explains the theory for this application:

• Each day counted represents four months or 33% of one year

• Two days represent eight months or 66% of a year and is rounded to the next number.

• When the percentage of months is greater than 50% the number is rounded up.

• When the number of days counted is two days or less use the following method:

   1. If born on the first or last solar day, in other words there are 0 days counted begin the first 10-Year Luck Cycle at birth, for example,
      0, 10, 20, 30, 40, 50, 60, 70, 80, 90

2. If the number of days is 2 the 10-Year Cycles are 1, 11, 21, 31, 41, 51, etc.

3. If the number of days is 1, the 10-Year Cycles are 1, 11, 21, 31, 41, 51, etc.

- The Month pillar is the Stem and Branch influence used for the time period from birth to the first 10-Year Luck Cycle, this pillar is the parent pillar and represents the most influential people in life.

8. Write numbers left to right

The first 10-Year Luck Cycle begins with the number calculated, in this case three, the following cycles represent 10-Year Cycles throughout this person's life.

0   3   13   23   33   43   53   63   73   83   93   103

In this case 0-2 years old will contain the Month Stem and Branch in the Four Pillars, you will learn this represents the parent's pillar and has the most influence during this time of life.

9. Finding the Stem and Branch for 10-Year Luck Cycles

- This always begins with the month binomial in the Four Pillars.

A *Yin Female* or *Yang Male* moves forward, refer to the 60-Stem and Branch cycle chart and find the *Birth Month Stem and Branch Binomial* and place this in age 0, move forward to the next binomial and place it in the first 10-Year cycle, continue to the next binomial and place it in the following 10-Year cycle, continue this process for as many cycles as you prefer.

A *Yang Female* and *Yin Male* moves backwards, refer to the 60-Stem and Branch cycle chart and find the *Birth Month Stem and Branch Binomial,* place it in age 0, move to the preceding binomial and place it in the first 10-Year cycle, continue moving backwards to the next binomial and place it in the following 10 Year cycle, continue this process for as many cycles as you prefer.

Summary

Type	Method of Counting 10-Year Luck Cycles
Yin Female or Yang Male	Count forward from the Birthday to the end of the solar month. <u>Do not</u> count the last solar day.
Yang Female or Yin Male	Count backwards from the Birthday to the first day of the solar month. <u>Do</u> count the first day of the solar month.
	In both cases <u>do</u> count the Birthday.
Counting Days	Divide the total number of days counting by three
Remainders	If the remainder is 1, do not round up, if the remainder is 2, round up one
The first binomial	It is always the Month binomial in the Four Pillars

Stem and Branch Cycle of 60

for Hours, Days, Months and Years

Number	1	2	3	4	5	6
Stem Branch	Yang Wood Rat	Yin Wood Ox	Yang Fire Tiger	Yin Fire Rabbit	Yang Earth Dragon	Yin Earth Snake
Number	7	8	9	10	11	12
Stem Branch	Yang Metal Horse	Yin Metal Sheep	Yang Water Monkey	Yin Water Cock	Yang Wood Dog	Yin Wood Pig
Number	13	14	15	16	17	18
Stem Branch	Yang Fire Rat	Yin Fire Ox	Yang Earth Tiger	Yin Earth Rabbit	Yang Metal Dragon	Yin Metal Snake
Number	19	20	21	22	23	24
Stem Branch	Yang Water Horse	Yin Water Sheep	Yang Wood Monkey	Yin Wood Cock	Yang Fire Dog	Yin Fire Pig
Number	25	26	27	28	29	30
Stem Branch	Yang Earth Rat	Yin Earth Ox	Yang Metal Tiger	Yin Metal Rabbit	Yang Water Dragon	Yin Water Snake
Number	31	32	33	34	35	36
Stem Branch	Yang Wood Horse	Yin Wood Sheep	Yang Fire Monkey	Yin Fire Cock	Yang Earth Dog	Yin Earth Pig
Number	37	38	39	40	41	42
Stem Branch	Yang Metal Rat	Yin Metal Ox	Yang Water Tiger	Yin Water Rabbit	Yang Wood Dragon	Yin Wood Snake
Number	43	44	45	46	47	48
Stem Branch	Yang Fire Horse	Yin Fire Sheep	Yang Earth Monkey	Yin Earth Cock	Yang Metal Dog	Yin Metal Pig
Number	49	50	51	52	53	54
Stem Branch	Yang Water Rat	Yin Water Ox	Yang Wood Tiger	Yin Wood Rabbit	Yang Fire Dragon	Yin Fire Snake
Number	55	56	57	58	59	60
Stem Branch	Yang Earth Horse	Yin Earth Sheep	Yang Metal Monkey	Yin Metal Cock	Yang Water Dog	Yin Water Pig

Branch	Pig	Rat	Ox	Tiger	Rabbit	Dragon	Snake	Horse	Sheep	Monkey	Cock	Dog
Main Element	Yang Water	Yin Water	Yin Earth	Yang Wood	Yin Wood	Yang Earth	Yang Fire	Yin Fire	Yin Earth	Yang Metal	Yin Metal	Yang Earth
Hidden Element	Yang Wood		Yin Water	Yang Fire		Yin Wood	Yang Earth	Yin Earth	Yin Fire	Yang Earth		Yin Metal
			Yin Metal	Yang Earth		Yin Water	Yang Metal		Yin Wood	Yang Water		Yin Fire

Example
A male born on June 30, 1957 at 6:30 am daylight savings time

Four Pillars

	Hour	Day	Month	Year
Stem	Yin Wood	Yin Water	Yang Fire	Yin Fire
Branch	Rabbit	Cock	Horse	Cock
Elements	Yin Wood	Yin Metal	Yin Fire Yin Earth	Yin Metal

10-Year Life Cycles

Age	0	8	18	28	38	48	58	68	78
Stem	Yang Fire	Yin Wood	Yang Wood	Yin Water	Yang Water	Yin Metal	Yang Metal	Yin Earth	Yang Earth
Branch	Horse	Snake	Dragon	Rabbit	Tiger	Ox	Rat	Pig	Dog
Main Element	Yin Fire	Yang Fire	Yang Earth	Yin Wood	Yang Wood	Yin Earth	Yin Water	Yang Water	Yang Earth
Hidden Elements	Yin Earth	Yang Earth Yang Metal	Yin Wood Yin Water		Yang Fire Yang Earth	Yin Water Yin Metal		Yang Wood	Yin Metal Yin Fire

The birthday is June 30, 1957

- This is Yin Cock or Yin Male, count backwards

- The solar month is June 6–July 7, count from June 30 to June 6 and include the first solar day and the birthday

- There are 25 days, divide 25 by 3 creating 8 with a remainder of 1, do not round up use 8. Eight years to 17 years is the first 10-Year Luck Cycle, see example above.

The Month Stem and Branch is Yang Fire/Horse or number 43 in the 60-Stem and Branch Cycle Chart, place this in the 0 time frame. This is a Yin Male move backward and place Binomial 42, Yin Wood/Snake in the first 10-Year cycle which is the 8-17 cycle, place Binomial 41 in the 18-27 cycle and continue for as many 10-year cycles as you prefer.

Stem Transformations

One of the underlying principles in Astrology is change. The Five-Element quality of Stems and Branches change with specific combinations, it is like mixing colors together, certain colors combine to create a new color. When certain elements mix they convert into a new element. In Four Pillars of Destiny, Stems may transform under specific conditions. Transformations can occur in the Four Pillars, 10-Year, Annual or Monthly cycles, if a transformation occurs in the Four Pillars the change exists for a lifetime. If an element from a future cycle of time combines with an element in the Four Pillars the transformation lasts for the duration of the cycle of time. When the time frame ends the transformed element reverts back to its original element, for example, it takes two Stems to cause a transformation and if one is in the Four Pillars and one appears in a particular year the transformation occurs for that year, after that year the new element reverts back to the original element.

Good fortune is when a new transformed element benefits the Self/Day Master.

Bad fortune is when a new transformed element hinders the Self/Day Master.

The following are Stem transformation combinations

Stem Combinations	Transforms into this New Element
Yang Wood and Yin Earth	Earth
Yang Metal and Yin Wood	Metal
Yang Fire and Yin Metal	Water
Yang Water and Yin Fire	Wood
Yang Earth and Yin Water	Fire

Each transformation includes the controlling Five-Element relationship, for example, Wood controls Earth and Metal controls Wood, the controlling element is always Yang (Yang Wood) and the element controlled is always Yin (Yin Earth).

Example
Yang Fire and Yin Metal

	Hour	Day	Month	Year
Stem	Yang Water	Yin Water	Yang Fire	Yin Metal
Branch				

Yang Fire and Yin Metal want to transform into Water, if they transform view both as Water. See the following Four Pillars.

	Hour	Day	Month	Year
Stem	Yang Water	Yin Water	Water	Water
Branch				

Yang Wood and Yin Earth may transform into Earth, if they do view both as Earth, see the following examples.

	Hour	Day	Month	Year
Stem	Yin Earth	Yin Metal	Yang Wood	Yin Earth
Branch				

	Hour	Day	Month	Year
Stem	Yin Earth	Yin Metal	Earth	Earth
Branch				

Transformation Rules

Transformations occur under specific conditions and all conditions must be present, if the conditions do not exist the elements combine but do not transform. The following are transformation guidelines:

1. Stems combine only when they are next to each other in the Four Pillars and include the following combinations:
   - Hour and Day
   - Day and Month
   - Month and Year

Day transformations have special rules that are presented later in this chapter.

2. If the Month and Year Stems have a transformation combination identify which element would be the new element, refer to the Month Branch and if the Month Branch provides root, which means it is the same element as the new transformed element, then the transformation will occur. This root can be Main or a Hidden element and provides the energy/Qi to allow the transformation to occur. Main root is the main element in the Month branch and Minor Root is a hidden element in the Month Branch.

Example
Yang Fire combines with Yin Metal

Four Pillars

	Hour	Day	Month	Year
Stem	Yin Wood	Yin Water	Yang Fire	Yin Metal
Branch	Rabbit	Cock	Pig	Cock
Elements	Yin Wood	Yin Metal	Yang Water Yang Wood	Yin Metal

Transforms to this Chart

	Hour	Day	Month	Year
Stem	Yin Wood	Yin Water	Water	Water
Branch	Rabbit	Cock	Pig	Cock
Elements	Yin Wood	Yin Metal	Yang Water Yang Wood	Yin Metal

Yang Fire in the Month Stem combines with Yin Metal in the Year Stem and wants to transform to Water, for the transformation to occur the Month Branch must provide root. The Month Branch is Pig and contains Yang Water and Yang Wood, Yang Water provides Main root because it is the main element of the Pig and this root is the catalyst for the transformation because it provides the energy to the Stem combination. The example above reflects the new transformed element.

3. When a Stem transforms it must have a polarity or gender, both transformed Stems take the gender or polarity of the Element that provides root.

4. *If two or more Stems combine and want to transform with one Stem it is called the "Jealousy" or "Competition" combination and is usually unfavorable. If two or more stems want to combine, it usually implies some type of unfavorable condition or activities, very often sexual affairs.*

5. If a minor/hidden element provides root and the main element of the month branch is its controlling element, the transformation does not occur. For example, if the potential transformed element would be Water and the Month Branch is Ox, which has hidden Water and would provide root, but the main element of the Ox is Earth, Earth controls Water preventing the transformation.

Day Master Transformations

The Day Stem requires special conditions for a transformation and all conditions must exist for it to occur, the following are the conditions:

- The Day Stem combines only with the Hour or Month Stem, the adjacent Pillars and may also transform with 10-Year, Annual and Monthly Cycles.
- The new element formed by the transformation must have root in the Month Branch, the root can be main or hidden.
- If the Day Stem element is also in the Hour, Month or Year Stems there *cannot* be a transformation, sibling elements in the Stems are not allowed.
- There cannot be the controlling or grandparent element of the new transformed element anywhere in the Four Pillars, this includes Stems and main elements in Branches, hidden elements are allowed in the hour, day and year branch but not the month.
- If a minor/hidden element in a branch provides root and the main element of the month branch is the controlling element, the transformation does not occur. For example, if the transformed element would be Water and the Month Branch is Ox, which has hidden Water providing root, but the main element is Earth, Earth controls Water preventing the transformation.

The following table summarizes each of the Day Stem transformation.

Day Stem Transformations

Element Combination	New Element	Month Branch (Must be present)	Controlling Element (not in FP)
Yang Metal & Yin Wood	Metal	Ox, Cock No Snake in month	Fire
Yang Wood & Yin Earth	Earth	Ox, Dragon, Sheep or Dog	Wood
Yang Fire & Yin Metal	Water	Rat, Monkey or Pig No Dragon and Ox in the Month	Earth
Yang Water & Yin Fire	Wood	Tiger, Rabbit, Sheep or Pig	Metal
Yang Earth & Yin Water	Fire	Tiger, Snake, Horse or Dog	Water

Day Master or Self

The Day Stem is considered the centerpiece of Four Pillars of Destiny because it reflects the "Self", some astrologers refer to this as the *Day Master*. The way other Stems, Branches and cycles of time affect the Day Stem/Self is a major focus of Zi Ping Chinese Astrology. In Chinese Astrology we refer to the condition of the Self Element, it can be a variation of strong, balanced or weak and is determined by the total mix and interaction of elements in the birth chart. This calculation is a critical aspect of Four Pillars of Destiny and begins with determining the relative condition of each element in the Four Pillars, then totaling elements that weaken and strengthen the day stem.

Determining the condition of each element within the Four Pillars is an art and science. The following is a quantitative method for calculating the strength of each element, in a short period of time you will be able to calculate this condition by understanding the Five-Element relationships of the Four Pillars. This formula is very accurate but no formula is 100% accurate, the key is to understand the mechanics of the formula and applying its principles without the formula structure. The following explains this procedure and examples follow which illustrate the process.

A critical element in determining the condition of the day stem is "Timeliness", this integral influence captures the condition of the vibrancy of energy for each element in Four Pillars of Destiny. The major tool used to determine the Timeliness of the Day Stem and Four Pillars is the 12-Stage Growth Cycle. The following is a quantitative method for determining the relative strength or Timeliness of each element in the Four Pillars:

1. Allocate the value of 100 to each of the Stems in the Four Pillars

2. In the Hidden Element table locate the element value in each of the Branches of the Four Pillars and include Hidden Elements.

3. Determine the 12-Stage Growth Cycle and percentage for each Element.

4. Multiply the element values found in step 2 by the percentages found in step 3, this determines the relative strength of each element.

Hidden Elements

Nine of the 12-Branches or Animals contain "Hidden Elements" which are minor elements inside a Branch, they exert an influence and must be evaluated. The Hidden Element chart shows the influence or strength of the main and hidden elements, they are fixed values and the bottom of each page in the "Chinese Calendar Made Easy" contains a box showing the main and hidden elements.

Hidden Elements

(Relative Weights)

Animal	Main Element	Hidden Element
Pig	Yang Water 70	Yang Wood 30
Rat	Yin Water 100	
Ox	Yin Earth 60	Yin Water 20, Yin Metal 20
Tiger	Yang Wood 60	Yang Fire 20, Yang Earth 20
Rabbit	Yin Wood 100	
Dragon	Yang Earth 60	Yin Wood 20, Yin Water 20
Snake	Yang Fire 60	Yang Earth 20, Yang Metal 20
Horse	Yin Fire 70	Yin Earth 30
Sheep	Yin Earth 60	Yin Fire 20, Yin Wood 20
Monkey	Yang Metal 60	Yang Earth 20, Yang Water 20
Cock	Yin Metal 100	
Dog	Yang Earth 60	Yin Metal 20, Yin Fire 20

12-Stage Growth Cycle

The 12-Stage Growth cycle is a more detailed variation of Yin-Yang and Five-Element cycles of expansion, peak, decline and regeneration or Waxing and Waning. In this analysis each element in the Four Pillars is compared to the element and energy of the Month Branch, which reflects the Season of birth. Each element represents a season and each season may nourish, support, weaken or control another element, this formula clearly illustrates how the Month Branch influences each of the elements in the Four Pillars. The following table shows each element and their corresponding season.

Element	Season
Wood	Spring
Fire	Summer
Earth	Indian Summer or the Transition time from Season to Season
Metal	Fall
Water	Winter

The 12-Stage Growth Cycle determines the actual degree of strength for those standard values of each Stem and Branch, it is the Elemental/Seasonal/Five-Element relationship that determines relative values.

How to use 12-Stage Growth Cycle

1. In the top row of the 12-Stage Growth Cycle Chart, locate each Element in the Four Pillars

2. Locate the Month Branch from the Four Pillars in the column directly beneath each element, the intersection box of the Element and Month Branch contains the percentage or strength of the 12-Stage Growth Cycle, use this percentage and multiply it by the Relative weights, the total is the actual strength of each element.

12 Stage Growth Cycle

Cycle Stage		Element ▼ Wood	Element ▼ Fire	Element ▼ Earth	Metal	Element ▼ Water
1	**Birth - Chang Sheng** Needs Energy	Pig 80 %	Tiger 80 %	Tiger 50 %	Snake 50%	Monkey 80%
2	**Childhood - Mu Yu** Needs Energy	Rat 50%	Rabbit 50%	Rabbit 50%	Horse 50%	Cock 50%
3	**Adolescence - Guan Dai** Needs Direction	Ox 50 %	Dragon 50%	Dragon 100%	Sheep 50%	Dog 50%
4	**Adulthood - Lin Guan** Rising, Growth	Tiger 100%	Snake 100%	Snake 100%	Monkey 100%	Pig 100%
5	**Prime - Di Wang** Peak	Rabbit 100%	Horse 100%	Horse 100%	Cock 100%	Rat 100%
6	**Decline - Sui** Harvest, Decline	Dragon 80%	Sheep 80%	Sheep 100%	Dog 80%	Ox 50%
7	**Aging - Bing** Weakening	Snake 50%	Monkey 50%	Monkey 50%	Pig 50%	Tiger 50%
8	**Death - Si** Depletion	Horse 50%	Cock 50%	Cock 50%	Rat 50%	Rabbit 50%
9	**Dormancy - Mu** Buried, Storing	Sheep 80%	Dog 80%	Dog 100%	Ox 80%	Dragon 50%
10	**Void - Jue** Preparation	Monkey 50%	Pig 50%	Pig 50%	Tiger 50%	Snake 50%
11	**Embryo - Tai** Beginning	Cock 50%	Rat 50%	Rat 50%	Rabbit 50%	Horse 50%
12	**Pregnancy - Yang** New creation has began	Dog 50%	Ox 50%	Ox 100%	Dragon 50%	Sheep 50%

Locate the Month Branch

Explanation of the Percentages

Stage	Condition
100%	Same Element
80%	Same Direction, Trinity/Element Frame, Yang Parent Element, except when the main element controls the designated element, for example, Metal and Snake, Water and Ox or Dragon.
50%	Not Same Element, Not Trinity
Earth	100% for all Earths, Snake and Horse
Adjustments	Add 20% to the values of the Hour and Month Stems and Day and Hour Branches, they are next to the Day Stem and have a stronger influence. Also elements that block elements form the Day Master. Also reduce the influence of Empty Branches in the Four Pillars

Example

Male born on June 30, 1957 at 6:30 am daylight savings time

Four Pillars

	Hour	Day	Month	Year
Stem	Yin Wood Offspring 100 X 50%	Yin Water Sibling 100 X 50%	Yang Fire Grandchild 100 X 100%	Yin Fire Grandchild 100 X 100%
Branch	Rabbit	Cock	Horse	Cock
Elements	Yin Wood Offspring 100 X 50%	Yin Metal Parent 100 X 50%	Yin Fire Grandchild 70 X 100% Yin Earth Grandparent 30 X 50%	Yin Metal Parent 100 X 50%

Heavenly Influences

"10-Gods or Deities"

Heavenly Influences or as they are traditionally known 10-Gods or 10-Deities reflect a major aspect of one's destiny, providing information revealing the blueprint of one's life. There are five aspects to this evaluation, each is based on the Five-Element relationship of the Day Stem to the Hour, Day, Month and Year Stems, as well as Branches and their hidden elements. The following chart summarizes each of the 10-Gods/Heavenly Influences and the detailed Heavenly Influence table lists more comprehensive aspects of these Influences.

Relationship to Day Stem	Heavenly Influence	Qualities of Relationships
Sibling Same as Day Stem	Friends	Represents friends, supporters, assistance, colleagues and competitors
Child	Expression	Represents creations, production, manifesting, talent, intelligence, performance and creativity
Grandchild	Wealth	Represents income, finances, materialism, family For males romance or spouse.
Grandparent	Power	Represents power, leadership, management, discipline, authority, entrepreneurship and ambition For females romance or spouse.
Parent	Resource	Represents love, nourishment, support, assistance and stability

Heavenly Influences / 10-Gods

Relationship	Type	Meaning
Mother Element of Day Stem **Resource**	1. **Primary Resource** "Zheng Yin" **Two different genders** Example: Yin Water and Yang Metal	**Primary Resource** represents love, nourishment, support and new opportunities; it can come from parents, relatives or superiors. If this influence has strong support they have a strong probability for achievement and the capacity to be a leader and achieve success. A lack of support requires time and preparation for success.
	2. **Inconsistent Resource** "Pian Yin" **Same gender** Example: Yang Water and Yang Metal	**Inconsistent Resource** represents inconsistent receiving of support or love, they have difficulties in relationships, may lack patience and are susceptible to jealousy; conditional love is or has been predominant during their life. This person should focus on overcoming the conditional nature of one's life and success can be achieved. **Too Much Resource** One can be very spoiled, arrogant, never satisfied and rigid. **Lack of Resource** One can be unfulfilled, lack patience, has a lack of love, often conditional love is a predominant theme in their life, difficulties in relationships and susceptible to jealousy.
Same Element as the Day Stem **Sibling**	3. **Friends-Competitors** "Jia Cai" **Opposite genders** Example: Yang Water and Yin Water	**Friends-Competitors** represent help, support or assistance from friends, family or superiors; it can also be competitors or enemies. Combined with a weak Day Stem this provides strong support. Combined with a strong Day Stem this creates competitors or enemies
	4. **Friends** "Bi Jian" **Two of the same sign** Example: Yang Water and Yang Water	**Friends** represent help, support or assistance from friends, family or superiors. Too much Friends can lead to competition Lack of Friends can lead to lack of support in work and personal life, as well as stress, pressure and obstacles.

Offspring of the Day Stem, the child. Expressions	5. Proper Expression "Shi Shen" **Same gender** Yang Wood and Yang Fire 6. Powerful Expression "Shang Guan" **Opposite genders** Yang Wood and Yin Fire.	**Proper Expression** represents creations, productions or achievements and is showing, displaying, performing or manifesting skills and abilities. **Powerful Expression** represents creations, productions or achievements and is showing, displaying, performing or manifesting skills and abilities. It is more aggressive and powerful than Proper Expression and tends to express itself in an abrasive way, lacking sensitivity for others. **Too Much Expressions** One can feel tired, fatigued and pressured to perform, they often spread themselves too thin. **Lack of Expression** One feels frustrated about not having outlets for expressing their feelings and creativity.
Grandparent is the controller of Day Stem Power For women this represents their Spouse and romance	7. Proper Power "Zheng Guan" **Opposite genders** Yang Metal and Yin Fire 8. Aggressive Power "Chi Sha" **Same gender** Yang Metal and Yang Fire	**Proper Power** represents leadership, control, authority, achievement, sophistication, ambition, responsibility, organization, entrepreneurship, honesty and the ability to organize resources and use power/influence in a positive way. **Aggressive Power** is similar to Proper Power but emphasizes aggressiveness, it reflects using power to achieve and often is exerted in an insensitive way. **Too Much Power** One feels lots of pressure and stress and too many constraints. They are susceptible to lawsuits. **Lack of Power** Leadership, management and authority come through hard work and great effort, it will not be obtained easily. This person may have difficulties dealing with authority.

Grandson of the Day Stem Wealth For men this represents their Spouse and romance	9. Primary Wealth "Zheng Cai" Opposite gender Example: Yang Earth and Yin Water 10. Dynamic Wealth " Pian Cai" Same Gender Example: Yang Earth and Yang Water	Primary Wealth reflects wealth, finances, planning and organization, as well as good planning and the capacity to develop a good career with a steady flow of income. Dynamic Wealth is similar to Primary Wealth but is more volatile regarding how wealth is obtained and managed, they obtain wealth but it is difficult to keep and they enjoy spending. Too Much Wealth Wealth will be very important, there will be numerous wealth opportunities throughout a lifetime. For males women will bring joy or great stress depending on the condition of the day master. Lack of Wealth Wealth is not a primary concern or they will have to work hard utilizing initiative to generate wealth.

The following illustrates the procedure to calculate these relationships

1. Compare the Hour Stem to the Day Stem and make note of the Five-Element relationship.

Example 1

	Hour	Day	Month	Year
Stem	Yang Metal	Yin Water		
Branch				

Hour Stem is Yang Metal and is the parent of the Day Stem and is Primary Resource

Repeat this process for the Day Stem to Month Stem, see example 2
Repeat this process for the Day Stem to Year and Hour Stems

Example 2

	Hour	Day	Month	Year
Stem		Yin Wood	Yin Fire	
Branch				

This is Proper Expression
This analysis is performed for all elements found in the Stems and Branches, see example 3.

Example 3

	Hour	Day	Month	Year
Stem	Yang Metal Primary Resource	Yin Water	Yang Earth Proper Power	Yang Fire Primary Wealth
Branch	Dog	Snake	Horse	Cock
Elements Hidden Elements	Yang Earth Proper Power Yin Metal Inconsistent Resource Yin Fire Dynamic Wealth	Yang Fire Dynamic Wealth Yang Earth Proper Power Yang Metal Primary Resource	Yin Fire Dynamic Wealth Yin Earth Aggressive Power	Yin Metal Inconsistent Resource

- The Hour Stem is Yang Metal, which is the Parent of the Day Stem Yin Water or Primary Resource.

- The Month Stem is Yang Earth, which is the grandparent of the Day Stem Yin Water, or Proper Power.

- The Year Stem is Yang Fire, which is the Grandchild of the Day Stem Yin Water or Primary Wealth.

- The Hour Branch is Dog and the main element is Yang Earth, it is the Grandparent of the Day Stem and or Proper Power.

  One Hidden element is Yin Metal which is the Mother of the Day Stem Element and is Yin-to-Yin or Inconsistent Resource.

  Another Hidden branch is Yin Fire which is the Grandchild of the Day Stem, this is Yin-to-Yin or Dynamic Wealth.

- The Day Branch is Snake and the main element is Yang Fire, which is the Grandchild of the Day Stem, it is Primary Wealth.

  One Hidden element is Yang Earth or the Grandparent of the Day Stem which is Proper Power.

  The other Hidden element is Yang Metal or Primary Resource.

- The Month Branch is Horse (Yin Fire), which is the grandchild of the Day Stem or Dynamic wealth.

  The Hidden element is Yin Earth which is the Grandparent or Aggressive Power.

- The Year Branch is Cock or Yin Metal and is Inconsistent Resource.

Example

A male born on June 30, 1957 at 6:30 am daylight savings time

Four Pillars

	Hour	Day	Month	Year
Stem	**Yin Wood** Proper Expressions	**Yin Water**	**Yang Fire** Primary Wealth	**Yin Fire** Dynamic wealth
Branch	**Rabbit**	**Cock**	**Horse**	**Cock**
Elements	**Yin Wood** Proper Expressions	**Yin Metal** Inconsistent Resource	**Yin Fire** Dynamic Wealth **Yin Earth** Aggressive Power	**Yin Metal** Inconsistent Resource

Heavenly Influence analysis:

Two Proper Expressions

Proper Expression represents creations, productions, intelligence or achievements; it is showing, displaying, performing or manifesting skills and abilities.

One Primary Wealth and Two Dynamic Wealth

Primary Wealth reflects wealth, finances, planning and organization; they have a good plan for life and the capacity to develop a good career and a steady flow of income. If they have strong support, a high level of success comes quickly and smoothly, if there is weak support it takes time to build career and wealth.

Dynamic Wealth represents money coming and going, they obtain money but it is difficult to keep and they enjoy spending. If they have strong support and a good luck cycle there is a great chance for quick money and it can be saved. If they have little or no support money comes and goes.

This person has a mixture of Primary Wealth and Dynamic Wealth. Wealth will be created in numerous ways and they have periods of steady income and variable income. The Month Branch is Horse or Yin Fire, it is the most influential aspect of the Four Pillars on the Day Stem, the Wealth aspect of life will create many opportunities and if a cycle of time provides a weak Day Stem Wealth will create great pressure, if the Day Stem or Self is strong there are many opportunities to build Wealth, timing will be crucial for this person.

Wealth or Fire has strong Support in the Hour Pillar because the two woods make Fire stronger, the Horse-Fire in the Month provides Root to the Fire in the Month and Year Stems, making Wealth the Predominant Heavenly Influence.

One Aggressive Power

They use power to achieve things even when not necessary and this power is often exerted in an abrasive way as they want people to follow them and they have a tendency to break rules to achieve their goals. If they obtain support and prepare for opportunities they can obtain success, if there is little support many challenges and obstacles will appear. The tendency is to be aggressive or manipulate others during pressure and stress.

This is a deceiving Influence as it is a Hidden Element in the Month Branch and has strong support from the three Fires in the Chart, this person has the capacity to lead and exert influence over others, he must be careful not to allow edginess or abrasiveness to dominate his actions. The best success will occur during times when the Day Master is strong allowing him to have the strength to handle pressure in a gentle way; if the Self is weak the pressure will allow aggressiveness or edginess to be overly expressed.

Two Inconsistent Resource

This person receives or gives mixed types of support in their life and has difficulties in relationships, he may lack patience and is susceptible to jealousy. Conditional love has been a major issue in their life. Challenges and obstacles confront them, they need to focus on overcoming the conditional nature of life and then success can be achieved.

The Cock or Inconsistent Resource is located in the Day and Year Branches providing nourishment to the Day Stem.

The Day Branch is close to the Day Stem and provides direct support.

The Year Branch Yin Metal/Cock is blocked by Fire in the Month Pillar and it does not fully nourish the Day Master, this person needs to focus on developing nurturing and unconditional relationships to feel complete and fulfilled, he will prefer a safe, calm and steady life.

Predominant Heavenly Influences

Heavenly Influences or 10-Gods are one of the most important aspects of analyzing a Four Pillars chart, the key is identifying the most influential ones for they reveal a predominant life path and suitable professions. The following describes a method for selecting these Influences.

An important principle when identifying predominant Heavenly Influences is "Root", when a Stem has a Branch of the same element the Stem has root. A Branch that provides root to a Stem offers support to Stems. Stems can have main or minor (hidden) root, main root is stronger as its energy is more potent. When a stem has root this Influence is more potent than a stem with no root or a branch with no matching Stem. Stems are heavenly influences and Branches are earthly influences, when a stem has root it is earth supporting heaven and reveals a major direction or aspect of life. Conceptually we can view this as Early Heaven and Later Haven are on harmony.

The following is the technique:

1. Identify the main Element in the Month Branch and if this element is also found in the Hour, Month or Year Stem, but not in the Day Stem this Element is a predominant Element. The Heavenly Influence it has with the Day Stem is a predominant influence.

2. If the main element of the Month Branch is not in the Stems look to the Hidden Elements, if the *first* Hidden Element is found in the Stems but not the Day Stem, that element and its Heavenly Influence with the Day Stem is a predominant influence.

3. If the main element and first hidden element of the month branch are not in the Stems and there is a second hidden element refer to it, if the second Hidden Element is found in the Stems but not the Day Stem this is a predominant Heavenly Influence.

4. If the main or Hidden Elements of the month branch are not in the Stems, use the main element of the month branch as a predominant element and its relationship with the day Stem as a predominant Heavenly Influence.

5. If any stem except the day stem has main or hidden root in any branch it is a predominant influence.

6. The month branch is the most potent single influence on the day stem, if it provides root to a stem it will stand out from other influences.

7. When the Day Stem has root in any branch and it is Timely, it is a powerful Influence, because the Qi is Timely and powerful.

Example
A male born on June 30, 1957 at 6:30 am daylight savings time

Four Pillars

	Hour	Day	Month	Year
Stem	**Yin Wood** Proper Expressions	**Yin Water**	**Yang Fire** Primary Wealth	**Yin Fire** Dynamic wealth
Branch	**Rabbit**	**Cock**	**Horse**	**Cock**
Elements	**Yin Wood** Proper Expressions	**Yin Metal** Inconsistent Resource	**Yin Fire** Dynamic Wealth **Yin Earth** Aggressive Power	**Yin Metal** Inconsistent Resource

- The main element in the Month Branch is Fire and it provides root in the Month and Year Stems, therefore Dynamic and Primary Wealth are the Predominant influences.

- The Hour Stem Yin Wood has Root in the Hour Branch that is Rabbit/Yin Wood. Expressions, performance and intelligence will be an important aspect of this person's life.

Favorable and Unfavorable Elements

Useful and Annoying Elements

A major principle of the Tao is balance and it is applied especially to the Day Stem, when an element brings a birth chart to balance it is a "favorable element", alternatively when an element causes the day stem to become too weak or too strong it is considered an "unfavorable element". When the most favorable element exists in the Four Pillars it is referred to as the "Useful Element/God/Influence" or "Yong Shen", also when an element brings balance, but is not in the Four Pillars it is referred to as the "Favorable Element/God/Influence". The Useful Element reveals the quality of a chart, if the Useful Element is in the Four Pillars and has a Stem with a main root this is a vibrant and favorable chart. If the Useful Element is in the 10-Year Luck Cycles during that cycle of time the chart is favorable. If the Useful Element is not in the Four Pillars or has minor root the chart is mediocre or challenging. The Useful Element is Qi in your birth chart and exists inside you, when nature's cycles of time provide this energy it combines with the energy within your body creating a synergy and potent influence. This is the most favorable influence one can receive and usually brings auspiciousness and prosperity.

The element/God/Influence that controls or dominates the Useful Element is referred to as the Annoying Element/God or Ji Shen, it is unfavorable and can diminish the Useful Element's influence. This element's influence exerts its greatest influence when it is combined with the useful element, for example, if water is the useful element then earth is the annoying element, it is always the controlling element or if the year binomial is Yang Water and Sheep/Earth, the Earth controls or dominates water preventing its favorable influence from manifesting.

Determining "Yong Shen" is a critical aspect of Zi Ping or Four Pillars of Destiny, one approach is to find the element that will reduce or enhance the entire elemental chart, regardless of its effect on the Day Master, for example, if a person was a weak metal Day Master with lots of Water, one approach would be to select Fire as Yong Shen, for it will warm and diminish the excess Water. Some might say the Fire would control and weaken the weak Metal Day Master, this is one approach. Another approach would be to select Earth, for it controls and weakens excess Water and nourishes the weak Day Master Metal. Generally, if one understands the five elements well, even if they select the wrong Yong Shen, they will be selecting a favorable element, the only real difference should be the level of effectiveness in predictions.

Special Day Master Types

Follow the Trend

Weak Day Masters

Four Pillars of Destiny contains two major types of Birth Charts, the first is a Normal Chart and the second includes a series of Special Charts. Special Charts or "Follow Types" occur when the Day Stem is so weak or strong they cannot retain balance in the normal way. In the first section we discuss weak "Follow Types", these Day Master types are so weak it cannot find balance in the normal way, the method is to follow the dominant element in the Four Pillars. This unique method is the way to balance and harmony. Specific conditions must exist for a chart to be classified as a "Follow Type" and they are listed below. There are three types of these charts, Follow Power, Follow Child and Follow Wealth. The "Follow Element" takes the place of the Day Master as the centerpiece of the Four Pillars. The following section describes each Special Types.

Special Type Rules

The following are general rules for all special types, additional guidelines for each type are located in their separate sections.

1. The Day Master has no *main* root in the Hour, Day, Month or Year Branches. Root is when the Day Stem element is also found in the Branches, if it is found in the main element of the Branch it is referred to as main root, if it is found in the Hidden element it is minor root.

2. Minor Root can exist in the Hidden Elements of the Hour, Day and Year Branches but not the Month Branch. The month branch is the most powerful of all Branches and this includes its hidden elements, the energy is strong and supports the Day Master and prevents this special chart from occurring.

3. The Day Master Element must not be in Cycle 4 or 5 in the 12-Stage Growth Cycle in relation to the Month Branch, Cycle 4 and 5 are referred to as being "Timely", this means the element is in a very strong stage and is powerful, too powerful to follow another element in the chart.

4. One of the Five-Elements must be dominant in the Chart, located in the Stems and in cycle 4 or 5 in the 12 Stage Growth Cycle in relation to the Month Branch. It must be timely.

5. The Day Master element cannot have the following:

    1. Stems cannot contain the resource element of the Day Master and have root in Branches. For example, if the Day Stem is Water and its parent Metal cannot be a Stem and have the Monkey, Cock, Ox, Snake or Dog in the Four Pillars, these Branches contain Metal as main or minor elements.

    2. The resource element of the Day Stem cannot have main root in the Branches, minor root is acceptable.

    3. The Dominant element cannot have its Power/Grandparent element anywhere in the Four Pillars because it weakens it, preventing it from having enough energy to change the chart. For example, if the dominant element is Wood, yin or yang

Metal cannot be in the Stems and the monkey, cock, dog, ox and snake cannot be in the Four Pillars.

4. Pay close attention to Trinity and Directional combinations as they may create a strong elemental influence preventing these Follow Types to manifest.

5. If Earth is the dominant element the month of birth must be Fire or Earth.

Follow Power

Follow Power has two types, Real Follow Power and Fake Follow Power. The following are guidelines for Real Follow Power.

Real Follow Power

- Power or Grandparent element is the dominant element in the Four Pillars and is timely or in stage 4 or 5 in the 12-Stage Growth Cycle in relation to the Day Stem.

- Expression or Child element cannot be in the Stems or as a main element in any Branch, this is because the expression element is the grandparent or controlling element of the power element preventing this condition.

- Day Stem element must not be stage 4 or 5 and cannot have main roots in the Four Pillars, minor roots may appear anywhere except the Month Branch.

- One Sibling element of the Day Stem may appear in the Stems but it cannot have any root.

- If Stems do not have a Sibling element minor root may exist in the Hour, Day or Year Branches.

- Favorable Influences are Wealth, Power, Sibling and Resource of the day stem.

- The Expression element of the day stem is unfavorable

Fake Follow Power is similar to Real Follow Power, the difference is the dominant element Power is Stage 1, 6, or 9 in the 12-Stage Growth Cycle not Stage 4 or 5. This type is very unbalanced, in good times great achievement and success can result, in unfavorable luck periods life is very detrimental. This chart is a great example of a roller-coaster life.

Follow Child

- Expression/child is the dominant element
- Expression is stage 4 or 5 in 12-Stage Growth Cycle, it is Timely
- Stems must have one Expression element
- Stems cannot contain the Resource element
- The main element in the Branches cannot be Resource
- Sibling with minor root is allowed
- Day Master can be any location in 12-Stage Growth Cycle
- Beneficial elements are Expression, Sibling and Wealth
- Resource and Power are unfavorable

Follow Wealth

- Day Master is untimely, it is not stage 4 or 5 in 12-Stage Growth Cycle
- Day Master cannot have root
- Wealth element is dominant element and is timely or in stage 4 or 5 in 12-Stage Growth Cycle
- Stems must have one Wealth element
- Branches must form a Trinity or Directional Wealth Element Frame combination
- Siblings cannot be present in Four Pillars
- Resource cannot be a Stem or a main element in any Branch
- Favorable elements include Wealth, Expression and Power
- Resource and Sibling elements are unfavorable

Follow Trend Types

Strong Day Masters

In these Follow Trend types the Day Master is too strong and the Four Pillars cannot obtain balance in traditional ways, the method to obtain balance is following the flow of the chart, which means the favorable element will be the Day Master element even though it is very strong. The following section lists each of the five Follow Trend Charts.

Wood

- Yin or Yang Wood is the Day Stem
- Birth Month is Pig, Tiger, Rabbit, Dragon or Sheep
- Branches must form a Trinity (Pig, Rabbit, Sheep) or Directional combination (Tiger, Rabbit, Dragon)
- Yin or Yang Metal are not in Stems
- Monkey or Rooster are not in Branches

Beneficial elements are Wood, Water, Fire; Earth is favorable when accompanied with Fire.
Unfavorable elements are Metal, and Earth without Fire
Useful God is Wood
Annoying God is Metal

Fire

- Yin or Yang Fire is the Day Stem
- Birth Month is Tiger, Snake, Horse, Sheep or Dog
- Branches form a Trinity (Tiger, Horse, Dog) or Directional combination (Snake, Horse, Sheep)
- Yang or Yin Water are not in the Stems
- Pig or Rat are not in Branches

Fire, Wood and Earth are beneficial
Water and Metal are unfavorable

Useful God is Fire
Annoying God is Water

Earth

- Yang or Yin Earth is the Day Stem
- Dragon, Sheep, Dog or Ox must be the Month Branch
- Pillar Branches must be Ox, Dragon, Sheep and Dog
- Stems cannot have Yang or Yin Wood or Branches containing Tiger or Rabbit

Earth, Fire and Metal and beneficial; Water is beneficial when companied with Metal
Wood and Metal are unfavorable
Useful God is Earth
Annoying God is Wood

Metal

- Yang or Yin Metal is Day Stem
- Birth Month is Snake, Monkey, Cock, Dog or Ox
- Branches form a Trinity (Snake, Cock, Ox) or Directional Combination (Tiger, Rabbit, Dragon)
- Stems cannot have Yang or Yin Fire
- Horse or Sheep cannot be in Branches

Metal, Earth and Water are beneficial; Wood accompanied with Water is beneficial
Wood and Fire are unfavorable
Useful God is Metal
Annoying God is Fire

Water

- Yang or Yin Water is the Day Stem
- Birth Month is Monkey, Pig, Rat, Ox or Dragon
- Branches form a Trinity: Monkey/Rat/Dragon or Directional Combination Pig/Rat/Ox
- No Yang or Yin Earth in the Stems
- No Sheep or Dog in the Branches

Wood, Water and Fire are beneficial; Earth accompanied with Fire is favorable
Metal and Earth are unfavorable
Useful God is Water
Annoying God is Earth

Empty-Void Branches

Empty or Void Branches are an important aspect of Four Pillars Astrology and reveal a profound influence in a life. We learned there are 10-Stems and 12- Branches, therefore there are two Branches that do not have a matching Stem, these two Branches are referred to as Empty or Void Branches. The following method explains the technique for identifying Empty Branches.

Method to calculate Empty Branches:

1. Locate the Year of birth Stem

2. Locate the Year of birth Branch

3. Locate your Year Stem in the table below and identify its number, subtract this number from 10 and call this number X

4. Locate your Year of birth Branch in table below, count X spaces after your Year Branch, the next two Branches after that are your Empty Branches

Empty Branch Table

Stems	Branches
1 Yang Wood	1 Rat
2 Yin Wood	2 Ox
3 Yang Fire	3 Tiger
4 Yin Fire	4 Rabbit
5 Yang Earth	5 Dragon
6 Yin Earth	6 Snake
7 Yang Metal	7 Horse
8 Yin Metal	8 Sheep
9 Yang Water	9 Monkey
10 Yin Water	10 Cock
	11 Dog
	12 Pig

Example

The person has a Yin Fire Year Stem and the Year Branch is the Cock

1. Yin Fire is number 4

   10-4=6

2. Count six Branches/Animals after the Cock (Year of birth Branch): Dog, Pig, Rat, Ox, Tiger, Rabbit, the next two Animals-Branches are the Empty Branches, they are Dragon and Snake.

Empty Branch Applications

1. If the Empty Branches are in your Four Pillars identify its Palace, it is unfavorably influenced and the energy or potency is reduced.

2. Any Branch combinations that include Empty Branches will be unfavorably influenced, for example, if the Empty Branch is Cock and the current Year is Rabbit this is a Clash and its effects are intensified. Another example is if the Empty Branch is the Tiger and the Monkey is the current Year, this is a Travel combination and Traveling will create problems. Follow this same logic for all Empty Branches combinations.

The following tables list some application of empty branches

Palace	Meaning
Year	Their entire life requires hard work, an unfavorable beginning in life or background, difficulties or unfavorable influences with Grandparents, aunts or uncles.
Month	Unfavorable influences from their parents and a difficult background
Day	Unfavorable influences in romance, marriage and relationships; probable separation, divorce and poor fortune.
Hour	Challenges with children and most likely not many grandchildren

Heavenly Influence	Meaning
Power	They do not achieve power only status. They fail easily and lack ambition. If this is a woman she has many obstacles and problems with her husband.
Wealth	They do not manage or control finances and wealth, they do not save money well. If this is a male their wife or partner is often ill and weak.
Resource	Difficulties relating with their mother and obtaining nourishing relationships.
Sibling	Obstacles with their siblings, subordinates or people that should provide assistance.
Offspring	Obstacles with their children and in their performance or output.

Five-Element Personalities

The following section includes general attributes for each of the Five-Elements. A Four Pillars chart contains a blend of Five-Elements but the most significant element is the Day Stem, it represents the Self and reveals the most accurate qualities about a person, for example, Fire represents charisma, energy and leadership. Often a chart will have predominant elements that are not the same as the Day Stem, refer to those elements for additional information about a person, it is common that a person is a mixture of personalities and this method reveals the multifaceted aspects of a person. The Day Stem element is the "True Self", when a person is in harmony with those qualities he or she is balanced and happy.

Water

Favorable:

Water people communicate well, are gentle and caring. They are not straightforward and prefer a soft, gentle and indirect way of interaction. Water people are good at both sides of communication, listening and talking. They can use their emotional sensitivity to influence people. Water people unify others with emotional energy and understanding. They trust their intuition, and use flexibility and perseverance to succeed.

Unfavorable:

Water people are very susceptible to fear and be greatly influenced by others and their environment, they can be too easily influenced by their emotions and must manage this area of life.

Element	Water
Movement	Adaptable, Flexible
Season	Winter
Direction	North
Planet	Mercury
Color	Blue, Black
Compatible Profession	Teaching, communication, transportation, fishing, divination, lecturing, healers
Relationships	Water is the sibling Wood is the child Fire is the grandchild Earth is the grandparent Metal is the parent
Organs	Kidneys – Rat Branch Urinary Bladder – Pig Branch
Emotions	Gentleness Fear
Sense Orifice	Hearing
Tissues	Bones
Taste	Salty
Spirit	Zhi – Will Power

Wood

Favorable:

Wood people can turn resources into products, ideas into profits, and believe expansion or growth will resolve any problems. Wood people are very sociable and are usually surrounded by others; they have good verbal skills. Woods are extroverted and love to accomplish or complete activities. Wood people are always looking to the future.

Unfavorable:

Wood people can have strong tempers and feel frustrated when other people fail to perform to their standards. They can be scattered, spreading themselves and their resources too thin. Wood types may find it difficult to express their inner emotions and often suffer from feelings of inadequacy.

Element	Wood
Movement	Growth, Ascension
Season	Spring
Direction	East
Planet	Jupiter
Color	Green
Compatible Profession	Education, writing, publishing, apparel manufacturing, fashion, herbal products, wood related industries
Relationships	Water is parent Wood is sibling Fire is child Earth is grandchild Metal is grandparent
Organs	Liver – Rabbit Branch Gallbladder – Tiger Branch
Sense	Vision
Taste	Sour
Tissues	Tendons
Emotions	Kindness Anger
Spirit	Hun – Direction, Planning

Fire

Favorable:

Change is a predominant theme for Fire people; they are leaders, motivators and take-charge people. Fire people are highly charismatic, very self-driven, and passionate. If nothing is going on, they will ignite a spark to create something. They are adventurous and are always looking for something new and want to be the center of attention. Fire people can be good speakers and are creators that think and act fast.

Unfavorable:

The often leap before looking and can be poor listeners. Fire people can be flamboyant, filled with passion and make life exciting but sometimes are too intense for others. The can be too verbose and demand to be the center of attention.

Element	Fire
Movement	Active, vitality
Season	Summer
Direction	South
Planet	Mars
Color	Red
Compatible Profession	Restaurant, alcohol, electricity, entertainment, power sources
Relationships	Wood is the parent Fire is sibling Earth is the child Metal is the grandchild Water is the grandparent
Organ	Heart – Horse Branch Small Intestine – Snake Branch
Sense	Taste
Taste	Bitter
Tissues	Blood Vessels
Emotions	Joy, Love Hastiness, Impatience, Hatred

Earth

Favorable:

Fairness is often a predominant quality in an Earth person, they tend to be steady and do not move as fast as others, but what they lack in speed, they make up with consistency and longevity. They do not like to waste their time in grand schemes or ideas; instead they plow through the realities of a situation. Earth people make wonderful managers or organizers, they can be trusted with implementing a plan. Earth people are not overly emotional, but are sensitive. They resolve emotional problems in practical, concrete ways.

Unfavorable:

They tend to be chronic worriers, in fact they may worry about everything, not only their direct life, but everything in the universe. The tend to be very focused, which may lead to a single-mindedness that hinders versatility and the ability to handle multiple factors simultaneously. Earth people expect the rest of the world to view life as they do, if they do not, they can become stubborn and rigid. They respond well to change, if the change is slow and gradual, abrupt change disturbs them.

Element	Earth
Movement	Stability, stillness
Season	Indian Summer
Direction	North East, South West, Center
Planet	Saturn
Color	Yellow, beige
Compatible Profession	Construction, real estate, attorney, judges, human resources, management, consultation
Relationships	Fire is the parent Earth is the sibling Metal is the child Water is the grandchild Wood is the grandparent
Organs	Spleen – Ox and Sheep Branches Stomach – Dragon and Dog Branches
Emotions	Openness and Fairness Worry
Spirit	Yi - Concentration

Metal

Favorable:

Metal people can organize others for positive goals or negative objectives. They can be focused, emotional, intuitive, confident and aggressive in pursuing objectives. Metals can be extremely driven to pursue their goals. Metals can be successful in any profession and can also motivate others to achieve common objectives.

Unfavorable:

Metals tend to be loners, isolated and often withdraw. Metal types may be stubborn and driven by an inner faith whether they are right or wrong. When problems arise, they will turn inward to find answers and cannot be expected to communicate their inner feelings. They are very susceptible to sadness, depression and loneliness, which can dominate their lives. If they become more flexible and open, they will develop loyal friendships.

Element	Metal
Movement	Inward
Season	Fall
Direction	West, North West
Planet	Venus
Color	White, Gold
Compatible Profession	Metal related industries, strategic management, automobile and jewelry industries
Relationships	Water is the child Wood is the grandchild Fire is the grandparent Earth is the parent Metal is the sibling
Organ	Lungs – Cock Branch Large Intestine – Monkey Branch
Emotions	Courage Sadness, Depression
Spirit	Po – Physical

Stem and Branch Combinations

The key to Chinese Astrology is determining the condition of the Day Stem, in general if the Day Stem receives detrimental energies negative aspects of Stem and Branch combinations manifest and that area of life will have stress, challenges and obstacles. If the Day Stem receives beneficial energies positive aspects will manifest. This principle is applied throughout this Chinese divination system.

Branches are the foundation and set the theme for any cycle of time.

Stems are variations within the general theme of a cycle, when a Stem and Branch are in harmony the effect is very potent.

The following section includes the most influential Branch-to-Branch combinations. These combinations are used in two major ways, the first is when combinations appear in the Four Pillars and in this case the influence lasts for a lifetime. The second is when a cycle of time Binomial, for instance, 10-Year Luck Cycle, Annual, Monthly or a Daily Binomials combine with the Four Pillars, in this case the influence lasts for that duration of time.

The following has two sections, the first describes combinations and the second is a summary table for quick and easy reference.

The following table summarizes general ways to interpret Stem and Branch influences.

Stem and Branch Type	Meaning
Beneficial Stem Beneficial Branch	Primarily good fortune and luck
Beneficial Stem Detrimental Branch	Primarily unlucky with periods of good fortune
Detrimental Stem Beneficial Branch	Primarily good fortune with periods of obstacles
Detrimental Stem and Branch	Primarily unlucky with many challenges

Good Partners

These Animals are located in the same geographical area and share the same element, they enjoy similar activities and have the potential to become good friends.

1. Snake and Horse

2. Monkey and Cock

3. Rat and Pig

4. Rabbit and Tiger

Trinity–Elemental Frame

Trinity/Frame Branches have a strong affinity and friendship with each other, they are used for romance, marriage and friendships and they also release a strong element influence, and the element released can provide beneficial or unfavorable influences depending on which elements help or hinder the Day Master.

Trinity relationships are Branches that are four locations from each other and there are four sets of three Branches, the following are Trinity relationships.

Branch Combinations	Releases
Cock-Ox-Snake	Metal
Rat-Dragon-Monkey	Water
Rabbit-Sheep-Pig	Wood
Horse-Dog-Tiger	Fire

- If two are together a mild force is created
- If three are together a strong force is created

Notice the geographical position of the first animal of each Trinity, (see the following diagrams) they are located in the cardinal or middle position, the second and third animals in a Trinity contain the element of the cardinal animal's element, it is their Hidden elements. When the three Branches of a Trinity combine it releases the Hidden elements and they become very strong and influential. For example, in the Cock-Snake-Ox combination,

Cock is Metal and the Cock-Ox-Snake Trinity releases Metal. The release of this influence can occur in the Four Pillars or two may appear in the Four Pillars and one in the 10-Year Luck, Annual or Monthly cycles.

Trinity Diagram

	South Red Snake Horse Sheep + Fire - Fire - Earth 6 7 8 **Summer**	
East Green Dragon + Earth 5 Rabbit - Wood 4 Tiger + Wood 3 **Spring**		**West** Gold-Silver Monkey + Metal 9 Cock - Metal 10 Dog + Earth 11 **Fall**
	North Black-Blue Ox Rat Pig - Earth - Water + Water 2 1 12 **Winter**	

Trinity relationships are every fourth Branch or Animal

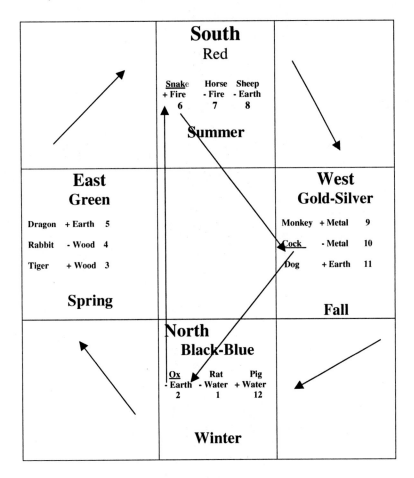

If the change occurs because it is triggered by future cycles of time, for example, two Branches are in the Four Pillars and one is in the Annual Branch an influence may occur which is very strong, for example, a major change from one's normal personality or emotional condition, for most people sudden change can be very traumatic.

Traveling

There will some traveling during these time frames

1. Snake and Pig
2. Tiger and Monkey

Playboy or Playgirl

These Branches are often called the four corners or four gates and reflects a person who is very sensual, romantic and sexual. If these combinations appear in the Four Pillars it represents their constitutional nature, additionally there can be three in the Pillars and one during a 10-Year Luck, Annual or Monthly cycles, when those conditions occur these qualities last for that time frame.

Each Animal sits in the cardinal or middle geographical location: Horse in South, Cock in West, Rat in North and Rabbit in East.

Opposites Attract

1. Horse and Rat or South to North
2. Rabbit and Cock or East to West

These Branches are opposite each other (Clash Combination) and provide a romantic spark, excitement and lots of activity, both favorable and unfavorable, it requires good discrimination skills to select favorable opportunities.

Arguing–Three Penalties

These combinations are also named the "Three Penalties"; this combination generates Arguing, Bickering and Fighting and may occur in a variety of ways, the first is when Branches or Animals are side-by-side in the Birth Pillars and the second is when Pillar Branches interact with 10-Year, Annual or Month cycles.

1. Two Horses/Wu
2. Two Cocks/Yu
3. Two Pigs/Hai
4. Two Dragons/Chen

Also:

1. Tiger, Snake and Monkey
2. Sheep, Dog and Ox

Example:

	Hour	Day	Month	Year
Stem	Yin Wood	Yin Water	Yang Fire	Yin Fire
Branch	Rabbit	Horse	Horse	Cock

If the four animals combine there will be a serious problem or challenge.

Six Combinations

These Branch combinations are attracted to each other and usually create auspicious and favorable activities.

1. Rat and Ox combine
2. Tiger and Pig combine
3. Rabbit and Dog combine
4. Dragon and Cock combine
5. Snake and Monkey combine
6. Horse and Sheep combine

Six Clashes

These combinations generate disruptions, challenges and confrontations; the Branches are in opposite geographical locations.

1. Rat and Horse
2. Ox and Sheep
3. Tiger and Monkey
4. Rabbit and Cock
5. Dragon and Dog
6. Snake and Pig

Branch Combinations

Branch - Animal	Combination	Meaning
Rat	Pig	Good Partner
	Ox	Six Combinations
	Horse	Opposites Attract, Travel, Clash
	Monkey, Dragon	Trinity
	Horse, Cock, Rabbit	Playboy-Playgirl

Ox	Snake, Cock	Trinity
	Sheep	Clash
	Rat	Six Combinations

Tiger	Rabbit	Travel, Good Partner
	Monkey	Travel, Clash
	Pig	Six Combinations
	Horse, Dog	Trinity

Rabbit	Tiger	Good Partners
	Sheep, Pig	Trinity
	Dog	Six Combinations
	Cock	Opposites Attract, Clash
	Horse, Cock, Rat	Playboy-Playgirl

Dragon	Dragon	Argue
	Dog	Clash
	Rat, Monkey	Trinity
	Cock	Six Combinations

Snake	Horse	Good Partners
	Ox, Cock	Trinity
	Monkey	Six Combinations
	Pig	Travel, Clash

Branch Combinations

Branch – Animal	Combination	Meaning
Horse	Horse	Argue
	Snake	Good Partner
	Dog, Tiger	Trinity
	Sheep	Six Combinations
	Rat	Opposite Attract, Clash
	Cock, Rat, Rabbit	Playboy-Playgirl

Sheep	Ox	Clash, stress in all aspects of life
	Dog	Conflict
	Rabbit, Pig	Trinity
	Horse	Six Combinations

Monkey	Cock	Good Partners
	Tiger	Travel, Clash, love is lost, a big misunderstanding
	Dragon, Rat	Trinity
	Snake	Six Combinations

Cock	Cock	Argue
	Monkey	Good Partners
	Rabbit	Opposites Attract, Clash
	Horse, Rat, Rabbit	Playboy-Playgirl
	Snake, Ox	Trinity
	Dragon	Six Combinations

Dog	Dragon	Clash
	Horse, Tiger	Trinity
	Rabbit	Six Combinations

Pig	Rat	Good Partners
	Snake	Travel, Clash
	Sheep, Rabbit	Trinity
	Tiger	Six Combinations
	Pig	Argue

Example

Yin Water Day Master

Male born on June 30, 1957 at 6:30 am daylight savings time

Four Pillars

	Hour	Day	Month	Year
Stem	Yin Wood Offspring 100 X 50%	Yin Water	Yang Fire Grandchild 100 X 100%	Yin Fire Grandchild 100 X 100%
Branch	Rabbit	Cock	Horse	Cock
Elements	Yin Wood Offspring 100 X 50%	Yin Metal Parent 100 X 50%	Yin Fire Grandchild 70 X 100% Yin Earth Grandparent 30 X 50%	Yin Metal Parent 100 X 50%

Branch Combination Analysis

- Rabbit and Cock: Opposites attract, Clash
- Rabbit, Cock and Horse are three parts of Playboy-Playgirl type, *Rat* is the fourth, predict a Rat 10-Year Luck Cycle, Rat Years or Rat Months as times for Romance.

Wealth

Wealth includes money, financial instruments, real estate, family, education or things of value and is reflected by the element the Day Master or Self controls, for example, a Yang Water Day Stem controls Fire, Fire is the Wealth generator. When Wealth generators appear one should be prepared by having the proper training, energy and resources to turn opportunities into success. Wealth generators can appear in the Four Pillars, 10-Year Luck Cycles, Yearly, Monthly or Daily cycles, the length of an opportunity lasts for the duration of the cycle.

The following are Wealth generators for each element

Element	Wealth Generator
Water	Fire
Wood	Earth
Fire	Metal
Earth	Water
Metal	Wood

Wealth generators can initiate both favorable and unfavorable activities; if one is strong and prepared Wealth generators create opportunities that may be realized. If there are too many opportunities it is possible one may be spread too thin creating stress and pressure. If the day stem is weak too many Wealth generators may cause stress, challenges, frustration and fatigue, the reason is it takes energy and resources to act on these Wealth generators. The key is to be prepared when opportunities occur, this is the strength of Chinese Astrology, doing the right thing at the right time.

Wealth generators in the Four Pillars provide wealth opportunities for a lifetime.

Wealth generators in 10-Year Luck Cycles provide opportunities for those 10-years.

Wealth generators in a Year provide wealth opportunities for that particular year.

Wealth generators for a Month provide wealth opportunities for that month.

Wealth generators for a Day provide wealth opportunities for that day.

An important aspect of Four Pillars of Destiny is for planning, for example, use time frames with wealth generators to begin or realize wealth activities. If a Wealth generator is in the Month Branch and the 12-Stage Growth cycle is strong there is great potential for Wealth, especially from the parents. See the table below to identify where wealth may originate.

	Hour	Day	Month	Year
Stem	Sons Younger Brothers	Self	Father Older Brothers	Granddad Uncles Relatives
Branch	Daughters Younger Sisters	Spouse	Mother Older Sisters	Grandmother Aunts, Relatives

If the Wealth generator is in the Year Palace a grandparent had wealth or provides wealth.

If the Month Palace contains the Wealth generator a parent had wealth or provides wealth.

If the Hour, Month and Year palaces contain Wealth generators there will be wealth in the family.

Romance

Romance and Marriage are one of the most important areas of interest of women and men and a priority during a Chinese Astrology consultation, there are a variety of methods to determine how and when Romance and Marriage will manifest in a lifetime. This topic is segmented into three methods:

1. Predicting the type of relationship one is most likely to obtain
2. Selecting most compatible partners
3. Predicting the timing of Romantic opportunities

Predicting the most likely type of relationship a person will select can be predicted based on the "Palace Method" and the Five-Element relationship between the Day Stem and a Branch. Below is a Four Pillars chart listing positions of family members, in this method the Day Branch represents Spouse and the Day Stem is Self, the Day Pillar or Palace is referred to as the Marriage Pillar or Palace.

	Hour	Day	Month	Year
Stem	Sons Younger Brothers	Self	Dad Older Brothers Mentors	Grandfather Uncles Relatives
Branch	Daughters Younger Sisters	Spouse Marriage	Mom Older Sisters Mentors	Grandmother Aunts Relatives

The Five-Element relationship between the Day Branch and Day Stem reveals the way in which a couple will interact as seen in the following example, the Cock is Yin Metal which is the parent element of the Day Stem Water, this person's spouse will be nourishing and supporting because Metal is the Parent/Resource of Water.

If the Day Branch were the Dog or Yang Earth it would control Water, therefore the spouse would be older, controlling, dominating or more intelligent.

	Hour	Day	Month	Year
Stem	Yin Wood Proper Expressions	Yin Water ↑	Yang Fire Primary Wealth	Yin Fire Dynamic wealth
Branch	Rabbit	Cock	Horse	Cock
Elements	Yin Wood Proper Expressions	Yin Metal Inconsistent Resource	Yin Fire Dynamic Wealth Yin Earth Aggressive Power	Yin Metal Inconsistent Resource

Compatibility

Determining compatibility and romantic opportunities includes two major methods, the traditional method begins by determining the condition and beneficial elements of the Day Stems of two people, if each person contains their partner's beneficial elements a deep connection and compatibility exists. This is the traditional method of arranged marriages, both charts are brought to an astrologer of which the favorable elements of each person is determined and if they match each other they have a deep affinity, essentially they fulfill each other providing energies that bring balance to their lives.

A common method for predicting compatibility is the Trinity or Harmonic relationship between branch Animals, listed below are the favorable combinations and they are based on the year of birth, for example, Horse gets along with the Dog and Tiger or the Tiger likes a Horse. The reason these Branch combinations create an attraction for each other is they share the same elements, by way of the hidden element or element frames.

Snake-Cock-Ox is the Metal frame
Horse- Dog-Tiger is the Fire frame
Rabbit- Sheep-Pig is the Wood frame
Rat-Monkey-Dragon is the Water frame

A second method includes Branches in the same geographical area because they comprise the directional combinations and share the same elements.

Horse-Snake, South
Monkey-Cock, West
Pig-Rat, North
Tiger-Rabbit, East

A third method is the "Six Combinations" which are based on the year of birth.

Rat and Ox
Tiger and Pig
Rabbit and Dog
Dragon and Cock
Snake and Monkey
Horse and Sheep

These three methods: Trinity, Same Directions and Six Combinations create an initial attraction that may or may not be on a deep level but a spark is usually felt, these methods are not as effective as the first method described.

There are two major methods to predict the timing of romantic opportunities and the first is based on the following Five-Element relationships.

1. *For males* the element the Self controls is the Wealth generator, it also represents Spouse and Romantic opportunities and when time frames with a Wealth/Romance generator occur there will be romantic opportunities.

   Example

   Fire is the Wealth and Romance generator of a Water Day Stem, and includes the Horse, Snake, Yang Fire and Yin Fire and can exist in the Four Pillars, 10- Year, Annual, Month or Day time frames. Predict romantic opportunities during these cycles of time.

2. *For females* the element that controls the Day Stem represents their spouse and romantic opportunities, for example, for a Wood Day Stem, Metal represents Romance.

Special Situation

The Rat/North, Rabbit/East, Horse/Fire and Cock/West are in cardinal geographical locations and each is considered to have "sexual charisma" more than the other branches. If a *Horse, Cock, Rat and Rabbit* are in the Four Pillars this person is a Playboy or Playgirl type, they flirt and have lots of sexual charisma, when these Branches are in the Four Pillars it will last throughout a lifetime, if there are three in the Pillars and the other appears in a 10-Year Luck cycle the influence last for that time frame. This principle applies to year and month cycles as well.

Family

A method for determining relationships between family members is based on the Five-Element relationship between the Day Stem element and each element in the Four Pillars. Example 1 is a Four Pillars chart listing family relationships based on the Four Pillars Palace method.

Example 1	Hour	Day	Month	Year
Stem	Sons Younger Brothers	Self	Dad Older Brothers	Grandfather Uncles, Male relatives
Branch	Daughters Younger Sisters	Spouse	Mom Older Sisters	Grandmother Aunts, Female relatives

Family relationships are revealed by evaluating the relationship between each element and the day stem, in example 2 the Parent Pillar has Yang Fire, Yin Fire and Yin Earth, they weaken the Day Stem Water, we predict parents create stress, obstacles, difficulties and pressure. Stems relate to males and Branches relate to females. The Month Stem is Yang Fire with a 100% strength factor, predict this person's father will creates stress and difficulties, this person's father died when he was an infant. The Month Branch or the Mother is Yin Fire with a weight of 70 and strength factor of 100%, it also contains a small amount of the controlling element Yin Earth, this person's mother died when he was 16.

The Year Pillar represents the Grandparents and contains Fire and Metal, the Stem is Fire and generates more weakness, stress and obstacles. This person never knew his Grandfather as he passed away before his birth. The Year Branch is Yin Metal and is the Parent or Resource of the Day Stem, this person had a wonderful relationship with his Grandmother and she was one of the most influential people in his life.

Example 2	Hour	Day	Month	Year
Stem	Yin Wood Offspring 100 X 50%	Yin Water	Yang Fire Grandchild 100 X 100%	Yin Fire Grandchild 100 X 100%
Branch	Rabbit	Cock	Horse	Cock
Elements	Yin Wood Offspring 100 X 50%	Yin Metal Parent 100 X 50%	Yin Fire Grandchild 70 X 100% Yin Earth Grandparent 30 X 50%	Yin Metal Parent 100 X 50%

An effective method to determine the relationship between family members is using Five-Element relationships and determining whether they are favorable or unfavorable to the Day Stem. The following examples explain these relationships.

Example 3

If the Day Stem is weak Water, Metal is favorable. If the Month Branch is Metal it is the resource of the Day Stem and provides nourishment.

Example 3	Hour	Day	Month	Year
Stem		Yin Water		
Branch			Mother Pillar Monkey Yin Metal	

Example 4.
   If the Self is weak and the Parents Pillar is the controlling element, Parents will exert a strong pressure, discipline and control and this situation can result in a negative way because the Self is weak and discipline or control may result in pressure.

Example 5.
If the Self is very strong and the Mother Pillar/Month Branch is the controlling element the Mother provides focus, direction and discipline and in this case the Self is strong enough to use control in a positive way.

Example 6.
If the Hour Stem is the mother element of the Self there is a nourishing relationship between Son and Self.

Example 6	Hour	Day	Month	Year
Stem	Yin Wood	Yang Fire		
Branch				

Applications of the Four Pillars

Hour	Day	Month	Year
Influential people, fellow workers, friends, children, spouse	Self	Environment, socialization, influences in childhood	Heritage, genetics, inheritance

Hour	Day	Month	Year
Inner-Self Internal Dynamics	Inner-self Internal Dynamics	Outer Self External Expression	Outer Self External Expression

Identify the impact of the Five-Elements on each area of life, for example, if this person was excess Fire and the Month branch was Horse/Yin Fire they would express themselves in a Fiery way, they would be very flamboyant, outgoing, verbal and intense.

If this same person had Yang Water and the Rat/Yin Water was in the Hour Pillar, their inner being would be calm and relaxed but they may act like an excess Fire person.

If the Month Pillar was Yang Wood/Tiger the environment during childhood created pressure and excitement, exacerbating the excess Fire condition.

Five-Element Relationships

When the strength of the Day Master is determined and favorable elements are identified universal Five-Element relationships that enhance the quality of life can be selected. For instance, a weak Water person can design Metal and Water wardrobes and living environments with beneficial elements, directions, colors and gemstones. The information in the following chart can be applied to one's life based on their Four Pillar astrology and these applications are examples of the integration of the Heaven, Human and Earth.

Element Relationship Chart

Element	Color Primary	Color Secondary	Direction	Organs	Gemstones	Planet
Wood	Green	Blue, Brown	East South East	Liver Gallbladder	Emerald, Jade, Green Opal	Jupiter
Fire	Red	Purple, Pink	South	Heart Small Intestine	Red Ruby	Mars
Earth	Yellow	Beige, Brown	North East South West Center	Spleen Stomach	Yellow Opal, Yellow Diamond	Saturn
Metal	White Gold	Gold Silver Sheen	North West West	Lungs Large Intestine	Pearl, Crystal, White Diamond	Venus
Water	Blue Black	Grey	North	Kidneys Urinary Bladder	White Opal, Blue Sapphire	Mercury

Example

Excess Metal may need Water or Fire, favorable Five-Element relationships include red or pink clothing, living in the Southern Hemisphere, southern part of a country, state or city and spend time in the southern part of their house or wear red ruby gems.

Four Pillars And Oriental Medicine

The Taoist view of the universe is one integrated life form, which is connected by an energy network with all parts influencing each other. Four Pillars and Oriental Medicine is an organic way to understand and harmonize these connections. Medical Four Pillars reveals the relationships between Stems, Branches and their related internal organs, acupuncture channels and areas of the body; each Stem and Branch relates to an internal organ and acupuncture channel. When Stems and Branches or their corresponding Five-Elements are in balance there is harmony and health and when Five-Elements are deficient or in excess, disharmony or disease is present or is likely to manifest. The following tables list each Stem and Branch and their related organ. A Four Pillars chart and its relationship to health originate by connecting Four Pillars Stems and Branches to their related organs.

Stems and Internal Organs

Stems	Related Organ -Channel-Area
Yang Wood	Gallbladder
Yin Wood	Liver
Yang Fire	Small Intestine
Yin Fire	Heart
Yang Earth	Stomach, Flank-Rib Cage Area
Yin Earth	Spleen, Abdomen
Yang Metal	Large Intestine, Navel Area
Yin Metal	Lungs, Buttocks
Yang Water	Urinary Bladder, Shins
Yin Water	Kidney, Lower Limb-Feet

Branches and Internal Organs

Branches-Animals	Organ-Channel-Area
Pig contains Yang Water	Urinary Bladder, Head, Scrotum, Feet
Rat contains Yin Water	Kidney, Genitals
Ox contains Yin Earth	Spleen, Abdomen, Feet
Tiger contains Yang Wood	Gallbladder, Hair, Hands, Legs
Rabbit contains Yin Wood	Liver, Fingers, Flank
Dragon contains Yang Earth	Stomach, Shoulders, Chest
Snake contains Yang Fire	Small Intestine, Face, Throat, Teeth, Genitals Anus
Horse contains Yin Fire	Heart, Eyes, Head
Sheep contains Yin Earth	Spleen, Diaphragm, Spine
Monkey contains Yang Metal	Large Intestine, Nerves
Cock contains Yin Metal	Lung, Sperm, Blood, Thorax
Dog contains Yang Earth	Stomach, Legs, Ankles, Feet

Four Pillars Constitutional Condition

Determining the health condition of a Four Pillars chart is a three-step process:

1. Calculate the Four Pillars
2. Determine the relative condition of each internal organ in the Four Pillars
3. Determine favorable and unfavorable elements

   - Favorable elements include elements that supplement weak, reduce excess or bring balance to elements.

   - Unfavorable elements are elements that alter balanced, reduce deficient or supplement excessive elements.

Once these steps are completed the prenatal condition has been determined, energetic conditions of the organs-channels revealed and favorable and unfavorable elements identified providing the foundation to predict constitutional health conditions.

Example

Four Pillars

	Hour	Day	Month	Year
Stem	Yin Wood Liver 100X 50%	Yin Water Kidney 100 X 50%	Yang Fire Small Intestine 100 X 100%	Yin Fire Heart 100 X 100%
Branch **Elements**	Rabbit Yin Wood Liver 100 X 50%	Cock Yin Metal Lung 100 X 50%	Horse Yin Fire Heart 70 X 100% Yin Earth Spleen 30 X 50%	Cock Yin Metal Lung 100 X 50%

Element	Organ	Relative Strength	Total Element	Percentage	Condition
Water	Kidney	50	50	9%	Weak
Wood	Liver	100	100	19%	Balanced
Fire	Small Intestine Heart	100 170	270	50%	Excess
Earth	Spleen	15	15	3%	Weak
Metal	Lung	100	100	19%	Balanced

Favorable Elements:

- *Water* controls excess Fire
- *Metal* supports deficient Metal
- *Earth* supports deficient Earth and reduces excess Fire

Unfavorable Elements:

- Fire is very excessive, additional Fire creates very unfavorable health influences
- Wood is balanced but makes Fire stronger exacerbating the excess condition

General Principles for Health

A profound principle in Oriental Medicine is balance for it leads to health. Learning to calculate or diagnose organ conditions is an integral aspect of Four Pillars and Oriental Medicine, it is the foundation for applying Four Pillars knowledge to health. The following are general principles for evaluating a Four Pillars chart.

- When an element is not present in the Four Pillars the related organ is weak or susceptible to disorders.

- When an element is controlled by a strong element it is very susceptible to disorders and when the controlling cycle causes a health problem the process is referred to as overacting, generally overacting leads to unfavorable health.

- If the Day Stem is weak illnesses tend to be of a chronic nature and require time to cure.

- If the Day Stem is strong illnesses tend to be acute and take a short time to cure.

- If the element causing the illness is weak the illness is not strong.

- If the element causing the illness is strong the illness is strong.

- Day, Month, Year and 10-Year Life/Luck cycles must be evaluated to predict how nature's energetic cycles affect Four Pillars and health at any given time.

Example
Male born on June 30, 1957 at 6:30 am, daylight saving time

Four Pillars

	Hour	Day	Month	Year
Stem	Yin Wood Liver 100X 50%	Yin Water Kidney 100 X 50%	Yang Fire Small Intestine 100 X 100%	Yin Fire Heart 100 X 100%
Branch **Elements**	Rabbit Yin Wood Liver 100 X 50%	Cock Yin Metal Lung 100 X 50%	Horse Yin Fire Heart 70 X 100% Yin Earth Spleen 30 X 50%	Cock Yin Metal Lung 100 X 50%

Element	Organ	Relative Strength	Total Element	Percentage	Condition
Water	Kidney	50	50	9%	Weak
Wood	Liver	100	100	19%	Balanced
Fire	Small Intestine Heart	100 170	270	50%	Excess
Earth	Spleen	15	15	3%	Weak
Metal	Lung	100	100	19%	Balanced

Analysis

- Excess Fire
- Deficient Earth
- Fire overacts on Metal creating potential Lung and Large Intestine conditions
- Deficient Earth receives some energy from its resource Fire, but Earth is still weak and this person is susceptible to Earth disorders
- Deficient Earth fails to nourish Metal contributing to Metal disharmonies
- Deficient Water obtains some energy from its resource Metal but is still deficient

Objective

- Clear excess Fire from Heart and Small Intestine
- Clear Fire from Metal organs (Lung and Large Intestine)
- Supplement Earth, Metal and Water organs

Day Stem is Water

Strengthening elements:
- Metal-parent 100
- Water-same 50
- Total is 150

Weakening elements:
- Wood 100
- Fire 270
- Earth 15
- Total 385

This is a weak Water Day Stem

A weak Water Day Master provides the environment for chronic illnesses, it is important to resolve any illnesses quickly preventing opportunities for an illness to develop and become chronic. It is very important to balance the Four Pillars condition.

- This person is very susceptible to developing chronic Fire, Earth and Metal conditions.
- Fire is very strong and its influence on Metal is very unfavorable, special focus must be used to balance this condition; this is an example of a very strong element controlling and unfavorably influencing another element.

Five-Element Organ Syndromes

The Five-Element Organ Syndromes below lists basic conditions for each of the internal organs when they are excess or deficient.

Five-Element Organ Syndromes

Element	Organ	Condition
Water	**Kidney**	**No Excess Conditions**
		Deficiency Conditions Dizziness, tinnitus, vertigo, deafness, poor memory, thirst, sore back, knee pain, night sweats, red cheek bones, insomnia, hyper-sexual activity, constipation Fatigue, frequent urination, diarrhea, cold limbs and back, pale face, impotence, premature ejaculation, edema of legs, infertility, loose stools, incontinence, spermatorrhea, shortness of breath, difficulty inhaling, cough, asthma Poor bone development, softening of bones, loose teeth, premature graying of hair, lack of sexual energy
	Urinary Bladder	**Excess Conditions** Frequent burning or difficult urination, dark-yellow or turbid urination, fever, thirst, copious and clear urine
		Deficiency Conditions Frequent, pale urination, incontinence, enuresis
Wood	**Liver**	**Excess Conditions** Distention or pain of the hypochondria and chest, sighing, hiccup, fluctuation of mental and emotional state, nausea, vomiting, poor appetite, a feeling of a lump in throat, irritability, anger, menstrual disorders, PMS, headache, digestive disorders, dizziness, convulsions, tremor of limbs, numbness of limbs, bitter taste, jaundice, vaginal discharge and itching
		Deficiency Conditions Anemia, menstrual disorders, numbness of limbs, weak nails, dizziness, blurred vision, menstrual irregularities, pale expressions, pale lips, muscular weakness, muscle spasms, cramps, brittle nails
	Gallbladder	**Excess Conditions** Hypochondriac pain, nausea, vomiting, inability to digest fats, yellow complexion and bitter taste
		Deficiency Conditions Dizziness, blurred vision, nervousness, timidity, lack of courage, sighing

Five-Element Organ Syndromes

Element	Organ	Condition
Fire	Heart	**Excess Conditions** Palpitations, thirst, mouth and tongue ulcers, mental restlessness, heat, insomnia, red face, bitter taste, dream disturbed sleep, incoherent speech, pain in the heart region which can radiate to inner aspect of the left arm, feeling of oppression of chest
		Deficiency Conditions Palpitations, shortness of breath on exertion, sweating, pallor, fatigue, listlessness, dizziness, insomnia, dream-disturbed sleep, poor memory, malar flushed face, low grade fever, feeling of heat
	Small Intestine	**Excess Conditions** Mental restlessness, tongue ulcers, pain in throat, abdominal pain, thirst, scanty and dark urine, painful urination, blood in urine. Lower abdominal twisting pain which may radiate to the back, abdominal distention, borborygmus, flatulence, pain in testis, dislike of abdominal pain, constipation, vomiting, diarrhea
		Deficiency Conditions Abdominal discomfort, borborygmus, scanty urination, flatulence and diarrhea
Earth	Spleen	**Excess Conditions** Lack of appetite, stuffiness of epigastrium, feeling of cold, heaviness sensation of the head, sweetish taste, loose stools, fatigue, feeling of heaviness of the body, thirst without a desire to drink, nausea, vomiting, burning sensation of the anus, edema
		Deficiency Conditions Lack of appetite, abdominal distention after eating, fatigue, sallow complexion, weakness of limbs, loose stools, shortness of breath, nausea, feeling of heaviness, chilliness, cold limbs, prolapsed of stomach/uterus/anus or vagina, blood spots under the skin, blood in the urine or stools, menorrhagia, varicose veins, edema
	Stomach	**Excess Conditions** Burning sensation in the epigastrium, thirst for cold liquids, constant hunger, swelling, pain or bleeding gums, nausea, vomiting after eating, bad breath. Sudden pain in the epigastrium, feeling of cold, vomiting of clear fluid
		Deficiency Conditions Lack of appetite, loose stools, fatigue, weak limbs, discomfort of epigastrium, nausea, belching, vomiting, hiccup Fever or feeling of heat in the afternoon, constipation, epigastric pain, dry mouth and throat, feeling of fullness after eating

Five-Element Organ Syndromes

Metal	Lung	**Excess Conditions** Chronic cough, phlegm/clear or yellow, stuffiness of chest, shortness of breath, asthma
		Deficiency Conditions Shortness of breath, cough, weak voice, catches colds easily, fatigue, dry throat, low-grade fever, night sweating, thirst
	Large Intestine	**Excess Conditions** Abdominal pain, diarrhea, mucous in blood, burning anus, smelly stools, fever, sweating, scanty dark urine, constipation, cold, diarrhea with pain, chronic diarrhea, prolapsed anus, hemorrhoids, cold limbs, borborygmus
		Deficiency Conditions Diarrhea, constipation, prolapsed anus, hemorrhoids, abdominal distention

When a color is predominant on the body it is often an indicator of a disharmony with its corresponding organ system, for example, if someone has a red face and eyes it may reflect excess Fire; if the lower eyelids are a dark shade, it may reflect a Water or Kidney disharmony. Connect the predominant color to the Organ-Element system and refer to the Five-Element-Organ System table to identify possible syndromes, if the syndromes, color and element match this confirms the organ is out of balance, use harmonizing techniques to promote balance and health.

Example

Four Pillars

	Hour	Day	Month	Year
Stem	Yin Wood Liver 100X 50%	Yin Water Kidney 100 X 50%	Yang Fire Small Intestine 100 X 100%	Yin Fire Heart 100 X 100%
Branch **Elements**	Rabbit Yin Wood Liver 100 X 50%	Cock Yin Metal Lung 100 X 50%	Horse Yin Fire Heart 70 X 100% Yin Earth Spleen 30 X 50%	Cock Yin Metal Lung 100 X 50%

Element	Organ	Relative Strength	Total Element	Percentage	Condition
Water	Kidney	50	50	9%	Weak
Wood	Liver	100	100	19%	Balanced
Fire	Small Intestine Heart	100 170	270	50%	Excess
Earth	Spleen	15	15	3%	Weak
Metal	Lung	100	100	19%	Balanced

Analysis

- Excess Fire

  Palpitations, thirst, mouth and tongue ulcers, mental restlessness, heat, insomnia, red face, bitter taste, dream disturbed sleep, incoherent speech, pain in the heart region which can radiate to inner aspect of the left arm, feeling of oppression of chest.

- Deficient Earth

  Lack of appetite, abdominal distention after eating, fatigue, sallow complexion, weakness of limbs, loose stools, shortness of breath, nausea, feeling of heaviness, chilliness, cold limbs, prolapse of stomach, uterus, anus or vagina, blood spots under the skin, blood in the urine or stools, menorrhagia, varicose veins.

  Lack of appetite, loose stools, fatigue, weak limbs, discomfort epigastrium, nausea, belching, vomiting, hiccup. Fever or feeling of heat in the afternoon, constipation, epigastric pain, dry mouth and throat, feeling of fullness after eating.

- Excess Fire overacts on Metal, creating potential Lung and Large Intestine syndromes. This is the most predominant constitutional condition. Chronic cough, phlegm-clear or yellow, stuffiness of chest, shortness of breath, asthma, weak voice, catches colds easily, fatigue, dry throat, low-grade fever, night sweating, thirst, diarrhea, constipation, prolapsed anus, hemorrhoids, abdominal distention

- Deficient Earth receives some energy from its resource Fire, but earth remains deficient and there is a high potential for digestive difficulties.

- Deficient Earth fails to nourish Metal contributing to Metal disharmonies.

- Water deficiency

  Dizziness, tinnitus, vertigo, deafness, poor memory, thirst, sore back, knee pain, night sweats, red cheek bones, insomnia, hypersexual activity, constipation.

Excess Fire dries up and weakens Water, while Water normally controls Fire, Water is weak and Fire is very strong overwhelming it creating Water syndromes. This is commonly referred to as the Insulting cycle, it is when the controlled element is so strong or there is a strong imbalance it attacks and negatively influences the controlling element.

Natural Harmonizing Techniques

Acupuncture Points

This chapter introduces a variety of basic practices and techniques to enhance health and includes traditional Acupuncture points, Qi Gong, Five-Element Cosmology and influences of the Seasons. The following table lists Acupuncture points for each element, as well as their corresponding organ and Acupuncture points for excess and deficient conditions. Please refer to any standard book on Acupuncture or Oriental Medicine as a reference.

Element	Organ	Excess	Deficiency
Water	Kidney	No Excess Syndromes	Kidney 3, 6, 7 Bladder 23 Ren 4 Spleen 6 Five-Element Treatment: Kidney 7
	Urinary Bladder	Bladder 28, 40, 58, 60, 62, 64 Five-Element Treatment: Bladder 65	Bladder 23, 40, 60, 62 Kidney 3, 6, 7 Ren 3 Five-Element Treatment: Bladder 67
Wood	Liver	Liver 2, 3, 5, 14 Pericardium 6 Bladder 18 Five-Element Treatment: Liver 2	Liver 3, 5, 8. 14 Bladder 18 Liver 8
	Gallbladder	Gallbladder 20, 24, 30, 31, 34, 40, 41 Bladder 19 Five-Element Treatment: GB 38	Gallbladder 20, 30, 31, 34, 41 Bladder 19 Five-Element Treatment: GB 43
Fire	Heart	Heart 3, 6, 7, 8 Ren 14, 17 Pericardium 6 Bladder 14, 15 Five-Element Treatment: Heart 7	Heart 1, 3, 7 Ren 14, 17 Pericardium 6 Bladder 14, 15 Five-Element Treatment: Heart 9
	Small Intestine	Small Intestine 3, 6, 7 Ren 4 Bladder 27 Five-Element Treatment: Small Intestine 8	Small Intestine 3, 7 Ren 4 Bladder 27 Five-Element Treatment: Small Intestine 3
Earth	Spleen	Spleen 4, 6, 9, 10 Ren 4, 12 Bladder 20, 21 Five-Element Treatment: Spleen 5	Spleen 3, 4, 6, 9, 10 Ren 4, 12 Stomach 36 Bladder 20, 21 Five-Element Treatment: Spleen 2
	Stomach	Stomach 21, 34, 36, 42, 44 Ren 12 Bladdder 21 Five-Element Treatment: Stomach 45	Stomach 21, 36 Ren 12 Spleen 6 Bladder 21 Five-Element Treatment: Stomach 41
Metal	Lung	Lung 1, 5, 6, 7, 10 Ren 17 Bladder 13 Five-Element Treatment: Lung 5	Lung 1, 7, 9 Ren 17 Bladder 13 Five-Element Treatment: Lung 9
	Large Intestine	Large Intestine 4, 6, 11, 15 Stomach 25, 37 Ren 12 Bladder 25 San Jiao 6 Kidney 6 Five-Element Treatment: Large Intestine 2	Large Intestine 4, 10 Stomach 25, 37 Ren 12 Bladder 25 Five-Element Treatment: Large Intestine 11

Five-Element Cosmology

Five-Element cosmology relates Five-Elements to space or direction, benefits are obtained by positioning oneself in specific geographical locations to absorb or bathe in a favorable Five-Element influence. The Five-Element Cosmology table lists the Five-Elements and directional relationships.

Five-Element Cosmology

Element	Direction	Element
Water	North	Water Fountain, Aquarium
Wood	East, South East	Plants
Fire	South	Red Candle, Red Items
Earth	South West, North East, Center	Ceramic, Porcelain, Crystals, Soil-based items
Metal	West, North West	Metal clocks, grandfather clocks, Metal items

Seasons

Each element corresponds to a season and the element for a particular season is the pre-dominant force during its cycle, this elemental force can be favorable or unfavorable depending on the Four Pillars condition of a person. The application of this knowledge is to predict how each season will affect a person's health and which techniques can be used to find balance during each season, the Five-Element Season table lists the element for each season and an example follows illustrating how to apply this knowledge.

Five-Elements Seasons

Season	Element
Winter	Water
Spring	Wood
Summer	Fire
Indian Summer	Earth
Fall	Metal

Example

Four Pillars

	Hour	Day	Month	Year
Stem	**Yin Wood Liver** 100X 50%	**Yin Water Kidney** 100 X 50%	**Yang Fire Small Intestine** 100 X 100%	**Yin Fire Heart** 100 X 100%
Branch **Elements**	**Rabbit** **Yin Wood Liver** 100 X 50%	**Cock** **Yin Metal Lung** 100 X 50%	**Horse** **Yin Fire Heart** 70 X 100% **Yin Earth Spleen** 30 X 50%	**Cock** **Yin Metal Lung** 100 X 50%

Element	Organ	Relative Strength	Total Element	Percentage	Condition
Water	Kidney	50	50	9%	Weak
Wood	Liver	100	100	19%	Balanced
Fire	Small Intestine Heart	100 170	270	50%	Excess
Earth	Spleen	15	15	3%	Weak
Metal	Lung	100	100	19%	Balanced

Analysis

- Excess Fire
- Deficient Earth
- Fire overacts on Metal creating potential Lung and Large Intestine syndromes
- The deficient Earth receives some energy from its resource Fire, promoting or supplementing Earth. Earth is weak making this person susceptible to Earth disorders.
- Deficient Earth falls to nourish Metal contributing to Metal disharmonies
- Deficient Water obtains some energy from its resource Metal

Objective

- Clear excess Fire from the Heart and Small Intestine
- Clear Fire from Metal organs, Lung and Large Intestine
- Supplement Earth, Metal and Water

Seasonal Analysis

- Spring and Summer increases the existing excess Fire, special emphasis must be placed on reducing Fire and increasing Metal and Water.
- Indian Summer brings some relief as the Earth element drains or reduces Fire.
- Fall and Winter representing Water and Metal are the best months for this person and they provide natural energies for naturally balancing the Four Pillars.

Traditional Time Acupuncture

"Ling Gui Ba Fa"

Lost in the modern day of Oriental Medicine is the ancient art of Time Acupuncture, one of the esoteric Branches of Taoist Healing. This art is based on the Waxing and Waning of Vital Substances throughout the body and identifying the proper time to needle specific acupuncture points for optimal treatment results. Ling Gua Ba Fa is based on the same principles as the Taoist arts of Feng Shui and Five-Element Chinese Astrology/Four Pillars of Destiny. This ancient form of acupuncture can enhance any acupuncture treatment and promotes the body's self-healing mechanisms.

Traditional Time Acupuncture is based on the natural cycles of Vital Substances within the body: Qi, Blood, Essence and Body Fluids, they make up the matrix of human life and are the basis of health and vitality. Vital Substances follow a specific pattern of circulation through Acupuncture channels during each day. There are a variety of systems in Traditional Time Acupuncture, some are practical and easily applied in modern society and others are impractical, in this book the ancient system of Ling Gui Ba Fa is introduced, it is a highly effective system using eight of the most powerful acupuncture points.

Ling Gui Ba Fa or The Eight Techniques of the Mysterious Turtle is an ancient Acupuncture technique for applying Stems, Branches, Eight Trigrams and the Master Points of the Eight Extraordinary Channels. The Eight Extraordinary channels influence the most profound levels of health. Classic texts state "The 360 Acupuncture points on the twelve regular channels are controlled by the 66 points on the extremities, the 66 points on the extremities are controlled by the 8 Master Points. These Master Points can treat 243 kinds of symptoms and diseases". The Eight Master Points are the key to utilizing the deepest aspects of Oriental Medicine.

The Nine Palaces or Magic Square are discussed in the "The Scripture of the Luo" and is the basis for Ling Gui Ba Fa. Odd numbers are Yang representing the Celestial and even numbers are Yin representing the terrestrial. The numbers in the four directions (South, West, North, East) are odd and relate to the celestial, numbers in the four corners (South East, South West, North West, North East) are even and relate to the terrestrial.

	South **Fire** **4, 9**	
East **Wood** **3, 8**	**Center** **Earth** **5, 10**	**West** **Metal** **2, 7**
	North **Water** **1, 6**	

The following tables list the Later Heaven Ba Gua, their related trigrams and command point for the eight extraordinary channels.

Table A

Later Heaven Arrangement of Gua

South East Wood 4	South Fire 9	South West Wood 2
Gallbladder 41	Lung 7	Kidney 6
East Wood 3	Center Earth 5	West Metal 7
San Jiao 5	Kidney 6	Small Intestine 3
North East 8	North Water 1	North West Metal 6
Pericardium 6	Bladder 62	Spleen 4

Table B

Ling Gui Ba Fa Numbers

Number	Trigram	Element	Master Point	Couple Point
1	Kan	Water	Bladder 62	Small Intestine 3
2 5	Gen	Earth	Kidney 6	Lung 7
3	Zhen	Wood Thunder	San Jiao 5	Gall Bladder 41
4	Xun	Wood Wind	Gallbladder 41	San Jiao 5
6	Metal	Metal Heaven	Spleen 4	Pericardium 6
7	Dui	Metal Lake	Small Intestine 3	Bladder 62
8	Ken	Earth Mountain	Pericardium 6	Spleen 3
9	Li	Fire	Lung 7	Kidney 6

The Ling Gui Ba Fa technique consists of a three-step process

1. Locate the Binomial number for the treatment Day, this is the Day Stem and Branch and is located in the Appendix (years 1920-2010)

2. Table C contains the 12-Double Hours along with every combination of Stems and Branches (Binomials)

   - Locate the Binomial number for the treatment Day in Table C, it is in the top row
   - Locate the treatment Hour in the first column
   - Identify the intersection of the treatment Hour and treatment Day Binomial, this is the Ling Gui Ba Fa number, refer to Table B for the related Master Point

Master Points of the Eight Extraordinary Channels are grouped in pairs and it is very effective to use the paired Master Point in a treatment, it is referred to as the Coupled Point, use the Ling Gui Ba Fa Master Point first then the paired Point, Table B list each combination of master and couple point.

How to use Table C

- Locate the Binomial for the treatment Day in the top row
- Locate the treatment Hour in the first column
- Locate the intersection of the Day Binomial and the treatment Hour, this is the Ling Gui Ba Fa number
- Refer to Table B for the Master Point

Table C

	Binomials				Binomials				Binomials				Binomials		
Hour	1	2	3	4	5	6	7	8	9	10	11	12	13	14	15
11pm-1am	8	5	2	3	5	5	5	1	7	1	2	2	1	5	3
1am-3am	6	3	5	1	3	3	3	4	5	5	9	6	4	3	1
3am-5am	4	1	3	5	6	1	1	2	3	2	7	4	2	1	4
5am-7am	2	4	1	3	4	5	4	6	1	6	5	1	9	5	2
7am-9am	9	2	8	6	2	3	2	4	4	4	3	5	7	2	9
9am-11am	3	6	6	4	9	6	9	2	2	2	6	3	5	6	7
11am-1pm	7	4	6	2	4	4	4	5	6	6	1	1	5	4	2
1pm-3pm	5	2	4	6	7	2	2	3	4	3	8	5	3	2	5
3pm-5pm	3	5	2	4	5	6	5	1	2	1	6	2	1	6	3
5pm-7pm	1	3	9	1	3	4	3	5	5	5	4	6	8	3	1
7pm-9pm	4	1	7	5	1	1	1	3	3	3	7	4	6	1	8
9pm-11pm	2	5	1	3	8	5	8	6	1	1	5	2	9	5	6

	Binomials				Binomials				Binomials				Binomials		
Hour	16	17	18	19	20	21	22	23	24	25	26	27	28	29	30
11pm-1am	6	8	4	5	2	1	4	4	2	2	2	6	5	8	5
1am-3am	4	6	1	3	6	8	2	7	6	9	6	4	2	6	3
3am-5am	2	4	5	1	3	6	6	5	4	3	4	2	6	4	6
5am-7am	6	7	6	8	1	4	3	3	2	1	2	5	4	2	4
7am-9am	4	5	1	3	5	2	1	1	5	8	6	3	2	5	2
9am-11am	1	3	5	9	3	5	5	8	3	6	3	1	6	3	6
11am-1pm	5	7	2	4	1	9	3	8	1	1	1	5	3	7	4
1pm-3pm	3	5	6	2	4	7	1	6	5	4	5	3	1	5	1
3pm-5pm	1	8	4	9	2	5	4	4	3	2	3	6	5	3	5
5pm-7pm	5	6	2	3	6	3	2	2	6	9	1	4	3	6	3
7pm-9pm	2	4	6	1	4	6	6	9	4	7	4	2	1	4	1
9pm-11pm	6	2	3	8	2	4	4	3	2	5	2	9	4	2	5

Table C

Hour	Binomials 31	32	33	34	Binomials 35	36	37	38	Binomials 39	40	41	42	Binomials 43	44	45
11pm-1am	8	5	3	4	5	5	5	1	6	6	2	2	1	5	4
1am-3am	6	3	6	2	3	3	3	4	4	4	9	6	4	3	2
3am-5am	4	1	4	6	6	1	1	2	2	1	7	4	2	1	5
5am-7am	2	4	2	4	4	5	4	6	9	5	5	1	9	5	3
7am-9am	9	2	9	1	2	3	2	4	3	3	3	5	7	2	1
9am-11am	3	6	7	5	9	6	9	2	1	1	6	3	5	6	8
11am-1pm	7	4	7	3	4	4	4	5	5	5	1	1	5	4	3
1pm-3pm	5	2	5	1	7	2	2	3	3	2	8	5	3	2	6
3pm-5pm	3	5	3	5	5	6	5	1	1	6	6	2	1	6	4
5pm-7pm	1	3	1	2	3	4	3	5	4	4	4	6	8	3	2
7pm-9pm	4	1	8	6	1	1	1	3	2	2	7	4	6	1	9
9pm-11pm	2	5	2	4	8	5	8	6	9	8	5	2	9	5	7

Hour	Binomials 46	47	48	49	Binomials 50	51	52	53	Binomials 54	55	56	57	Binomials 58	59	60
11pm-1am	1	8	4	5	2	9	3	4	2	2	2	7	6	8	5
1am-3am	5	6	1	3	6	7	1	7	6	9	6	5	3	6	3
3am-5am	3	4	5	1	3	5	5	5	4	3	4	3	1	4	6
5am-7am	1	7	3	8	1	3	2	3	2	1	2	6	5	2	4
7am-9am	5	5	1	2	5	1	6	1	5	8	6	4	3	5	2
9am-11am	2	3	5	9	3	4	4	8	3	6	3	2	1	3	6
11am-1pm	6	7	2	4	1	8	2	8	1	1	1	6	4	7	4
1pm-3pm	4	5	6	2	4	6	6	6	5	4	5	4	2	5	1
3pm-5pm	2	8	4	9	2	4	3	4	3	2	3	7	6	3	5
5pm-7pm	6	6	2	3	6	2	1	2	6	9	1	5	4	6	3
7pm-9pm	3	4	6	1	4	5	5	9	4	7	4	3	2	4	1
9pm-11pm	1	2	3	8	2	8	3	3	2	5	2	1	5	2	5

Example 1
    Treatment Day is March 5, 1987 at 8:30 am

    Treatment Day Binomial is 50, Yin Water/Ox
    Treatment Hour is 8:30am
    Table C at 8:30 am contains Binomial five
    Table B revels #5 is Kidney 6, the Coupled Master Point is Lung 7

Example 2
    Treatment Day is April 8, 1985 at Noon

    Treatment Day Binomial is 14, Yin Fire/Ox
    Treatment Hour is Noon
    Table C at Noon contains Binomial #4
    Table B reveals #4 is Gallbladder 41, the Coupled Master Point is San Jiao 5

Spiritual Qi Gong

Taoist Alchemy

Spiritual Qi Gong reveals the ancient Taoist system of internal alchemy for Health, Longevity and Spiritual Development. The practices contained in this book have been kept a closely guarded secret for centuries, Taoist internal alchemy or spiritual cultivation has historically been written in ambiguous and obtuse forms primarily to retain the true meaning from being revealed to the public and they have been cloaked in secrecy even within the Taoist community. My primary objective in writing this book is to communicate these ancient meditations in an easily understandable method; the benefits obtained from these practices include emotional harmony, physical health, vitality, longevity and spiritual development.

The information being presented is the result of thousands of years of human spiritual development and is derived from ancient Taoist cannons which are esoteric books explaining Asian Arts. The classic books Pao Pu Tze and Can Tong Qi are the major basis of this book and the Taoist spiritual alchemical formulas contained in this book are the Five-Elements Organ Rejuvenation, Heavenly Orbit, Eight Treasures and Shen-Spirit Realization (Kan and Li cultivations). The presentation of this material is based on my twenty-five years of studying, practicing and teaching Asian arts, I have retained the essence of the traditional practices while presenting them in a clear, easily understandable format for modern society. People of all philosophical, spiritual or educational backgrounds can practice these meditations, it is a path that reveals spiritual truth common to all human life.

A key element within Spiritual Qi Gong is human life is integrated and consists of three major influences: Physical, Mental and Spiritual, they are one undivided whole. Each type of Qi Gong affects all aspects of life, while some Qi Gong forms may focus more on one area than another, all aspects of life are affected by these practices. There are common experiences for all who practice these meditations, but each person is unique and may

261

experience different levels and depths, additionally each practice is inter-connected often activating or stimulating an experience explained in another Qi Gong section, this is normal and an example of the integration of human life. Follow the practices in a gentle and relaxed way and you will taste the fruit of Spiritual Qi Gong.

The desire to understand the meaning of life can be found in cultures throughout the world, each has developed practices, techniques, philosophies and religions that reveal the relationship between human life and the creator of all life. In ancient China, a system of spiritual cultivation evolved, "Spiritual Qi Gong", which comprises numerous styles of meditations. The ancients developed these practices with the goal of achieving physical, mental and spiritual development. Spiritual Qi Gong practices begin with promoting physical health and emotional well being, if one chooses he or she can pursue the spiritual goal of the direct realization of one's true spiritual nature. There is one integral requirement for obtaining the fruit of Spiritual Qi Gong, a person must be virtuous, and without virtue the fruit of this work cannot be achieved. Virtue is a magnet that attracts energies necessary to refine and cultivate body, mind and spirit. These practices begin a process of refinement and transformation, the key is to relax and have an open, virtuous heart, as you practice the fruit will appear.

Spiritual Qi Gong consists of cultivating the three treasures of life: Jing, Qi and Shen. Jing is essence or the base energy of life, it can also be called biological or reproductive energy, Qi is vitality or life force and Shen is Spirit. Jing or essence is the densest and most physical of the three, it is the foundation for the two other treasures. Qi is created from the transformation of Jing and Qi nourishes Shen/Spirit, they are one undivided whole. This transformation process occurs naturally but stress, tension, emotional and mental disharmony can slow, block or cause an imbalance among the Three Treasures, for instance, to much emphasis can be placed on material or sexual interests, this causes one's life force to be directed towards those areas of life and away from the natural transformation and evolution towards spiritual growth. Spiritual Qi Gong gently guides transformation of Jing to Qi and Qi to spiritual consciousness and development, these practices restore the natural rhythm of life where the root, foundation or biological energy supports spirit.

Universal Cosmology

The Universe is self-generating and eternal. One integral principle which permeates the Universe is "root always exists within a branch", this root to branch relationship is the basis of Spiritual Qi Gong. One application of this root to branch interaction is explained by the ancient Chinese Tai Chi symbol. Tai Chi consists of a trinity: Early-Heaven or Yang, Later-Heaven or Yin and the integration of the two, Tai Chi. The Early Heaven condition is life before time, space and the dimension of duality, it is an eternal, self-generating, undivided unity. The Later Heaven stage is the stage of transformation, it is reflected by the principles of Yin-Yang, and the physical, dual world. The dimensions of polarity: time and space form this Later Heaven condition and the interaction of Early Heaven and Later Heaven energies create human life or Tai Chi, these three aspects of life exist simultaneously, they are one undivided whole. Spiritual Qi Gong is designed to guide a person to realize the unity of Early Heaven and Later Heaven life, revealing their true spiritual nature.

Tai Chi

Early Heaven or subtle realm is referred to as the Mysterious Mother, like a Mother it gives birth to life. The subtle realm includes pure, undivided energy and is the destination or fruit of Spiritual Qi Gong. The process of "connecting" to the subtle realm begins with the unification of the physical, emotional, energetic and spiritual aspects of one's life and is the goal of Taoist Qi Gong or Taoist Alchemy.

The subtle realm is the Early Heaven or Godly realm and the root of life, it is also the vitality contained within all Branches of life. Later Heaven includes Branches of the subtle realm, they are direct extensions of the subtle realm and comprise the manifest, dual world. Branches are always connected to root, it is within these Branches Spiritual Qi Gong reconnects a person to the source of life, Branches are pathways to root, subtle realm or God. From a Universal perspective, root and branch are one undivided reality and this realization and experience is the fruit of Spiritual Qi Gong.

The subtle realm expanded itself to create the universe and the following introduces this process:

- The first expression or branch of the subtle realm includes *Immortal Divine Beings*, they are pure spirits, fully God conscious and guides for humans. They are the source of Spiritual Qi Gong.

- The second expression or branch includes *Solar Beings or Natural Deities*, they are locations in the Universe that gather and store subtle energy. These categories of life include Stars and Planets and are transmitters for receiving and distributing pure, unaltered energy of the Subtle Realm. These living entities are centers of energy which humans can develop relationships, acting as pathways that guide aspiring humans to the subtle realm or God consciousness. Solar Beings or Natural Deities act as spiritual compasses, guiding human life to their final destination, human life benefits by connecting, communicating and absorbing their energy, nourishing and revitalizing human consciousness, providing energy and guidance for spiritual evolution.

- Immortal Spirits are another expression of the subtle realm. Immortality is a state of consciousness or awareness of the subtle realm, human life has the opportunity to cultivate and refine themselves to become an Immortal or aware of their true nature. In this awareness, time and space or the polar dimension is transcended and one merges with the undivided, original, subtle realm. An Immortal, at will, enters and exits the Early Heaven and Later Heaven dimensions, in reality for an Immortal, there is no difference between the Early and Later Heaven, they are one undivided whole.

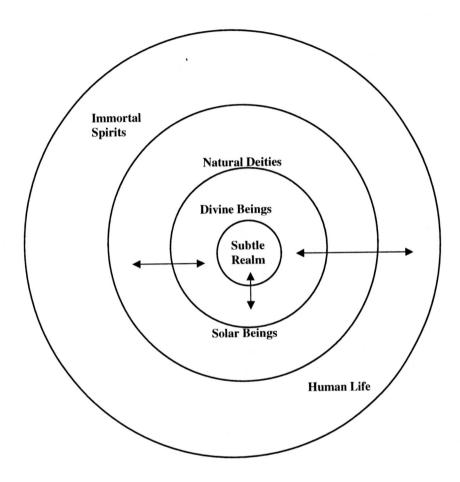

A major goal of Spiritual Qi Gong is realizing Early and Later Heaven life exist simultaneously, this is why humans can experience the Subtle Realm in this life, it is not required to wait for another life. These ancient Qi Gong practices assist in the evolution of human consciousness and remove the veil people wear, not only revealing their true spiritual nature, but also causing a permanent transformation into a new dimension of awareness. This dimension is the integration of Early Heaven and Later Heaven life, in essence realizing Heaven within Earth. This process begins by harmonizing our emotions to find peace and balance in daily life.

Emotional Harmony Qi Gong

Five-Element Organ Rejuvenation

The Mysterious Mother is the source of Qi Gong,
 know the offspring but stay with the Mysterious Mother,
 health and spiritual growth will be assured.

Emotional Harmony Qi Gong is a simple but powerful form of Qi Gong and has two major goals, the first is detoxification and second is achieving emotional harmony. When practicing each Qi Gong meditation spend as much time as necessary during each stage until you experience the described feeling, sensation or process; spend weeks to a year at any stage until the benefits are achieved and you feel ready to move to the next practice. Each person is unique and there is no set duration of time to practice that fits all people, your daily experience determines your level of cultivation. The fruit of these practices appear through consistent dedicated practice, theoretical mastery has no true benefit without actually experiencing these meditations, practice leads to direct experience and achievement.

The Universe is an integrated living being and this principle applies to all of life. There are a variety of Qi Gong practices presented in this book, even though the following meditations will have clear descriptions of each specific practice, due to the integrated nature of life one mediation can activate benefits that are listed in other practices. Each person is unique and one practice may influence a person differently than another, they may have "advance" experiences with basic mediations, this is normal and should be viewed as healthy and positive. One of the most important things to remember during all these practices is to be relaxed, gentle and breathe naturally.

266

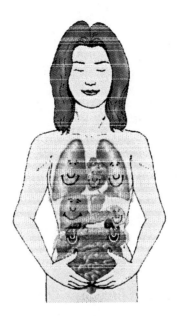

Emotional Harmony Qi Gong

Part 1 – Five-Element Healing Sounds

Benefits:

- Detoxifies the organs and acupuncture channels
- Cools the body
- Clears heat trapped in the organs and channels
- Releases negative emotions
- Transforms negative emotions/Qi into positive/Qi

See the Five-Element Rejuvenation table for the organs and their correspondences
General Principle:
The form for each of the Healing Sounds is one long inhale and one long exhale, the breath is in the lower belly, fill this area on the inhale.

1. Begin by sitting naturally in a chair, open your eyes and place your mind's attention in the Lungs, take a slow deep inhale breathing into the abdomen, think of sadness and depression, as you exhale make the SSSSSSSSSSSSSSSS sound releasing sadness and depression, when finished, move your attention into the Lungs, smile and repeat the word courage, feel courage in the Lungs. To enhance this process when you smile into the Lungs place your hands over the Lungs, palms touching the body, you may do this for all the organs, maintain this smiling feeling for one to three minutes. Repeat this process 1-3 times.

2. Open your eyes and place your mind's attention in the Kidneys, take a deep inhale breathing into the lower abdomen, think of fear and make the Chuuuu sound releasing fear during the exhale. When finished move your attention into the Kidneys, smile and repeat the word gentleness, feel gentleness in the Kidneys. To enhance this process when you smile into the Kidneys place your hands over the Kidneys, maintain this feeling for one to three minutes. Repeat this process 1-3 times.

3. Open your eyes and place your mind's attention in the Liver, take a full inhale breathing into the abdomen, think of anger and make the Shhhhhh sound releasing anger during the exhale. When finished move your attention into the Liver, smile and repeat the word Kindness, feel Kindness in the Liver. To enhance this process when you smile into the Liver place your hands over the Liver, maintain this feeling for 1-3 minutes. Repeat this process 1-3 times.

4. Open your eyes and place your mind's attention in the Heart, take a full inhale breathing into the abdomen, think of Hastiness, Impatience and Hatred and make the Haw sound releasing Hastiness, Impatience and Hatred during the exhale. When finished move your attention into the Heart, smile and repeat the words Joy and Love, feel Joy and Love in the Heart. To enhance this process when you smile into the Heart place your hands over the Heart, maintain this feeling for 1-3 minutes. Repeat this process 1-3 times.

5. Open your eyes and place your mind's attention in the Spleen, take a full inhale breathing into the abdomen, think of Worry and make the Whooo sound releasing Worry during the exhale. When finished move your attention into the Spleen, smile and repeat the word Openness. To enhance this process when you smile into the Spleen place your hands over the Spleen, maintain this feeling for 1-3 minutes. Repeat this process 1-3 times.

6. Open your eyes and take a full inhale breathing into the abdomen, make the Hee sound when exhaling. There is no emotion or organ related to this sound, it balances all organs. Repeat this process 1-3 times.

Part 2 – Five-Element Healing Smile

- Smile and place your mind's attention or "Yi" at the top of your head at the vertex, crown or acupuncture point Du 20.

- Smile at the top of you head for a moment or two and repeat to yourself smiling, loving energy

- Like a waterfall let this smiling, loving energy or feeling gently flow down the front of your face and back of the head filling your head with smiling, loving energy.

- Guide this smiling, loving energy down the neck and into the Heart

- Smile into the Heart and say the words Joy and Love for 30 seconds to a few minutes, say the words silently to your self, feel Joy and Love.

- Move your attention into the Spleen and repeat the word Openness for 30 seconds to a few minutes, feel Openness.

- Move to the Lungs and repeat Courage for 30 seconds to a few minutes, feel Courage.

- Move to the Kidneys and repeat Gentleness for 30 seconds to a few minutes, feel Courage.

- Move to the Liver and repeat Kindness for 30 seconds to a few minutes, feel Kindness.

- Repeat this process for 1 to 5 minutes and finish with the Kidneys, then move your attention behind the navel and concentrate there for 1 to 5 minutes.

Achieving emotional harmony and balance is the initial aspect of Spiritual Qi Gong and the refinement of a person, the ups and downs of life are often great motivators but when that lifestyle is the normal everyday way of living, growth and transformation does not occur. Transformation implies a change in the way one lives life, the foundation cultivation practice "Emotional Harmony" calms, relaxes and harmonizes emotions providing the opportunity to approach daily life in a balanced and healthy way.

Organ	Sound	Positive Emotions	Negative Emotions
Kidney Bladder	Chuuu The sound of a wave	Gentleness	Fear
Liver Gallbladder	Shhhh Like Shhhhhhing a little child	Kindness	Anger
Heart Small Intestine	Haw	Joy, Love	Hastiness Hate
Spleen Stomach	Whooo The sound comes from the throat	Openness	Worry
Lung Large Intestine	SSSSS	Courage	Sadness Depression
Three Centers	Heeeee		

Eight Treasures Qi Gong

Cultivating the Eight Extraordinary-Psychic Channels

Self-generation and transformation are expressions of the subtle realm.
Guided by the subtle realm,
  heavenly stars and planets circulate in natural rhythm.
Spiritual Qi Gong follows this heavenly rhythm,
  circulating cosmic forces within generates vitality and longevity,
  and reveals the eternal nature of human spirit.

Stars, planets and human life exist within a Universal energy web, paralleling this Universal structure is a human web comprised of acupuncture channels or pathways. These networks of energy channels contain eight special pathways, which are the eight extraordinary or psychic channels. These channels are the first channels developed in the body and function at the deepest, most constitutional level and have a special relationship with the three treasures: Essence, Qi and Spirit, the energetic DNA of human life. Similar to an astrological birth chart, the Eight Extraordinary channels reveal the constitutional condition of a person and reflect the Karmic or constitutional blueprint of life. Below is a table that lists applicable Qi Gong information for each of the Eight Extraordinary channels. While practicing Qi Gong meditations one goal is harmonizing these Eight Extraordinary channels and their current conditions. From a Spiritual Qi Gong perspective transformation must occur in these channels for a person to change, the channels are a reflection of a person's spiritual, mental and physical condition.

Eight Treasures Qi Gong is the entry practice for cultivating a change in the focus from Physical and Emotional to Spiritual, this meditation refines physical/root/sexual energy into Spiritual energy and vitalizes all the energy pathways, creating awareness that we are not solely our physical body, that these other aspects of our life are as real as the physical body.

One important benefit of this practice is enjoying our physical body more when we practice Eight Treasures Qi Gong because our bodies become stronger and healthier.

Eight Extraordinary Channels

Channel	Qualities
Center Channel "Chong"	Relates to destiny, revealing the blueprint of life and how we relate to ourselves. This is the center or "Yuan" channel, it reflects the center or original condition and is integral in Taoist cultivation.
Front Channel "Ren"	Relates to bonding with the world and our connection to life, including parents, intimate relationships and self.
Back Channel "Du"	Relates to independence, movement and separation from parents or dependencies, it includes the ability to make these changes in a healthy way.
Belt Channel "Dai"	Relates to holding, retaining and releasing, when issues of these eight channels are not resolved they can be retained in this channel.
Interior Leg Channel "Yin Qiao"	Relates to how we stand up to ourselves, seeing our role in life with clarity and obtaining an understanding of the meaning and purpose of life. It is how well we feel comfortable in our position in life, dealing with what is, not what could be.
Lateral Leg Channel "Yang Qiao"	Relates to how we stand up to the world and how we present ourselves to the world. Issues relating to the external world can manifest from these channels.
Interior Arm Channel "Yin Wei"	Relates to how one deals with stages of life, these issues relate to the past and future and how one feels about their place and role in life, including family and society. Its focus is on position or space in life.
Lateral Arm Channel "Yang Wei"	Relates to how one responds to day-to-day activities and dealing with time issues, for example, death, achievement levels in giving time frames.

Qi or energy naturally flows throughout the body and channels and when stress, pressure or trauma occurs, whether emotional or physical, a blockage of this energy occurs, causing physical or emotional stagnation resulting in discomfort or pain, most importantly, Qi is not circulating properly failing to nourish and energize the body. This lack of nourishment can lead to chronic illness and depression of the immune system, when Qi flows normally all of the body is nourished and energized. The eight special channels control and manage other channels in the body, they are functionally similar to reservoirs, gathering, storing and distributing energy to other channels, internal organs, glands, lymphatic, central nervous and skeletal systems. The Heavenly Orbit meditation enhances energy flow through two of these major channels, they have a profound influence on recycling energy, preventing loss of life force and increasing vitality. The Heavenly Orbit is the foundation for all Qi Gong practices and the basis of Spiritual Qi Gong. There are many ways to practice the Orbit meditation, in my experience the following technique is simple, efficient and very effective.

Eight Treasures Qi Gong

The Heavenly Orbit or Small Wheel

The beauty of the solar system with its planets and stars floating throughout space in endless cycles is a magnificent example of the Universe's maco cycle. Mirroring this universal flow is a micro flow of Qi within each person, it circulates through meridians connecting every tendon, muscle, organ and cell throughout the body. There are many types of meridians or pathways, two special ones are the major Yang (Back) and Yin (Front) channels or pathways. The Yang channel emerges at the perineum (about one inch about the anus), connects to the bottom of the spine, rises up the spine into the brain and then down into the palate. The major Yin channel begins at the perineum, moves up the front of the body and into the palate and meets with the Yang Channel. These two channels are really one channel, orbit or circuit. Energy or Qi flows or circulates through this orbit in the same way planets circulate through space; this orbit has many names, for example, Heavenly Orbit, Orbit, Microcosmic Orbit or Dharma Wheel.

Energy Centers

Energy Centers are areas located in the body that influence physical, mental, emotional and spiritual energy, they are also referred to as Tan Tiens or Chakras. In Spiritual Qi Gong there are three major Energy Centers: Lower or Navel center, Middle or Solar Plexus and Heart centers and Upper/ Third Eye center. The Lower/Navel Center is the most common known in Qi Gong, it is a meeting location of the Eight Extra Ordinary channels, a matrix of acupuncture pathways that can gather, store and distribute energy, it is a primary location for Spiritual Qi Gong and alchemy. Energy Centers are refinement areas, in all mediations we begin and end by placing our attention in the lower Energy Center to collect and store energy.

Energy Centers are also connectors and passageways to the deepest aspects of the Universe, it is in these areas one can experience the infinite and eternal nature of life, God or Tao. Each person has the creator or God within, by looking inward we can merge with God and experience this reality in this lifetime, this is the major goal of Spiritual Qi Gong.

Heavenly Orbit Qi Gong – Ren and Du channels

1. Sit in a chair or on the floor in a cross-legged or lotus position, your back should be straight and fold your hands together. One way to fold your hands is like clapping your hands while holding them in your lap. Place the tip of your tongue to the palate-roof of the mouth in a comfortable position. The most important thing is to relax and be comfortable.

2. Guide your mind's attention behind the navel and breath into the lower Energy Center for a few minutes, breath normally but keep all your attention behind the navel.

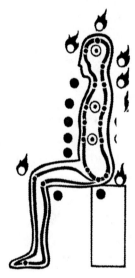

3. Guide your mind's attention to the perineum, it is located a few inches above the anus, gently inhale from the perineum up the inside of the spine to the top of the head while inhaling count one, exhale from the top of the head down to the perineum while counting two. Inhale from the perineum to the top of the head counting three and exhale down to the perineum counting four. Do not guide the energy in the spine, but in the channel that runs just inside it, basically move your Yi or mind's

attention 3-6 inches inside the skin of the body and circuit the energy through this orbit. Repeat this process until you reach the count of ten, breathing should be natural and comfortable.

Breathing up and down the Orbit guides energy/kundalini/prajna through the acupuncture channels and chakra system causing it to circulate smoothly clearing blockages or points of stagnation. Common sensations are tingling, pulsating, vibrating or electric feelings throughout the body, these are all favorable sensations, as the channels become clearer and more open the energy circulation and accumulation becomes increasingly favorable and enjoyable.

This meditation should be practiced for 5-20 minutes, it can be practiced longer or shorter depending on your schedule, be flexible and relaxed about this practice and its duration, create a realistic plan that meets your individual needs.

When you are ready to stop, place one hand over your navel palm facing the navel and the other over the first. Concentrate your mind's attention behind your navel, about an inch or two and circulate your mind's attention around the inside of the navel like a small circle, spiraling can be horizontal or vertical. Do this 18-36 times clockwise, then 18-36 times counterclockwise. The spiraling gathers energy and stores it in the lower Energy Center. This Energy Center is like a battery for the body as it safely stores energy for future usage. If energy is not stored in this Energy Center it may be stored or trapped in areas or Acupuncture points that could cause physical or emotional stress, it is vital to always finish each Qi Gong meditation by storing Qi behind the Navel in the lower Energy Center. When spiraling to collect Qi you can form it into a small energy pearl.

Eight Treasures Qi Gong
Center - Yuan Channel

The Center Channel–Chong Mai

1. Place your mind's attention behind the navel and feel the energy or pearl, guide it through the Orbit 18-36 times.

2. Move your attention or pearl into the perineum and center channel, this channel is in the middle of body and runs from the perineum to the crown. Begin by moving your attention into the center channel and guiding the pearl or Yi from bottom to top, then back down to the perineum, repeat this pattern nine to eighteen times and utilize your breath to enhance the effect of this meditation. Place your attention in the perineum, inhale as you move up the channel and exhale when moving down the channel, breathing should be gentle and at a normal pace.

Finish this section by moving your attention to the lower Energy Center, spiral and store the energy into a pearl.

Eight Treasures Qi Gong
The Belt Channel–Dai Mai

The next channel is the Belt or Girdle channel, it wraps around the body like an energy belt and extends from below your feet to above your head.

1. Continuing from the Center or Yuan channel cultivation, move your Yi/attention a few feet below your body and spiral your attention around your body, wrapping the energy around yourself like bandages on a mummy, work your way up your body until you reach the top of your head, when spiraling upward spiral in a clockwise direction. When you reach the top, spiral in a counter-clockwise direction to below your feet. Repeat this process 9-18 times or until you feel energy as you spiral up and down.

   Spiral clockwise when ascending

   Spiral counterclockwise descending

2. End this stage by collecting energy in the lower Energy Center

Eight Treasures Qi Gong
Interior and Exterior Limbs
Yin and Yang Wei
Yin and Yang Qiao

1. This section includes the Yin and Yang aspects of the arms and legs, both the interior and exterior aspects of the limbs.

2. Begin by focusing in the center behind the navel inside the cauldron, exhale while moving your attention from the navel center down to the perineum, split your attention into two parts and move it down the inside of the legs to the bottom of the feet.

3. Inhale while you move up and around the toes and the lateral aspects of the legs to the waist and to cervical vertebrae seven, the big bone between the shoulders, which is acupuncture point Du 14, this completes the inhale.

4. Exhale from Du 14 down the back of the arms to the fingers, this completes one exhale.

5. Inhale your attention into the palm of the hands and up the inside of the arms to Du 14, to the neck and top of the head, this completes the inhale.

6. Exhale down the front of the body following the nipple line to the perineum.

7. This represents one cycle, repeat this circulation 9-18 times or until you feel the energy.

End this meditation by collecting energy in the lower Energy Center behind the navel.

This completes the Eight Treasures Qi Gong, it is a profound meditation that clears these constitutional channels and refines one's energy and essence. These special energy channels comprise the "spiritual womb" for refinement and preparation for union with our highest nature. When practicing it is normal to feel very light and subtle and a powerful connection to the Universe. This refinement process transcends the physical and emotional body and is the entry to an expanded awareness of our spiritual nature. This cultivation can be practiced ten minutes to an hour depending on your schedule.

Three Treasures Qi Gong

Spirit Realization
Kan and Li Enlightenment

Turning inward reveals the essence and origin of the Universe.
The three treasures are the substances for transformation,
  essence is the foundation,
  energy generates vitality,
  spirit is the expression.
Integrate and refine the three treasures and your eternal spirit will be revealed.

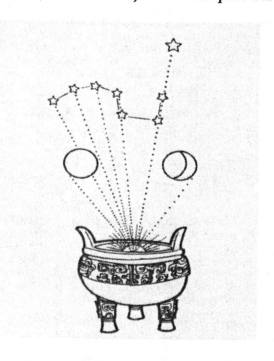

Navel Energy Center
Lesser Kan and Li

Three Treasures Qi Gong cultivation focuses on cultivating biological, sexual or kundalini energy, transforming it into a subtle energy vitalizing the body, particularly glands, organs, brain and nervous system. This refined energy becomes spiritual energy and provides the basis for spiritual growth. Spirit Realization as expressed in Kan and Li cultivation begins by creating the cauldron in the lower Tan Tien (behind the navel), in this cauldron Essence or Jing is steamed releasing enormous amounts of energy and vitality, particularly glands, organs, brain and central nervous system. This process also begins the process of transcending the physical body and resolving karmic conditions. The following is the process:

Part 1

1. Be aware of the cauldron behind the navel in the lower Tan Tien

2. Focus your attention in the Kidneys, they are directly connected to the planet Mercury, North direction, Water element and Moon, be aware of these correspondences. Place your attention in the Moon above and gather its Yin essence and place it into the Kidneys. Feel the cold-essence of the Kidneys, spend as much time as necessary to feel it, when there is a strong feeling move the essence and cold into the cauldron, spiral, collect and form this energy into the pearl.

3. Focus your attention in the adrenals and feel it's Heat-Yang, the adrenals are located above the Kidneys. Place your attention in the Sun above and move the Yang essence of the Sun underneath the cauldron, see and feel the Fire underneath the cauldron.

4. Feel the Yang-Fire heat up the cauldron and cook the Water-Yin-Cold-Essence, as the Yin-Essence heats up it will begin to steam; this process is the first goal, the fire must be strong enough to cook and steam the Yin-essence. This steaming process is a refinement of one's energy, it is transforming Essence or Jing into Qi or Vitality.

5. When steam appears guide it into the Kidneys, Liver, Pancreas, Spleen, Lungs, Heart, Thymus, Thyroid, Parathyroid, Pituitary Gland, Pineal Gland and the entire brain,

follow this exact sequence for the steaming process. Spiral the steam in each area for 30 seconds to one minute.

6. Finish this stage by gathering steam and guide it into the cauldron, spiral and collect it in the center of the cauldron and form it into the pearl. Spend as much time as necessary at each stage until you feel and experience each step.

Part 2

1. Continue from stage 1 and guide the steam into the Orbit, Center/Yuan, Belt, Arm and Leg channels 18-36 times.

2. Focus your attention in the cauldron and feel the Yin-Essence inside and the Yang-Fire underneath, move the cauldron underneath the spine and feel the Yang-Fire cook the Yin-Essence, feel the essence cook and become steam, guide the steam into the spine and up into the brain, feel the steam move up and down the spine totally steaming it.

3. Guide the steam into the spine and spinal nerves, these nerves connect to the whole body, feel steam spread through all nerves, organs, glands, skeletal, musculature and vascular systems.

4. Guide steam into the center of the cauldron, spiral and collect the steam-energy into the pearl.

Three Treasures Qi Gong

Spirit Realization

Solar Plexus Center
Greater Kan and Li

Solar Plexus Center cultivation is a practice of consciously integrating our life with subtle energy from universal forces, in this practice the Five-Elements and their corresponding directions, organs and planets nourish and transform consciousness to a subtler level. This center is located behind the solar plexus and a few inches behind the skin. Greater Kan and Li expands upon the Navel Center cultivation and involves the integration of physical and spiritual energy leading to the direct realization of the undivided nature of life.

The Practice

1. Continue from the Navel Center cultivation, move your attention from the navel center to behind the solar plexus and concentrate there until you feel energy or the pearl.

2. When you feel the pearl move it down your body and deep into the Earth below your feet, place all your attention into the Earth and feel its energy nourish this pearl, the pearl is your consciousness. Ask mother Earth to heal any illnesses or provide direction to your life. Stay here until you feel this healing energy.

3. When you are ready gently move your consciousness back to the solar plexus center and concentrate there forming the pearl and feel the energy.

4. Gently move your attention above your head into the sky, connect your consciousness, attention or Yi with the Sun and Moon, then planets Mercury, Jupiter, Saturn, Venus, Mars, Big Dipper and North Star. These planets are part of the universal energy matrix and are connected to each person. Feel the connection to these planets and stay focused here until you feel this reality undivided nature of human and planetary life.

5. Slowly move your attention and the pearl back to the Solar Plexus center

6. Feel the pearl in the Solar Plexus center, be aware of the stars and planets above and slowly guide their energy into the Solar Plexus and into the Pearl, feel the pearl nourished by these Stars and Planetary energy. Do this for a moment or two until you feel energy or pearl in the center.

7. When finished collect and gather the energy into the pearl

Three Treasures Qi Gong

Spirit Realization

Heart Center
Greatest Kan and Li

Heart Center cultivation unifies refined Essence or Biological/Sexual Energy and Spirit and reflects a person's conscious desire to apply their energy and efforts for spiritual awareness and development. This practice requires a level of refinement of emotions and desires for the fruit to manifest, which is experiencing unconditional divine love and bliss. By letting go of attachment to the physical world and emotions, conditions are ripe for this experience. Emotional Harmony and Eight Treasures Qi Gong contribute towards creating the "ripe" conditions for this experience.

The Practice

1. Continue from the Navel and Solar Plexus Center cultivations and place your attention in the Heart center, between the nipples or behind the sternum, feel Qi or energy build. Smile into the Heart Center and Spiral the energy to enhance the process. When you feel this Qi allow it to intensify and with time and practice feelings of divine love and bliss will appear, as this feeling grows allow it to spread throughout your body from head to toes including skin, organs, nerves and all energy channels.

   Finish by bringing your attention back to the Heart Center. A method to enhance this process is chanting a mantra or name of the creator of life, select any name that you feel comfortable with and repeat the name throughout this meditation.

The Heart is the seat of spirit or emotions, fill your spirit with this Qi and allow divine, unconditional love and bliss to manifest; you're physical, mental and emotional energy will nourish your spiritual energy, acting as a "Magnet" attracting Divine, Unconditional Love.

2. Feel the energy in the Heart Center and be aware of the entire Universe and the Creator of all life. With each inhale merge with the Universe and with each exhale feel bliss and divine love in the Heart Center, allow this feeling to grow and stay focused in this feeling until you begin to transcend the physical body, the limits of time and space will dissolve as you feel the eternal nature of spirit. This is individual spirit unifying with Universal Spirit and the direct realization of the undivided nature of life.

3. End this meditation by bring one's attention to the lower Energy Center and collect energy into a pearl.

Three Treasures Qi Gong

Spirit Realization

Third Eye Energy Center

The subtle realm nurtures its offspring,
know the world but live in the subtle realm,
individual spirit uniting with the subtle realm is Heaven in Earth,
and the ancient formula for Self-Realization.

Third Eye Center is an area in the head that is behind the third eye and extends to the crown at the top of the head, it includes the pituitary and pineal glands. This center/chakra is a spiritual location in the human body and a high level of refinement is necessary for this practice to be effective. A person's awareness and energy must be refined to be able to access, absorb and utilize the benefits of this spiritual center. This meditation is dependent on the body's ability to naturally direct all its energies: sexual, mental and emotional to support spiritual consciousness, when this is achieved individual spirit and collective spirit unite (union of God and human life). This cultivation reveals the undivided spiritual unity of life and provides a method to directly experience our true nature in this lifetime. The greatest achievement is integrating and applying this spiritual realization into daily life.

The process

Beginning

1. Be aware of the lower Energy Center behind the navel and feel the Qi pearl

2. Guide your attention into the Solar Plexus Center and feel the Qi pearl

3. Guide your attention into the Heart Center and feel the Qi pearl. Feel divine, unconditional love grow and fill the Heart center.

4. When you feel this divine love in the Heart center guide your attention into the Third Eye center.

5. Focus all your attention into this Energy Center, you may visualize the Earth below and the planets above, especially the Sun, Moon, North Star and Big Dipper, as you inhale draw energies from below and above into the Third Eye Center and as you exhale condense and store them in the Center. Repeat this process until you feel Universal Energy fill your Upper Energy Center. Breath gently, softly and naturally. There are many phenomenon that may occur, for example, some people may see colors, especially white, yellow or purple, some feel a profound release and connection to life and God, some feel the barriers of time and space dissolve and feel their immortal nature, whatever occurs, it is important to stay relaxed and focused on the Third Eye Center.

6. A method to enhance this process is to chant a mantra or name of the creator of life, select any name that you feel comfortable with and repeat the name throughout this meditation.

7. When you want to end the meditation gently move your attention to the lower Energy Center behind the navel and spiral collecting Qi into the pearl.

Advanced Practice

1. Be aware of the cauldron in the lower Tan Tien, behind the navel, feel all the organ's energies and the Five Shen beam into the center of the cauldron; feel the Earth, Sun, Moon and the entire solar system beam their energy into the cauldron, nourishing the pearl.

2. Repeat this process for the cauldron and the pearl at the level of the solar plexuses and Heart center.

3. Move the cauldron to the crystal palace and be aware of the pearl in the cauldron. See the Moon in the right eye and the Sun in the left eye, draw their energy into the cauldron.

4. Be aware of the mouth, connect the I-Spleen to the mouth and draw its energy into the cauldron.

5. Be aware of the ears, connect the Zhi-Kidneys to the ears and draw its energy into the cauldron.

6. Be aware of the tongue, connect the Shen-Heart to the tongue and draw its energy into the cauldron.

7. Be aware of the nose, connect the Po-Lungs to the nose and draw its energy into the cauldron.

8. Be aware of the eyes, connect the Hun-Liver to the eyes and draw the energy into the cauldron.

9. Be aware of the eyes, ears, nose, tongue and mouth and their respective organs and energies and draw their energy into the cauldron, nourishing the pearl.

10. Be aware of the North Star and Big Dipper, draw energy from the Big Dipper and North Star into the cauldron nourishing the pearl.

11. Be aware of the four cauldrons: navel, solar plexus, Heart and crystal palace centers, feel them radiate.

12. Relax in this conscious state of bliss and joy, this is experiencing one's true spiritual nature, it is the fruit of Spiritual Qi Gong and Kan and Li cultivation. Consistent

practice leads to deeper levels of awareness of this unity, creating a new dimension for experiencing daily life. The highest achievement is applying this experience into normal, regular daily life.

Portal	Aspect of Spirit	Organ
Right Eye	Moon, Ethereal, Hun Spirit	Liver
Left Eye	Sun, Hun, Ethereal Spirit	Liver
Nose	Po, Corporeal Spirit	Lungs
Ears	Zhi, Will Power	Kidneys
Mouth	I, Focus	Spleen
Tongue	Shen, Spirit	Heart

Chinese Astrology Calendar

by
David Twicken

1921

Find your Day Here	Month Stem	Branch	Year Stem	Branch	Day	Day	Time
February 4 - March 6	Yang Metal	Tiger	Yin Metal	Cock	Feb	31	16:20
March 6 - April 5	Yin Metal	Rabbit	Yin Metal	Cock	Mar	59	10:36
April 5 - May 6	Yang Water	Dragon	Yin Metal	Cock	April	30	16:03
May 6– June 6	Yin Water	Snake	Yin Metal	Cock	May	0	10:06
June 6 - July 8	Yang Wood	Horse	Yin Metal	Cock	June	31	14:51
July 8 - August 8	Yin Wood	Sheep	Yin Metal	Cock	July	1	1:24
August 8 - September 8	Yang Fire	Monkey	Yin Metal	Cock	Aug	32	11:17
September 8 – October 9	Yin Fire	Cock	Yin Metal	Cock	Sep	3	14:04
October 9 - November 8	Yang Earth	Dog	Yin Metal	Cock	Oct	33	5:22
November 8 - December 7	Yin Earth	Pig	Yin Metal	Cock	Nov	4	7:58
December 7– January 6	Yang Metal	Rat	Yin Metal	Cock	Dec	34	0:07

Branch	Pig	Rat	Ox	Tiger	Rabbit	Dragon	Snake	Horse	Sheep	Monkey	Cock	Dog
Main Element	Yang Water	Yin Water	Yin Earth	Yang Wood	Yin Wood	Yang Earth	Yang Fire	Yin Fire	Yin Earth	Yang Metal	Yin Metal	Yang Earth
Hidden Elements	Yang Wood		Yin Water	Yang Fire		Yin Wood	Yang Earth	Yin Earth	Yin Fire	Yang Earth		Yin Metal
			Yin Metal	Yang Earth		Yin Water	Yang Metal		Yin Wood	Yang Water		Yin Fire

1922

Find your Day Here	Month Stem	Branch	Year Stem	Branch	Day	Day	Time
January 6 – February 4	Yin Metal	Ox	Yin Metal	Cock	Jan	5	10:42
February 4 - March 6	Yang Water	Tiger	Yang Water	Dog	Feb	36	22:09
March 6 - April 5	Yin Water	Rabbit	Yang Water	Dog	Mar	4	16:25
April 5 - May 6	Yang Wood	Dragon	Yang Water	Dog	April	35	21:52
May 6 – June 6	Yin Wood	Snake	Yang Water	Dog	May	5	15:55
June 6 - July 8	Yang Fire	Horse	Yang Water	Dog	June	36	20:40
July 8- August 8	Yin Fire	Sheep	Yang Water	Dog	July	6	7:13
August 8 - September 8	Yang Earth	Monkey	Yang Water	Dog	Aug	37	17:05
September 8 – October 9	Yin Earth	Cock	Yang Water	Dog	Sep	8	19:52
October 9 - November 8	Yang Metal	Dog	Yang Water	Dog	Oct	38	11:11
November 8- December 8	Yin Metal	Pig	Yang Water	Dog	Nov	9	13:47
December 8 – January 6	Yang Water	Rat	Yang Water	Dog	Dec	39	5:57

1923

Find your Day Here	Month Stem	Branch	Year Stem	Branch	Day	Day	Time
January 6 – February 5	Yin Water	Ox	Yang Water	Dog	Jan	10	16:33
February 5 - March 6	Yang Wood	Tiger	Yin Water	Pig	Feb	41	3: 58
March 6 - April 6	Yin Wood	Rabbit	Yin Water	Pig	Mar	9	22:25
April 6 - May 6	Yang Fire	Dragon	Yin Water	Pig	April	40	21:41
May 6 – June 6	Yin Fire	Snake	Yin Water	Pig	May	10	21:28
June 7 - July 8	Yang Earth	Horse	Yin Water	Pig	June	41	2:27
July 8 - August 8	Yin Earth	Sheep	Yin Water	Pig	July	11	13:01
August 8 - September 9	Yang Metal	Monkey	Yin Water	Pig	Aug	42	22:53
September 9 – October 9	Yin Metal	Cock	Yin Water	Pig	Sep	13	1:41
October 9 - November 8	Yang Water	Dog	Yin Water	Pig	Oct	43	17:00
November 8 - December 8	Yin Water	Pig	Yin Water	Pig	Nov	14	19:30
December 8 – January 6	Yang Wood	Rat	Yin Water	Pig	Dec	44	11:47

Branch	Pig	Rat	Ox	Tiger	Rabbit	Dragon	Snake	Horse	Sheep	Monkey	Cock	Dog
Main Element	Yang Water	Yin Water	Yin Earth	Yang Wood	Yin Wood	Yang Earth	Yang Fire	Yin Fire	Yin Earth	Yang Metal	Yin Metal	Yang Earth
Hidden Elements	Yang Wood		Yin Water	Yang Fire		Yin Wood	Yang Earth	Yin Earth	Yin Fire	Yang Earth		Yin Metal
			Yin Metal	Yang Earth		Yin Water	Yang Metal		Yin Wood	Yang Water		Yin Fire

1924

Find your Day Here	Month Stem	Branch	Year Stem	Branch	Day	Day	Time
January 6 – February 5	Yin Wood	Ox	Yin Water	Pig	Jan	15	22:24
February 5-29 - March 6	Yang Fire	Tiger	Yang Wood	Rat	Feb	46	9:49
March 6 - April 5	Yin Fire	Rabbit	Yang Wood	Rat	Mar	15	4:13
April 5 - May 6	Yang Earth	Dragon	Yang Wood	Rat	April	46	9:34
May 6 – June 6	Yin Earth	Snake	Yang Wood	Rat	May	16	3:26
June 6 - July 7	Yang Metal	Horse	Yang Wood	Rat	June	47	8:02
July 7 - August 8	Yin Metal	Sheep	Yang Wood	Rat	July	17	18:30
August 8 - September 8	Yang Water	Monkey	Yang Wood	Rat	Aug	48	4:13
September 8 – October 8	Yin Water	Cock	Yang Wood	Rat	Sep	19	6:46
October 8 - November 8	Yang Wood	Dog	Yang Wood	Rat	Oct	49	9:53
November 8 - December 7	Yin Wood	Pig	Yang Wood	Rat	Nov	20	: 30
December 7 – January 6	Yang Fire	Rat	Yang Wood	Rat	Dec	50	16:54

1925

Find your Day Here	Month Stem	Branch	Year Stem	Branch	Day	Day	Time
January 6 – February 4	Yin Fire	Ox	Yang Wood	Rat	Jan	21	3:54
February 4 - March 6	Yang Earth	Tiger	Yin Wood	Ox	Feb	52	15:37
March 6 - April 5	Yin Earth	Rabbit	Yin Wood	Ox	Mar	20	10:00
April 5 - May 6	Yang Metal	Dragon	Yin Wood	Ox	April	51	15:23
May 6 – June 6	Yin Metal	Snake	Yin Wood	Ox	May	21	9:18
June 6 - July 8	Yang Water	Horse	Yin Wood	Ox	June	52	13:57
July 8 - August 8	Yin Water	Sheep	Yin Wood	Ox	July	22	0:25
August 8 - September 7	Yang Wood	Monkey	Yin Wood	Ox	Aug	53	10:08
September 8 – October 9	Yin Wood	Cock	Yin Wood	Ox	Sep	24	12:40
October 9 - November 8	Yang Fire	Dog	Yin Wood	Ox	Oct	54	3:48
November 8 - December 7	Yin Fire	Pig	Yin Wood	Ox	Nov	25	6:27
December 7 – January 6	Yang Earth	Rat	Yin Wood	Ox	Dec	55	22:53

Branch	Pig	Rat	Ox	Tiger	Rabbit	Dragon	Snake	Horse	Sheep	Monkey	Cock	Dog
Main Element	Yang Water	Yin Water	Yin Earth	Yang Wood	Yin Wood	Yang Earth	Yang Fire	Yin Fire	Yin Earth	Yang Metal	Yin Metal	Yang Earth
Hidden Elements	Yang Wood		Yin Water	Yang Fire		Yin Wood	Yang Earth	Yin Earth	Yin Fire	Yang Earth		Yin Metal
			Yin Metal	Yang Earth		Yin Water	Yang Metal		Yin Wood	Yang Water		Yin Fire

1926

Find your Day Here	Month Stem	Branch	Year Stem	Branch	Day	Day	Time
January 6 – February 4	Yin Earth	Ox	Yin Wood	Ox	Jan	26	9:55
February 4 - March 6	Yang Metal	Tiger	Yang Fire	Tiger	Feb	57	21:39
March 6 - April 5	Yin Metal	Rabbit	Yang Fire	Tiger	Mar	25	15:49
April 5 - May 6	Yang Water	Dragon	Yang Fire	Tiger	April	56	21:19
May 6– June 6	Yin Water	Snake	Yang Fire	Tiger	May	26	15:09
June 6 - July 8	Yang Wood	Horse	Yang Fire	Tiger	June	57	19:42
July 8 - August 8	Yin Wood	Sheep	Yang Fire	Tiger	July	27	6:06
August 8 - September 8	Yang Fire	Monkey	Yang Fire	Tiger	Aug	58	15:45
September 8 – October 9	Yin Fire	Cock	Yang Fire	Tiger	Sep	29	18:16
October 9 - November 8	Yang Earth	Dog	Yang Fire	Tiger	Oct	59	9:25
November 8 - December 8	Yin Earth	Pig	Yang Fire	Tiger	Nov	30	12:08
December 8 – January 6	Yang Metal	Rat	Yang Fire	Tiger	Dec	60	4:39

1927

Find your Day Here	Month Stem	Branch	Year Stem	Branch	Day	Day	Time
January 6 – February 5	Yin Metal	Ox	Yang Fire	Tiger	Jan	31	15:45
February 5 - March 6	Yang Water	Tiger	Yin Fire	Rabbit	Feb	2	3:10
March 6 - April 6	Yin Water	Rabbit	Yin Fire	Rabbit	Mar	30	21:51
April 6 - May 6	Yang Wood	Dragon	Yin Fire	Rabbit	April	1	3:07
May 6 – June 7	Yin Wood	Snake	Yin Fire	Rabbit	May	31	20:54
June 7 - July 8	Yang Fire	Horse	Yin Fire	Rabbit	June	2	1:25
July 8 - August 8	Yin Fire	Sheep	Yin Fire	Rabbit	July	32	11:50
August 8 - September 8	Yang Earth	Monkey	Yin Fire	Rabbit	Aug	3	21:32
September 8 – October 9	Yin Earth	Cock	Yin Fire	Rabbit	Sep	34	0:06
October 9 - November 8	Yang Metal	Dog	Yin Fire	Rabbit	Oct	4	15:16
November 8 - December 8	Yin Metal	Pig	Yin Fire	Rabbit	Nov	35	17:57
December 8 – January 6	Yang Water	Rat	Yin Fire	Rabbit	Dec	5	10:27

Branch	Pig	Rat	Ox	Tiger	Rabbit	Dragon	Snake	Horse	Sheep	Monkey	Cock	Dog
Main Element	Yang Water	Yin Water	Yin Earth	Yang Wood	Yin Wood	Yang Earth	Yang Fire	Yin Fire	Yin Earth	Yang Metal	Yin Metal	Yang Earth
Hidden Elements	Yang Wood		Yin Water	Yang Fire		Yin Wood	Yang Earth	Yin Earth	Yin Fire	Yang Earth		Yin Metal
			Yin Metal	Yang Earth		Yin Water	Yang Metal		Yin Wood	Yang Water		Yin Fire

1928

Find your Day Here	Month Stem	Branch	Year Stem	Branch	Day	Day	Time
January 6 – February 5	Yin Water	Ox	Yin Fire	Rabbit	Jan	36	21:32
February 5-29 - March 6	Yang Wood	Tiger	Yang Earth	Dragon	Feb	7	9:17
March 6 - April 5	Yin Wood	Rabbit	Yang Earth	Dragon	Mar	36	3:38
April 5 - May 6	Yang Fire	Dragon	Yang Earth	Dragon	April	7	8:55
May 6 – June 6	Yin Fire	Snake	Yang Earth	Dragon	May	37	2:44
June 6 - July 7	Yang Earth	Horse	Yang Earth	Dragon	June	8	7:18
July 7 - August 8	Yin Earth	Sheep	Yang Earth	Dragon	July	38	17:45
August 8 - September 8	Yang Metal	Monkey	Yang Earth	Dragon	Aug	9	3:28
September 8 – October 8	Yin Metal	Cock	Yang Earth	Dragon	Sep	40	6:02
October 8 - November 7	Yang Water	Dog	Yang Earth	Dragon	Oct	10	21:11
November 7 - December 7	Yin Water	Pig	Yang Earth	Dragon	Nov	41	23:50
December 7 – January 6	Yang Wood	Rat	Yang Earth	Dragon	Dec	11	16:18

1929

Find your Day Here	Month Stem	Branch	Year Stem	Branch	Day	Day	Time
January 6 – February 4	Yin Wood	Ox	Yang Earth	Dragon	Jan	42	3:23
February 4 - March 6	Yang Fire	Tiger	Yin Earth	Snake	Feb	13	15:09
March 6 - April 5	Yin Fire	Rabbit	Yin Earth	Snake	Mar	41	9:32
April 5 - May 6	Yang Earth	Dragon	Yin Earth	Snake	April	12	14:52
May 6 – June 6	Yin Earth	Snake	Yin Earth	Snake	May	42	8:41
June 6 - July 7	Yang Metal	Horse	Yin Earth	Snake	June	13	13:11
July 7 - August 8	Yin Metal	Sheep	Yin Earth	Snake	July	43	23:32
August 8 - September 8	Yang Water	Monkey	Yin Earth	Snake	Aug	14	9:09
September 8 – October 9	Yin Water	Cock	Yin Earth	Snake	Sep	45	11:40
October 9 - November 8	Yang Wood	Dog	Yin Earth	Snake	Oct	15	2:48
November 8 - December 7	Yin Wood	Pig	Yin Earth	Snake	Nov	46	5:28
December 7 – January 6	Yang Fire	Rat	Yin Earth	Snake	Dec	16	21:57

Branch	Pig	Rat	Ox	Tiger	Rabbit	Dragon	Snake	Horse	Sheep	Monkey	Cock	Dog
Main Element	Yang Water	Yin Water	Yin Earth	Yang Wood	Yin Wood	Yang Earth	Yang Fire	Yin Fire	Yin Earth	Yang Metal	Yin Metal	Yang Earth
Hidden Elements	Yang Wood		Yin Water	Yang Fire		Yin Wood	Yang Earth	Yin Earth	Yin Fire	Yang Earth		Yin Metal
			Yin Metal	Yang Earth		Yin Water	Yang Metal		Yin Wood	Yang Water		Yin Fire

1930

Find Your Day Here	Month Stem	Branch	Year Stem	Branch	Day	Day	Time
January 6 – February 4	Yin Fire	Ox	Yin Earth	Snake	Jan	47	9: 03
February 4 - March 6	Yang Earth	Tiger	Yang Metal	Horse	Feb	18	20: 52
March 6 - April 5	Yin Earth	Rabbit	Yang Metal	Horse	Mar	46	15: 17
April 5 - May 6	Yang Metal	Dragon	Yang Metal	Horse	April	17	20: 38
May 6– June 6	Yin Metal	Snake	Yang Metal	Horse	May	47	14: 28
June 6 - July 8	Yang Water	Horse	Yang Metal	Horse	June	18	18: 58
July 8 - August 8	Yin Water	Sheep	Yang Metal	Horse	July	48	5: 20
August 8 - September 8	Yang Wood	Monkey	Yang Metal	Horse	Aug	19	14: 58
September 8 – October 9	Yin Wood	Cock	Yang Metal	Horse	Sep	50	17:29
October 9 - November 8	Yang Fire	Dog	Yang Metal	Horse	Oct	20	8:38
November 8 - December 8	Yin Fire	Pig	Yang Metal	Horse	Nov	51	11: 21
December 8 – January 6	Yang Earth	Rat	Yang Metal	Horse	Dec	21	3:51

1931

Find Your Day Here	Month Stem	Branch	Year Stem	Branch	Day	Day	Time
January 6 – February 5	Yin Earth	Ox	Yang Metal	Horse	Jan	52	14:56
February 5 - March 6	Yang Metal	Tiger	Yin Metal	Sheep	Feb	23	2: 41
March 6 - April 6	Yin Metal	Rabbit	Yin Metal	Sheep	Mar	51	21: 03
April 6 - May 6	Yang Water	Dragon	Yin Metal	Sheep	April	22	2: 21
May 6 – June 7	Yin Water	Snake	Yin Metal	Sheep	May	52	20: 10
June 7 - July 8	Yang Wood	Horse	Yin Metal	Sheep	June	23	: 42
July 8 - August 8	Yin Wood	Sheep	Yin Metal	Sheep	July	53	11: 06
August 8 - September 8	Yang Fire	Monkey	Yin Metal	Sheep	Aug	24	20: 45
September 8 – October 9	Yin Fire	Cock	Yin Metal	Sheep	Sep	55	23:18
October 9 - November 8	Yang Earth	Dog	Yin Metal	Sheep	Oct	25	14:27
November 8 - December 8	Yin Earth	Pig	Yin Metal	Sheep	Nov	56	17: 10
December 8 – January 6	Yang Metal	Rat	Yin Metal	Sheep	Dec	26	9: 41

Branch	Pig	Rat	Ox	Tiger	Rabbit	Dragon	Snake	Horse	Sheep	Monkey	Cock	Dog
Main Element	Yang Water	Yin Water	Yin Earth	Yang Wood	Yin Wood	Yang Earth	Yang Fire	Yin Fire	Yin Earth	Yang Metal	Yin Metal	Yang Earth
Hidden Elements	Yang Wood		Yin Water	Yang Fire		Yin Wood	Yang Earth	Yin Earth	Yin Fire	Yang Earth		Yin Metal
			Yin Metal	Yang Earth		Yin Water	Yang Metal		Yin Wood	Yang Water		Yin Fire

1932

Find Your Day Here	Month Stem	Branch	Year Stem	Branch	Day	Day	Time
January 6– February 5	Yin Metal	Ox	Yin Metal	Sheep	Jan	57	20:46
February 5-29, - March 6	Yang Water	Tiger	Yang Water	Monkey	Feb	28	8:30
March 6 - April 5	Yin Water	Rabbit	Yang Water	Monkey	Mar	57	2:50
April 5 - May 6	Yang Wood	Dragon	Yang Water	Monkey	April	28	8:07
May 6 – June 6	Yin Wood	Snake	Yang Water	Monkey	May	58	1:55
June 6 - July 7	Yang Fire	Horse	Yang Water	Monkey	June	29	6:28
July 7 - August 8	Yin Fire	Sheep	Yang Water	Monkey	July	59	16:53
August 8 - September 8	Yang Earth	Monkey	Yang Water	Monkey	Aug	30	2:32
September 8 – October 8	Yin Earth	Cock	Yang Water	Monkey	Sep	1	5:03
October 8 - November 7	Yang Metal	Dog	Yang Water	Monkey	Oct	31	20:10
November 7 - December 7	Yin Metal	Pig	Yang Water	Monkey	Nov	2	22:50
December 7 – January 6	Yang Water	Rat	Yang Water	Monkey	Dec	32	15:19

1933

Find Your Day Here	Month Stem	Branch	Year Stem	Branch	Day	Day	Time
January 6 – February 4	Yin Water	Ox	Yang Water	Monkey	Jan	57	2:24
February 4 - March 6	Yang Wood	Tiger	Yin Water	Cock	Feb	28	14:10
March 6 – April 5	Yin Wood	Rabbit	Yin Water	Cock	Mar	57	8:32
April 5 – May 6	Yang Fire	Dragon	Yin Water	Cock	April	28	13:51
May 6 – June 6	Yin Fire	Snake	Yin Water	Cock	May	58	7:42
June 6 – July 7	Yang Earth	Horse	Yin Water	Cock	June	29	12:18
July 7 – August 8	Yin Earth	Sheep	Yin Water	Cock	July	59	22:45
August 8– September 8	Yang Metal	Monkey	Yin Water	Cock	Aug	30	8:26
September 8 – October 9	Yin Metal	Cock	Yin Water	Cock	Sep	1	10:58
October 9 – November 8	Yang Water	Dog	Yin Water	Cock	Oct	31	2:08
November 8 – December 7	Yin Water	Pig	Yin Water	Cock	Nov	2	4:44
December 7 – January 6	Yang Wood	Rat	Yin Water	Cock	Dec	32	21:12

Branch	Pig	Rat	Ox	Tiger	Rabbit	Dragon	Snake	Horse	Sheep	Monkey	Cock	Dog
Main Element	Yang Water	Yin Water	Yin Earth	Yang Wood	Yin Wood	Yang Earth	Yang Fire	Yin Fire	Yin Earth	Yang Metal	Yin Metal	Yang Earth
Hidden Elements	Yang Wood		Yin Water	Yang Fire		Yin Wood	Yang Earth	Yin Earth	Yin Fire	Yang Earth		Yin Metal
			Yin Metal	Yang Earth		Yin Water	Yang Metal		Yin Wood	Yang Water		Yin Fire

1934

Find Your Day Here	Month Stem	Branch	Year Stem	Branch	Day	Day	Time
January 6– February 4	Yin Wood	Ox	Yin Water	Cock	Jan	8	8: 17
February 4 - March 6	Yang Fire	Tiger	Yang Wood	Dog	Feb	39	20: 04
March 6 - April 5	Yin Fire	Rabbit	Yang Wood	Dog	Mar	7	14: 27
April 5 - May 6	Yang Earth	Dragon	Yang Wood	Dog	April	38	19: 44
May 6 – June 6	Yin Earth	Snake	Yang Wood	Dog	May	8	13: 31
June 6 - July 8	Yang Metal	Horse	Yang Wood	Dog	June	39	18: 02
July 8 - August 8	Yin Metal	Sheep	Yang Wood	Dog	July	9	4: 25
August 8 - September 8	Yang Water	Monkey	Yang Wood	Dog	Aug	40	14:04
September 8 – October 9	Yin Water	Cock	Yang Wood	Dog	Sep	11	16: 37
October 9 - November 8	Yang Wood	Dog	Yang Wood	Dog	Oct	41	7: 45
November 8 - December 8	Yin Wood	Pig	Yang Wood	Dog	Nov	12	10: 27
December 8 – January 6	Yang Fire	Rat	Yang Wood	Dog	Dec	42	2:57

1935

Find your Day Here	Month Stem	Branch	Year Stem	Branch	Day	Day	Time
January 6– February 5	Yin Fire	Ox	Yang Wood	Dog	Jan	13	14: 03
February 5 - March 6	Yang Earth	Tiger	Yin Wood	Pig	Feb	44	1: 49
March 6 - April 6	Yin Earth	Rabbit	Yin Wood	Pig	Mar	12	20: 11
April 6 - May 6	Yang Metal	Dragon	Yin Wood	Pig	April	43	1: 27
May 6– June 6	Yin Metal	Snake	Yin Wood	Pig	May	13	19:12
June 6 - July 8	Yang Water	Horse	Yin Wood	Pig	June	44	23:42
July 8 - August 8	Yin Water	Sheep	Yin Wood	Pig	July	14	10: 06
August 8 - September 8	Yang Wood	Monkey	Yin Wood	Pig	Aug	45	19: 48
September 8 – October 9	Yin Wood	Cock	Yin Wood	Pig	Sep	16	22: 25
October 9 - November 8	Yang Fire	Dog	Yin Wood	Pig	Oct	46	13: 36
November 8 - December 8	Yin Fire	Pig	Yin Wood	Pig	Nov	17	16: 18
December 8 – January 6	Yang Earth	Rat	Yin Wood	Pig	Dec	47	8: 45

Branch	Pig	Rat	Ox	Tiger	Rabbit	Dragon	Snake	Horse	Sheep	Monkey	Cock	Dog
Main Element	Yang Water	Yin Water	Yin Earth	Yang Wood	Yin Wood	Yang Earth	Yang Fire	Yin Fire	Yin Earth	Yang Metal	Yin Metal	Yang Earth
Hidden Elements	Yang Wood		Yin Water	Yang Fire		Yin Wood	Yang Earth	Yin Earth	Yin Fire	Yang Earth		Yin Metal
			Yin Metal	Yang Earth		Yin Water	Yang Metal		Yin Wood	Yang Water		Yin Fire

1936

	Month		Year				
Find your Day Here	**Stem**	**Branch**	**Stem**	**Branch**	**Day**	**Day**	**Time**
January 6 – February 5	Yin Earth	Ox	Yin Wood	Pig	Jan	18	19: 47
February 5 - 29, - March 6	Yang Metal	Tiger	Yang Fire	Rat	Feb	49	7: 29
March 6 - April 5	Yin Metal	Rabbit	Yang Fire	Rat	Mar	18	1: 50
April 5 - May 6	Yang Water	Dragon	Yang Fire	Rat	April	49	7: 07
May 6 – June 6	Yin Water	Snake	Yang Fire	Rat	May	19	: 57
June 6 - July 7	Yang Wood	Horse	Yang Fire	Rat	June	50	5: 31
July 7 - August 8	Yin Wood	Sheep	Yang Fire	Rat	July	20	15: 59
August 8 - September 8	Yang Fire	Monkey	Yang Fire	Rat	Aug	51	1: 43
September 8 – October 8	Yin Fire	Cock	Yang Fire	Rat	Sep	22	4:21
October 8 - November 7	Yang Earth	Dog	Yang Fire	Rat	Oct	52	19: 33
November 7 - December 7	Yin Earth	Pig	Yang Fire	Rat	Nov	23	22:15
December 7 – January 6	Yang Metal	Rat	Yang Fire	Rat	Dec	53	14:43

1937

	Month		Year				
Find your Day Here	**Stem**	**Branch**	**Stem**	**Branch**	**Day**	**Day**	**Time**
January 6 - February 4	Yin Metal	Ox	Yang Fire	Rat	Jan	24	1: 44
February 4 - March 6	Yang Water	Tiger	Yin Fire	Ox	Feb	55	13: 26
March 6 – April 5	Yin Water	Rabbit	Yin Fire	Ox	Mar	23	7: 45
April 5 – May 6	Yang Wood	Dragon	Yin Fire	Ox	April	54	13: 02
May 6 – June 6	Yin Wood	Snake	Yin Fire	Ox	May	24	6: 51
June 6 – July 7	Yang Fire	Horse	Yin Fire	Ox	June	55	11: 23
July 7– August 8	Yin Fire	Sheep	Yin Fire	Ox	July	25	21: 46
August 8– September 8	Yang Earth	Monkey	Yin Fire	Ox	Aug	56	7: 26
September 8 – October 9	Yin Earth	Cock	Yin Fire	Ox	Sep	27	10: 00
October 9 – November 8	Yang Metal	Dog	Yin Fire	Ox	Oct	57	1: 11
November 8 – December 7	Yin Metal	Pig	Yin Fire	Ox	Nov	28	3: 46
December 7 – January 6	Yang Water	Rat	Yin Fire	Ox	Dec	58	20: 27

Branch	Pig	Rat	Ox	Tiger	Rabbit	Dragon	Snake	Horse	Sheep	Monkey	Cock	Dog
Main Element	Yang Water	Yin Water	Yin Earth	Yang Wood	Yin Wood	Yang Earth	Yang Fire	Yin Fire	Yin Earth	Yang Metal	Yin Metal	Yang Earth
Hidden Elements	Yang Wood		Yin Water	Yang Fire		Yin Wood	Yang Earth	Yin Earth	Yin Fire	Yang Earth		Yin Metal
			Yin Metal	Yang Earth		Yin Water	Yang Metal		Yin Wood	Yang Water		Yin Fire

1938

Find your Day Here	Month Stem	Branch	Year Stem	Branch	Day	Day	Time
January 6 – February 4	Yin Water	Ox	Yin Fire	Ox	Jan	29	7: 32
February 4 - March 6	Yang Wood	Tiger	Yang Earth	Tiger	Feb	60	19:15
March 6 - April 5	Yin Wood	Rabbit	Yang Earth	Tiger	Mar	28	13: 34
April 5 - May 6	Yang Fire	Dragon	Yang Earth	Tiger	April	59	18: 49
May 6– June 6	Yin Fire	Snake	Yang Earth	Tiger	May	29	12: 36
June 6 - July 8	Yang Earth	Horse	Yang Earth	Tiger	June	60	17: 07
July 8 - August 8	Yin Earth	Sheep	Yang Earth	Tiger	July	30	3: 32
August 8 - September 8	Yang Metal	Monkey	Yang Earth	Tiger	Aug	1	13: 13
September 8 – October 9	Yin Metal	Cock	Yang Earth	Tiger	Sep	32	15: 49
October 9 - November 8	Yang Water	Dog	Yang Earth	Tiger	Oct	2	7: 02
November 8 - December 8	Yin Water	Pig	Yang Earth	Tiger	Nov	33	9: 49
December 8 – January 6	Yang Wood	Rat	Yang Earth	Tiger	Dec	3	2: 23

1939

Find your Day Here	Month Stem	Branch	Year Stem	Branch	Day	Day	Time
January 6 – February 5	Yin Wood	Ox	Yang Earth	Tiger	Jan	34	13: 23
February 5 - March 6	Yang Fire	Tiger	Yin Earth	Rabbit	Feb	5	1: 11
March 6 - April 6	Yin Fire	Rabbit	Yin Earth	Rabbit	Mar	33	19: 27
April 6 - May 6	Yang Earth	Dragon	Yin Earth	Rabbit	April	4	: 38
May 6 – June 6	Yin Earth	Snake	Yin Earth	Rabbit	May	34	18: 21
June 6 - July 8	Yang Metal	Horse	Yin Earth	Rabbit	June	5	22: 52
July 8 - August 8	Yin Metal	Sheep	Yin Earth	Rabbit	July	35	9: 19
August 8 - September 8	Yang Water	Monkey	Yin Earth	Rabbit	Aug	6	19: 04
September 8 – October 9	Yin Water	Cock	Yin Earth	Rabbit	Sep	37	21: 42
October 9 - November 8	Yang Wood	Dog	Yin Earth	Rabbit	Oct	7	12: 57
November 8 - December 8	Yin Wood	Pig	Yin Earth	Rabbit	Nov	38	15: 40
December 8 – January 6	Yang Fire	Rat	Yin Earth	Rabbit	Dec	8	8:18

Branch	Pig	Rat	Ox	Tiger	Rabbit	Dragon	Snake	Horse	Sheep	Monkey	Cock	Dog
Main Element	Yang Water	Yin Water	Yin Earth	Yang Wood	Yin Wood	Yang Earth	Yang Fire	Yin Fire	Yin Earth	Yang Metal	Yin Metal	Yang Earth
Hidden Elements	Yang Wood		Yin Water	Yang Fire		Yin Wood	Yang Earth	Yin Earth	Yin Fire	Yang Earth		Yin Metal
			Yin Metal	Yang Earth		Yin Water	Yang Metal		Yin Wood	Yang Water		Yin Fire

1940

Find your Day Here	Month Stem	Branch	Year Stem	Branch	Day	Day	Time
January 6 – February 5	Yin Fire	Ox	Yin Earth	Rabbit	Jan	39	19:24
February 5 - 29, March 6	Yang Earth	Tiger	Yang Metal	Dragon	Feb	10	7:08
March 6 - April 5	Yin Earth	Rabbit	Yang Metal	Dragon	Mar	39	1:24
April 5 – May 6	Yang Metal	Dragon	Yang Metal	Dragon	April	10	6:35
May 6 – June 6	Yin Metal	Snake	Yang Metal	Dragon	May	40	:16
June 6 – July 7	Yang Water	Horse	Yang Metal	Dragon	June	11	4:44
July 7 – August 8	Yin Water	Sheep	Yang Metal	Dragon	July	41	15:08
August 8 – September 8	Yang Wood	Monkey	Yang Metal	Dragon	Aug	12	:52
September 8 – October 8	Yin Wood	Cock	Yang Metal	Dragon	Sep	43	3:30
October 8 – November 7	Yang Fire	Dog	Yang Metal	Dragon	Oct	13	18:43
November 7 – December 7	Yin Fire	Pig	Yang Metal	Dragon	Nov	44	21:27
December 7 – January 6	Yang Earth	Rat	Yang Metal	Dragon	Dec	14	13:58

1941

Find your Day Here	Month Stem	Branch	Year Stem	Branch	Day	Day	Time
January 6 – February 4	Yin Earth	Ox	Yang Metal	Dragon	Jan	45	1:04
February 4 – March 6	Yang Metal	Tiger	Yin Metal	Snake	Feb	16	12:50
March 6 – April 5	Yin Metal	Rabbit	Yin Metal	Snake	Mar	44	7:10
April 5 – May 6	Yang Water	Dragon	Yin Metal	Snake	April	15	12:25
May 6 – June 6	Yin Water	Snake	Yin Metal	Snake	May	45	6:10
June 6 – July 7	Yang Wood	Horse	Yin Metal	Snake	June	16	10:40
July 7 – August 8	Yin Wood	Sheep	Yin Metal	Snake	July	46	21:03
August 8 – September 8	Yang Fire	Monkey	Yin Metal	Snake	Aug	17	6:46
September 8 – October 9	Yin Fire	Cock	Yin Metal	Snake	Sep	48	9:24
October 9 – November 8	Yang Earth	Dog	Yin Metal	Snake	Oct	18	:39
November 8 – December 7	Yin Earth	Pig	Yin Metal	Snake	Nov	49	3:25
December 7 – January 6	Yang Metal	Rat	Yin Metal	Snake	Dec	19	19:57

Branch	Pig	Rat	Ox	Tiger	Rabbit	Dragon	Snake	Horse	Sheep	Monkey	Cock	Dog
Main Element	Yang Water	Yin Water	Yin Earth	Yang Wood	Yin Wood	Yang Earth	Yang Fire	Yin Fire	Yin Earth	Yang Metal	Yin Metal	Yang Earth
Hidden Elements	Yang Wood		Yin Water	Yang Fire		Yin Wood	Yang Earth	Yin Earth	Yin Fire	Yang Earth		Yin Metal
			Yin Metal	Yang Earth		Yin Water	Yang Metal		Yin Wood	Yang Water		Yin Fire

1942

Find your Day Here	Month Stem	Branch	Year Stem	Branch	Day	Day	Time
January 6 – February 4	Yin Metal	Ox	Yin Metal	Snake	Jan	50	7:03
February 4 – March 6	Yang Water	Tiger	Yang Water	Horse	Feb	21	18:49
March 6 – April 5	Yin Water	Rabbit	Yang Water	Horse	Mar	49	13:10
April 5 – May 6	Yang Wood	Dragon	Yang Water	Horse	April	20	18:24
May 6 – June 6	Yin Wood	Snake	Yang Water	Horse	May	50	12:07
June 6 – July 8	Yang Fire	Horse	Yang Water	Horse	June	21	16:37
July 8 – August 8	Yin Fire	Sheep	Yang Water	Horse	July	51	2:52
August 8 – September 8	Yang Earth	Monkey	Yang Water	Horse	Aug	22	12:31
September 8 – October 9	Yin Earth	Cock	Yang Water	Horse	Sep	53	15:07
October 9 – November 8	Yang Metal	Dog	Yang Water	Horse	Oct	23	6:22
November 8 – December 8	Yin Metal	Pig	Yang Water	Horse	Nov	54	9:12
December 8 – January 6	Yang Water	Rat	Yang Water	Horse	Dec	24	1:47

1943

Find your Day Here	Month Stem	Branch	Year Stem	Branch	Day	Day	Time
January 6 –February 5	Yin Water	Ox	Yang Water	Horse	Jan	55	12:55
February 5 – March 6	Yang Wood	Tiger	Yin Water	Sheep	Feb	26	: 40
March 6 – April 6	Yin Wood	Rabbit	Yin Water	Sheep	Mar	54	18: 59
April 6 – May 6	Yang Fire	Dragon	Yin Water	Sheep	April	25	: 12
May 6 – June 6	Yin Fire	Snake	Yin Water	Sheep	May	55	17:54
June 6 – July 8	Yang Earth	Horse	Yin Water	Sheep	June	26	22:19
July 8 – August 8	Yin Earth	Sheep	Yin Water	Sheep	July	56	8:39
August 8 – September 8	Yang Metal	Monkey	Yin Water	Sheep	Aug	27	18: 19
September 8 – October 9	Yin Metal	Cock	Yin Water	Sheep	Sep	58	20: 56
October 9 – November 8	Yang Water	Dog	Yin Water	Sheep	Oct	28	12: 11
November 8 – December 8	Yin Water	Pig	Yin Water	Sheep	Nov	59	14: 59
December 8 – January 6	Yang Wood	Rat	Yin Water	Sheep	Dec	29	7: 33

Branch	Pig	Rat	Ox	Tiger	Rabbit	Dragon	Snake	Horse	Sheep	Monkey	Cock	Dog
Main Element	Yang Water	Yin Water	Yin Earth	Yang Wood	Yin Wood	Yang Earth	Yang Fire	Yin Fire	Yin Earth	Yang Metal	Yin Metal	Yang Earth
Hidden Elements	Yang Wood		Yin Water	Yang Fire		Yin Wood	Yang Earth	Yin Earth	Yin Fire	Yang Earth		Yin Metal
			Yin Metal	Yang Earth		Yin Water	Yang Metal		Yin Wood	Yang Water		Yin Fire

1944

Find your Day Here	Month Stem	Branch	Year Stem	Branch	Day	Day	Time
January 6 – February 5	Yin Wood	Ox	Yin Water	Sheep	Jan	60	18: 40
February 5-29, March 6	Yang Fire	Tiger	Yang Wood	Monkey	Feb	31	6: 23
March 6 - April 5	Yin Fire	Rabbit	Yang Wood	Monkey	Mar	60	: 41
April 5 - May 6	Yang Earth	Dragon	Yang Wood	Monkey	April	31	5: 54
May 5 - June 6	Yin Earth	Snake	Yang Wood	Monkey	May	1	23: 40
June 6 - July 7	Yang Metal	Horse	Yang Wood	Monkey	June	32	4: 11
July 7 - August 8	Yin Metal	Sheep	Yang Wood	Monkey	July	2	14: 37
August 8 - September 8	Yang Water	Monkey	Yang Wood	Monkey	Aug	33	: 19
September 8 - October 8	Yin Water	Cock	Yang Wood	Monkey	Sep	4	2:56
October 8 - November 7	Yang Wood	Dog	Yang Wood	Monkey	Oct	34	18:09
November 7 - December 7	Yin Wood	Pig	Yang Wood	Monkey	Nov	5	20: 55
December 7 - January 6	Yang Fire	Rat	Yang Wood	Monkey	Dec	35	13: 28

1945

Find your Day Here	Month Stem	Branch	Year Stem	Branch	Day	Day	Time
January 6 – February 4	Yin Fire	Ox	Yang Wood	Monkey	Jan	6	:35
February 4 - March 6	Yang Earth	Tiger	Yin Wood	Cock	Feb	37	12:20
March 6 - April 5	Yin Earth	Rabbit	Yin Wood	Cock	Mar	5	6:38
April 5 - May 6	Yang Metal	Dragon	Yin Wood	Cock	April	36	11:52
May 6 – June 6	Yin Metal	Snake	Yin Wood	Cock	May	6	5:37
June 6 – July 7	Yang Water	Horse	Yin Wood	Cock	June	37	10:06
July 7 - August 8	Yin Water	Sheep	Yin Wood	Cock	July	7	20:27
August 8 - September 8	Yang Wood	Monkey	Yin Wood	Cock	Aug	38	6:06
September 8 - October 8	Yin Wood	Cock	Yin Wood	Cock	Sep	9	8:39
October 8 - November 8	Yang Fire	Dog	Yin Wood	Cock	Oct	39	23:50
November 8 - December 7	Yin Fire	Pig	Yin Wood	Cock	Nov	10	2:35
December 7 - January 6	Yang Earth	Rat	Yin Wood	Cock	Dec	40	19:08

Branch	Pig	Rat	Ox	Tiger	Rabbit	Dragon	Snake	Horse	Sheep	Monkey	Cock	Dog
Main Element	Yang Water	Yin Water	Yin Earth	Yang Wood	Yin Wood	Yang Earth	Yang Fire	Yin Fire	Yin Earth	Yang Metal	Yin Metal	Yang Earth
Hidden Elements	Yang Wood		Yin Water	Yang Fire		Yin Wood	Yang Earth	Yin Earth	Yin Fire	Yang Earth		Yin Metal
			Yin Metal	Yang Earth		Yin Water	Yang Metal		Yin Wood	Yang Water		Yin Fire

1946

| | Month | | Year | | | | |
Find your Day Here	Stem	Branch	Stem	Branch	Day	Day	Time
January 6 – February 4	Yin Earth	Ox	Yin Wood	Cock	Jan	11	6:17
February 4 - March 6	Yang Metal	Tiger	Yang Fire	Dog	Feb	42	18:04
March 6 - April 5	Yin Metal	Rabbit	Yang Fire	Dog	Mar	10	12:25
April 5 - May 6	Yang Water	Dragon	Yang Fire	Dog	April	41	17:39
May 6 – June 6	Yin Water	Snake	Yang Fire	Dog	May	11	11:22
June 6 – July 8	Yang Wood	Horse	Yang Fire	Dog	June	42	15:49
July 8 - August 8	Yin Wood	Sheep	Yang Fire	Dog	July	12	2:11
August 8 - September 8	Yang Fire	Monkey	Yang Fire	Dog	Aug	43	11:52
September 8 - October 9	Yin Fire	Cock	Yang Fire	Dog	Sep	14	14:28
October 9 - November 8	Yang Earth	Dog	Yang Fire	Dog	Oct	44	5:42
November 8 - December 8	Yin Earth	Pig	Yang Fire	Dog	Nov	15	8:28
December 8 - January 6	Yang Metal	Rat	Yang Fire	Dog	Dec	45	1:01

1947

| | Month | | Year | | | | |
Find your Day Here	Stem	Branch	Stem	Branch	Day	Day	Time
January 6 – February 5	Yin Metal	Ox	Yang Fire	Dog	Jan	16	12:11
February 4 - March 6	Yang Water	Tiger	Yin Fire	Pig	Feb	47	23:55
March 6 - April 5	Yin Water	Rabbit	Yin Fire	Pig	Mar	15	18:12
April 5 - May 6	Yang Wood	Dragon	Yin Fire	Pig	April	46	23:23
May 6 - June 6	Yin Wood	Snake	Yin Fire	Pig	May	16	17:05
June 6 - July 8	Yang Fire	Horse	Yin Fire	Pig	June	47	21:33
July 8 - August 8	Yin Fire	Sheep	Yin Fire	Pig	July	17	7:56
August 8 - September 8	Yang Earth	Monkey	Yin Fire	Pig	Aug	48	17:39
September 8 - October 9	Yin Earth	Cock	Yin Fire	Pig	Sep	19	20:17
October 9 - November 8	Yang Metal	Dog	Yin Fire	Pig	Oct	49	11:32
November 8 - December 8	Yin Metal	Pig	Yin Fire	Pig	Nov	20	14:19
December 8 - January 6	Yang Water	Rat	Yin Fire	Pig	Dec	50	6:53

Branch	Pig	Rat	Ox	Tiger	Rabbit	Dragon	Snake	Horse	Sheep	Monkey	Cock	Dog
Main Element	Yang Water	Yin Water	Yin Earth	Yang Wood	Yin Wood	Yang Earth	Yang Fire	Yin Fire	Yin Earth	Yang Metal	Yin Metal	Yang Earth
Hidden Elements	Yang Wood		Yin Water	Yang Fire		Yin Wood	Yang Earth	Yin Earth	Yin Fire	Yang Earth		Yin Metal
			Yin Metal	Yang Earth		Yin Water	Yang Metal		Yin Wood	Yang Water		Yin Fire

1948

Find your Day Here	Month Stem	Branch	Year Stem	Branch	Day	Day	Time
January 6 – February 5	Yin Water	Ox	Yin Fire	Pig	Jan	21	18:01
February 5 - 29, March 5	Yang Wood	Tiger	Yang Earth	Rat	Feb	52	5:42
March 5 - April 5	Yin Wood	Rabbit	Yang Earth	Rat	Mar	21	23:58
April 5 - May 5	Yang Fire	Dragon	Yang Earth	Rat	April	52	5:10
May 5 - June 6	Yin Fire	Snake	Yang Earth	Rat	May	22	22:53
June 6 - July 7	Yang Earth	Horse	Yang Earth	Rat	June	53	3:21
July 7 - August 7	Yin Earth	Sheep	Yang Earth	Rat	July	23	13:44
August 7 - September 8	Yang Metal	Monkey	Yang Earth	Rat	Aug	54	23:27
September 8 - October 8	Yin Metal	Cock	Yang Earth	Rat	Sep	25	2:06
October 8 - November 7	Yang Water	Dog	Yang Earth	Rat	Oct	55	17:21
November 7 - December 7	Yin Water	Pig	Yang Earth	Rat	Nov	26	20:07
December 7 - January 6	Yang Wood	Rat	Yang Earth	Rat	Dec	56	12:38

1949

Find your Day Here	Month Stem	Branch	Year Stem	Branch	Day	Day	Time
January 6 – February 4	Yin Wood	Ox	Yang Earth	Rat	Jan	27	23:42
February 4 - March 6	Yang Fire	Tiger	Yin Earth	Ox	Feb	58	11:23
March 6 - April 5	Yin Fire	Rabbit	Yin Earth	Ox	Mar	26	5:40
April 5 - May 6	Yang Earth	Dragon	Yin Earth	Ox	April	57	10:52
May 6 - June 6	Yin Earth	Snake	Yin Earth	Ox	May	27	4:37
June 6 - July 7	Yang Metal	Horse	Yin Earth	Ox	June	58	9:07
July 7 - August 8	Yin Metal	Sheep	Yin Earth	Ox	July	28	19:32
August 8 - September 8	Yang Water	= Monkey	Yin Earth	Ox	Aug	59	5:16
September 8 - October 8	Yin Water	Cock	Yin Earth	Ox	Sep	30	7:55
October 8 – November 8	Yang Wood	Dog	Yin Earth	Ox	Oct	60	23:12
November 8 – December 7	Yin Wood	Pig	Yin Earth	Ox	Nov	31	2:00
December 7 – January 6	Yang Fire	Rat	Yin Earth	Ox	Dec	1	18:34

Branch	Pig	Rat	Ox	Tiger	Rabbit	Dragon	Snake	Horse	Sheep	Monkey	Cock	Dog
Main Element	Yang Water	Yin Water	Yin Earth	Yang Wood	Yin Wood	Yang Earth	Yang Fire	Yin Fire	Yin Earth	Yang Metal	Yin Metal	Yang Earth
Hidden Elements	Yang Wood		Yin Water	Yang Fire		Yin Wood	Yang Earth	Yin Earth	Yin Fire	Yang Earth		Yin Metal
			Yin Metal	Yang Earth		Yin Water	Yang Metal		Yin Wood	Yang Water		Yin Fire

1950

Find your Day Here	Month Stem	Branch	Year Stem	Branch	Day	Day	Time
January 6- February 4	Yin Fire	Ox	Yin Earth	Ox	Jan	32	5: 39
February 4 – March 6	Yang Earth	Tiger	Yang Metal	Tiger	Feb	3	17: 21
March 6 – April 5	Yin Earth	Rabbit	Yang Metal	Tiger	Mar	31	11: 36
April 5 – May 6	Yang Metal	Dragon	Yang Metal	Tiger	April	2	16: 45
May 6 – June 6	Yin Metal	Snake	Yang Metal	Tiger	May	32	10: 25
June 6 – July 8	Yang Water	Horse	Yang Metal	Tiger	June	3	14: 52
July 8 – August 8	Yin Water	Sheep	Yang Metal	Tiger	July	33	1: 14
August 8 – September 8	Yang Wood	Monkey	Yang Metal	Tiger	Aug	4	10:56
September 8 – October 9	Yin Wood	Cock	Yang Metal	Tiger	Sep	35	13: 34
October 9 – November 8	Yang Fire	Dog	Yang Metal	Tiger	Oct	5	4:52
November 8 – December 8	Yin Fire	Pig	Yang Metal	Tiger	Nov	36	7: 44
December 8 – January 6	Yang Earth	Rat	Yang Metal	Tiger	Dec	6	: 22

1951

Find your Day Here	Month Stem	Branch	Year Stem	Branch	Day	Day	Time
January 6- February 4	Yin Earth	Ox	Yang Metal	Tiger	Jan	37	11:31
February 4 – March 7	Yang Metal	Tiger	Yin Metal	Rabbit	Feb	8	23:14
March 7 – April 5	Yin Metal	Rabbit	Yin Metal	Rabbit	Mar	36	17:27
April 6 – May 7	Yang Water	Dragon	Yin Metal	Rabbit	April	7	22:33
May 7 – June 7	Yin Water	Snake	Yin Metal	Rabbit	May	37	16:10
June 7 – July 8	Yang Wood	Horse	Yin Metal	Rabbit	June	8	20:33
July 8 – August 8	Yin Wood	Sheep	Yin Metal	Rabbit	July	38	6:54
August 8 – September 8	Yang Fire	Monkey	Yin Metal	Rabbit	Aug	9	16:38
September 8 – October 9	Yin Fire	Cock	Yin Metal	Rabbit	Sep	40	19:19
October 9 – November 8	Yang Earth	Dog	Yin Metal	Rabbit	Oct	10	10:37
November 8 – December 8	Yin Earth	Pig	Yin Metal	Rabbit	Nov	41	13:27
December 8 – January 6	Yang Metal	Rat	Yin Metal	Rabbit	Dec	11	6:03

Branch	Pig	Rat	Ox	Tiger	Rabbit	Dragon	Snake	Horse	Sheep	Monkey	Cock	Dog
Main Element	Yang Water	Yin Water	Yin Earth	Yang Wood	Yin Wood	Yang Earth	Yang Fire	Yin Fire	Yin Earth	Yang Metal	Yin Metal	Yang Earth
Hidden Elements	Yang Wood		Yin Water	Yang Fire		Yin Wood	Yang Earth	Yin Earth	Yin Fire	Yang Earth		Yin Metal
			Yin Metal	Yang Earth		Yin Water	Yang Metal		Yin Wood	Yang Water		Yin Fire

1952

Find your Day Here	Month Stem	Branch	Year Stem	Branch	Day	Day	Time
January 6- February 5	Yin Metal	Ox	Yin Metal	Rabbit	Jan	42	17:10
February 5 – 29, March 5	Yang Water	Tiger	Yang Water	Dragon	Feb	13	4:53
March 5 – April 5	Yin Water	Rabbit	Yang Water	Dragon	Mar	42	23:08
April 5 – May 5	Yang Wood	Dragon	Yang Water	Dragon	April	13	4:16
May 5 – June 6	Yin Wood	Snake	Yang Water	Dragon	May	43	21:54
June 6 – July 7	Yang Fire	Horse	Yang Water	Dragon	June	14	2:21
July 7 – August 7	Yin Fire	Sheep	Yang Water	Dragon	July	44	12:45
August 7 – September 8	Yang Earth	Monkey	Yang Water	Dragon	Aug	15	22:32
September 8 – October 8	Yin Earth	Cock	Yang Water	Dragon	Sep	46	1:14
October 8 – November 7	Yang Metal	Dog	Yang Water	Dragon	Oct	16	16:33
November 7 – December 7	Yin Metal	Pig	Yang Water	Dragon	Nov	47	19:22
December 7 – January 5	Yang Water	Rat	Yang Water	Dragon	Dec	17	11:56

1953

Find your Day Here	Month Stem	Branch	Year Stem	Branch	Day	Day	Time
January 5- February 4	Yin Water	Ox	Yang Water	Dragon	Jan	48	23:03
February 4 – March 6	Yang Wood	Tiger	Yin Water	Snake	Feb	19	10:46
March 6 – April 5	Yin Wood	Rabbit	Yin Water	Snake	Mar	47	5:03
April 5 – May 6	Yang Fire	Dragon	Yin Water	Snake	April	18	10:13
May 6 – June 6	Yin Fire	Snake	Yin Water	Snake	May	48	3:53
June 6 – July 7	Yang Earth	Horse	Yin Water	Snake	June	19	8:17
July 7 – August 8	Yin Earth	Sheep	Yin Water	Snake	July	49	18:36
August 8 – September 8	Yang Metal	Monkey	Yin Water	Snake	Aug	20	4:15
September 8 – October 8	Yin Metal	Cock	Yin Water	Snake	Sep	51	6:54
October 8 – November 8	Yang Water	Dog	Yin Water	Snake	Oct	21	22:11
November 8 – December 7	Yin Water	Pig	Yin Water	Snake	Nov	52	1:02
December 7 – January 6	Yang Wood	Rat	Yin Water	Snake	Dec	22	17:38

Branch	Pig	Rat	Ox	Tiger	Rabbit	Dragon	Snake	Horse	Sheep	Monkey	Cock	Dog
Main Element	Yang Water	Yin Water	Yin Earth	Yang Wood	Yin Wood	Yang Earth	Yang Fire	Yin Fire	Yin Earth	Yang Metal	Yin Metal	Yang Earth
Hidden Elements	Yang Wood		Yin Water	Yang Fire		Yin Wood	Yang Earth	Yin Earth	Yin Fire	Yang Earth		Yin Metal
			Yin Metal	Yang Earth		Yin Water	Yang Metal		Yin Wood	Yang Water		Yin Fire

1954

Find your Day Here	Month Stem	Branch	Year Stem	Branch	Day	Day	Time
January 6- February 4	Yin Wood	Ox	Yin Water	Snake	Jan	53	4:46
February 4 – March 6	Yang Fire	Tiger	Yang Wood	Horse	Feb	24	16:31
March 6 – April 5	Yin Fire	Rabbit	Yang Wood	Horse	Mar	52	10:49
April 5 – May 6	Yang Earth	Dragon	Yang Wood	Horse	April	23	16:00
May 6 – June 6	Yin Earth	Snake	Yang Wood	Horse	May	53	9:39
June 6 – July 8	Yang Metal	Horse	Yang Wood	Horse	June	24	14:02
July 8 – August 8	Yin Metal	Sheep	Yang Wood	Horse	July	54	:20
August 8 – September 8	Yang Water	Monkey	Yang Wood	Horse	Aug	25	10:00
September 8 – October 9	Yin Water	Cock	Yang Wood	Horse	Sep	56	12:39
October 9 – November 8	Yang Wood	Dog	Yang Wood	Horse	Oct	26	3:58
November 8 – December 7	Yin Wood	Pig	Yang Wood	Horse	Nov	57	6:51
December 7 – January 6	Yang Fire	Rat	Yang Wood	Horse	Dec	27	23:29

1955

Find your Day Here	Month Stem	Branch	Year Stem	Branch	Day	Day	Time
January 6- February 4	Yin Fire	Ox	Yang Wood	Horse	Jan	58	10: 36
February 4 – March 6	Yang Earth	Tiger	Yin Wood	Sheep	Feb	29	22: 18
March 6 – April 5	Yin Earth	Rabbit	Yin Wood	Sheep	Mar	57	16: 32
April 5 – May 6	Yang Metal	Dragon	Yin Wood	Sheep	April	28	21: 39
May 6 – June 6	Yin Metal	Snake	Yin Wood	Sheep	May	58	15: 18
June 6 – July 8	Yang Water	Horse	Yin Wood	Sheep	June	29	19: 44
July 8 – August 8	Yin Water	Sheep	Yin Wood	Sheep	July	59	6: 07
August 8 – September 8	Yang Wood	Monkey	Yin Wood	Sheep	Aug	30	15: 50
September 8 – October 9	Yin Wood	Cock	Yin Wood	Sheep	Sep	1	18: 32
October 9 – November 8	Yang Fire	Dog	Yin Wood	Sheep	Oct	31	9: 53
November 8 – December 8	Yin Fire	Pig	Yin Wood	Sheep	Nov	2	12: 46
December 8 – January 6	Yang Earth	Rat	Yin Wood	Sheep	Dec	32	5: 23

Branch	Pig	Rat	Ox	Tiger	Rabbit	Dragon	Snake	Horse	Sheep	Monkey	Cock	Dog
Main Element	Yang Water	Yin Water	Yin Earth	Yang Wood	Yin Wood	Yang Earth	Yang Fire	Yin Fire	Yin Earth	Yang Metal	Yin Metal	Yang Earth
Hidden Elements	Yang Wood		Yin Water	Yang Fire		Yin Wood	Yang Earth	Yin Earth	Yin Fire	Yang Earth		Yin Metal
			Yin Metal	Yang Earth		Yin Water	Yang Metal		Yin Wood	Yang Water		Yin Fire

1956

Find your Day Here	Month Stem	Branch	Year Stem	Branch	Day	Day	Time
January 6 – February 5	Yin Earth	Ox	Yin Wood	Sheep	Jan	3	16: 31
February 5 – 29, March 5	Yang Metal	Tiger	Yang Fire	Monkey	Feb	34	4: 12
March 5 – April 5	Yin Metal	Rabbit	Yang Fire	Monkey	Mar	3	22: 25
April 5 – May 5	Yang Water	Dragon	Yang Fire	Monkey	April	34	3: 32
May 5 – June 6	Yin Water	Snake	Yang Fire	Monkey	May	4	21: 11
June 6 – July 7	Yang Wood	Horse	Yang Fire	Monkey	June	35	1: 36
July 7 – August 7	Yin Wood	Sheep	Yang Fire	Monkey	July	5	11: 59
August 7 – September 8	Yang Fire	Monkey	Yang Fire	Monkey	Aug	36	9: 41
September 8 – October 8	Yin Fire	Cock	Yang Fire	Monkey	Sep	7	: 20
October 8 – November 7	Yang Earth	Dog	Yang Fire	Monkey	Oct	37	15: 37
November 7 – December 7	Yin Earth	Pig	Yang Fire	Monkey	Nov	8	18: 27
December 7 – January 5	Yang Metal	Rat	Yang Fire	Monkey	Dec	38	11: 03

1957

Find your Day Here	Month Stem	Branch	Year Stem	Branch	Day	Day	Time
January 5 – February 4	Yin Metal	Ox	Yang Fire	Monkey	Jan	4	22: 11
February 4 - March 6	Yang Water	Tiger	Yin Fire	Cock	Feb	40	9: 55
March 6 - April 5	Yin Water	Rabbit	Yin Fire	Cock	Mar	8	4: 11
April 5 - May 6	Yang Wood	Dragon	Yin Fire	Cock	April	39	9: 19
May 6 - June 6	Yin Wood	Snake	Yin Fire	Cock	May	9	2: 59
June 6 - July 7	Yang Fire	Horse	Yin Fire	Cock	June	40	7: 25
July 7 - August 8	Yin Fire	Sheep	Yin Fire	Cock	July	10	17: 49
August 8 - September 8	Yang Earth	Monkey	Yin Fire	Cock	Aug	41	3: 33
September 8 - October 8	Yin Earth	Cock	Yin Fire	Cock	Sep	12	6: 13
October 8 - November 7	Yang Metal	Dog	Yin Fire	Cock	Oct	42	21: 31
November 8 - December 7	Yin Metal	Pig	Yin Fire	Cock	Nov	13	12: 21
December 7 - January 6	Yang Water	Rat	Yin Fire	Cock	Dec	43	16:57

Branch	Pig	Rat	Ox	Tiger	Rabbit	Dragon	Snake	Horse	Sheep	Monkey	Cock	Dog
Main Element	Yang Water	Yin Water	Yin Earth	Yang Wood	Yin Wood	Yang Earth	Yang Fire	Yin Fire	Yin Earth	Yang Metal	Yin Metal	Yang Earth
Hidden Elements	Yang Wood		Yin Water	Yang Fire		Yin Wood	Yang Earth	Yin Earth	Yin Fire	Yang Earth		Yin Metal
			Yin Metal	Yang Earth		Yin Water	Yang Metal		Yin Wood	Yang Water		Yin Fire

1958

		Month		Year				
Find your Day Here	**Stem**	**Branch**	**Stem**	**Branch**	**Day**	**Day**	**Time**
January 6 - February 4	Yin Water	Ox	Yin Fire	Cock	Jan	14	4 : 05
February 4 – March 6	Yang Wood	Tiger	Yang Earth	Dog	Feb	45	15 : 49
March 6 – April 5	Yin Wood	Rabbit	Yang Earth	Dog	Mar	13	10 : 06
April 5 – May 6	Yang Fire	Dragon	Yang Earth	Dog	April	44	15 : 13
May 6 – June 6	Yin Fire	Snake	Yang Earth	Dog	May	14	8 : 50
June 6 – July 8	Yang Earth	Horse	Yang Earth	Dog	June	45	13 : 13
July 7 – August 8	Yin Earth	Sheep	Yang Earth	Dog	July	15	23 : 34
August 8 – September 8	Yang Metal	Monkey	Yang Earth	Dog	Aug	46	9 : 18
September 8 – October 9	Yin Metal	Cock	Yang Earth	Dog	Sep	17	12 : 00
October 9 – November 8	Yang Water	Dog	Yang Earth	Dog	Oct	47	3 : 20
November 8 – December 7	Yin Water	Pig	Yang Earth	Dog	Nov	18	6 : 13
December 7 – January 6	Yang Wood	Rat	Yang Earth	Dog	Dec	48	22 : 50

1959

		Month		Year				
Find your Day Here	**Stem**	**Branch**	**Stem**	**Branch**	**Day**	**Day**	**Time**
January 6 – February 4	Yin Wood	Ox	Yang Earth	Dog	Jan	19	9 : 59
February 4 - March 6	Yang Fire	Tiger	Yin Earth	Pig	Feb	50	21 : 42
March 6 - April 5	Yin Fire	Rabbit	Yin Earth	Pig	Mar	18	15 : 57
April 5 - May 6	Yang Earth	Dragon	Yin Earth	Pig	April	49	21 : 04
May 6 – June 6	Yin Earth	Snake	Yin Earth	Pig	May	19	14 : 39
June 6 - July 8	Yang Metal	Horse	Yin Earth	Pig	June	50	19 : 01
July 8 - August 8	Yin Metal	Sheep	Yin Earth	Pig	July	20	5 : 21
August 8 - September 8	Yang Water	Monkey	Yin Earth	Pig	Aug	51	15 : 05
September 8 - October 8	Yin Water	Cock	Yin Earth	Pig	Sep	22	17 : 49
October 9 - November 8	Yang Wood	Dog	Yin Earth	Pig	Oct	52	9 : 11
November 8 - December 8	Yin Wood	Pig	Yin Earth	Pig	Nov	23	12 : 03
December 8 - January 6	Yang Fire	Rat	Yin Earth	Pig	Dec	53	4 : 38

Branch	Pig	Rat	Ox	Tiger	Rabbit	Dragon	Snake	Horse	Sheep	Monkey	Cock	Dog
Main Element	Yang Water	Yin Water	Yin Earth	Yang Wood	Yin Wood	Yang Earth	Yang Fire	Yin Fire	Yin Earth	Yang Metal	Yin Metal	Yang Earth
Hidden Elements	Yang Wood		Yin Water	Yang Fire		Yin Wood	Yang Earth	Yin Earth	Yin Fire	Yang Earth		Yin Metal
			Yin Metal	Yang Earth		Yin Water	Yang Metal		Yin Wood	Yang Water		Yin Fire

1960

Find your Day Here	Month Stem	Branch	Year Stem	Branch	Day	Day	Time
January 6 – February 5	Yin Fire	Ox	Yin Earth	Pig	Jan	24	15: 43
February 5 –29, March 5	Yang Earth	Tiger	Yang Metal	Rat	Feb	55	3: 24
March 5 - April 5	Yin Earth	Rabbit	Yang Metal	Rat	Mar	24	21: 36
April 5 - May 5	Yang Metal	Dragon	Yang Metal	Rat	April	55	2: 44
May 5 - June 6	Yin Metal	Snake	Yang Metal	Rat	May	25	20: 23
June 6 - July 7	Yang Water	Horse	Yang Metal	Rat	June	56	: 49
July 7 - August 7	Yin Water	Sheep	Yang Metal	Rat	July	26	11: 13
August 7 - September 7	Yang Wood	Monkey	Yang Metal	Rat	Aug	57	21: 00
September 7 - October 8	Yin Wood	Cock	Yang Metal	Rat	Sep	28	23: 46
October 8 - November 7	Yang Fire	Dog	Yang Metal	Rat	Oct	58	15: 09
November 7 - December 7	Yin Fire	Pig	Yang Metal	Rat	Nov	29	18: 02
December 7 - January 5	Yang Earth	Rat	Yang Metal	Rat	Dec	59	10:38

1961

Find your Day Here	Month Stem	Branch	Year Stem	Branch	Day	Day	Time
January 5 – February 4	Yin Earth	Ox	Yang Metal	Rat	Jan	30	21: 43
February 4 - March 6	Yang Metal	Tiger	Yin Metal	Ox	Feb	1	9: 22
March 6 - April 5	Yin Metal	Rabbit	Yin Metal	Ox	Mar	29	3: 35
April 5 - May 6	Yang Water	Dragon	Yin Metal	Ox	April	60	8: 42
May 6 - June 6	Yin Water	Snake	Yin Metal	Ox	May	30	2: 21
June 6 - July 7	Yang Wood	Horse	Yin Metal	Ox	June	1	6: 46
July 7 - August 8	Yin Wood	Sheep	Yin Metal	Ox	July	31	17: 07
August 8 - September 8	Yang Fire	Monkey	Yin Metal	Ox	Aug	2	2: 49
September 8 - October 8	Yin Fire	Cock	Yin Metal	Ox	Sep	33	5: 29
October 8 - November 7	Yang Earth	Dog	Yin Metal	Ox	Oct	3	20: 51
November 7 - December 7	Yin Earth	Pig	Yin Metal	Ox	Nov	34	23: 46
December 7 - January 6	Yang Metal	Rat	Yin Metal	Ox	Dec	4	16: 26

Branch	Pig	Rat	Ox	Tiger	Rabbit	Dragon	Snake	Horse	Sheep	Monkey	Cock	Dog
Main Element	Yang Water	Yin Water	Yin Earth	Yang Wood	Yin Wood	Yang Earth	Yang Fire	Yin Fire	Yin Earth	Yang Metal	Yin Metal	Yang Earth
Hidden Elements	Yang Wood		Yin Water	Yang Fire		Yin Wood	Yang Earth	Yin Earth	Yin Fire	Yang Earth		Yin Metal
			Yin Metal	Yang Earth		Yin Water	Yang Metal		Yin Wood	Yang Water		Yin Fire

1962

Find your Day Here	Month Stem	Branch	Year Stem	Branch	Day	Day	Time
January 6 – February 4	Yin Metal	Ox	Yin Metal	Ox	Jan	35	3: 35
February 4 - March 6	Yang Water	Tiger	Yang Water	Tiger	Feb	6	15: 18
March 6 - April 5	Yin Water	Rabbit	Yang Water	Tiger	Mar	6	9: 30
April 5 - May 6	Yang Wood	Dragon	Yang Water	Tiger	April	6	14: 34
May 6 – June 6	Yin Wood	Snake	Yang Water	Tiger	May	35	8: 10
June 6 - July 7	Yang Fire	Horse	Yang Water	Tiger	June	6	12: 31
July 7 - August 8	Yin Fire	Sheep	Yang Water	Tiger	July	36	22: 51
August 8 - September 8	Yang Earth	Monkey	Yang Water	Tiger	Aug	7	8: 34
September 8 - October 9	Yin Earth	Cock	Yang Water	Tiger	Sep	38	11: 16
October 9 - November 8	Yang Metal	Dog	Yang Water	Tiger	Oct	8	2: 38
November 8 - December 7	Yin Metal	Pig	Yang Water	Tiger	Nov	39	5: 35
December 7 - January 6	Yang Water	Rat	Yang Water	Tiger	Dec	9	22: 17

1963

Find your Day Here	Month Stem	Branch	Year Stem	Branch	Day	Day	Time
January 6 – February 4	Yin Water	Ox	Yang Water	Tiger	Jan	40	9: 27
February 4 - March 6	Yang Wood	Tiger	Yin Water	Rabbit	Feb	11	21: 08
March 6 - April 5	Yin Wood	Rabbit	Yin Water	Rabbit	Mar	39	15: 17
April 5 - May 6	Yang Fire	Dragon	Yin Water	Rabbit	April	10	20: 19
May 6 – June 6	Yin Fire	Snake	Yin Water	Rabbit	May	40	13: 52
June 6 - July 7	Yang Earth	Horse	Yin Water	Rabbit	June	11	18: 15
July 8 - August 8	Yin Earth	Sheep	Yin Water	Rabbit	July	41	4: 38
August 8 - September 8	Yang Metal	Monkey	Yin Water	Rabbit	Aug	12	14: 26
September 8 – October 9	Yin Metal	Cock	Yin Water	Rabbit	Sep	43	17: 12
October 9 - November 8	Yang Water	Dog	Yin Water	Rabbit	Oct	13	8: 36
November 8 - December 8	Yin Water	Pig	Yin Water	Rabbit	Nov	44	11: 32
December 8 - January 6	Yang Wood	Rat	Yin Water	Rabbit	Dec	14	4: 13

Branch	Pig	Rat	Ox	Tiger	Rabbit	Dragon	Snake	Horse	Sheep	Monkey	Cock	Dog
Main Element	Yang Water	Yin Water	Yin Earth	Yang Wood	Yin Wood	Yang Earth	Yang Fire	Yin Fire	Yin Earth	Yang Metal	Yin Metal	Yang Earth
Hidden Elements	Yang Wood		Yin Water	Yang Fire		Yin Wood	Yang Earth	Yin Earth	Yin Fire	Yang Earth		Yin Metal
			Yin Metal	Yang Earth		Yin Water	Yang Metal		Yin Wood	Yang Water		Yin Fire

1964

Find your Day Here	Month Stem	Branch	Year Stem	Branch	Day	Day	Time
January 6- February 5	Yin Wood	Ox	Yin Water	Rabbit	Jan	45	15: 22
February 5-29, - March 5	Yang Fire	Tiger	Yang Wood	Dragon	Feb	16	3: 05
March 5 – April 5	Yin Fire	Rabbit	Yang Wood	Dragon	Mar	45	21: 16
April 5 – May 5	Yang Earth	Dragon	Yang Wood	Dragon	April	16	2: 18
May 5 – June 6	Yin Earth	Snake	Yang Wood	Dragon	May	46	19: 51
June 6 – July 7	Yang Metal	Horse	Yang Wood	Dragon	June	17	: 12
July 7 – August 7	Yin Metal	Sheep	Yang Wood	Dragon	July	47	10: 32
August 7 – September 7	Yang Water	Monkey	Yang Wood	Dragon	Aug	18	20: 16
September 7 – October 8	Yin Water	Cock	Yang Wood	Dragon	Sep	49	23:00
October 8 – November 7	Yang Wood	Dog	Yang Wood	Dragon	Oct	19	14: 22
November 7 – December 7	Yin Wood	Pig	Yang Wood	Dragon	Nov	50	17: 15
December 7 – January 5	Yang Fire	Rat	Yang Wood	Dragon	Dec	20	9: 53

1965

Find your Day Here	Month Stem	Branch	Year Stem	Branch	Day	Day	Time
January 5 – February 4	Yin Fire	Ox	Yang Wood	Dragon	Jan	51	21: 02
February 4 - March 6	Yang Earth	Tiger	Yin Wood	Snake	Feb	27	8: 46
March 6 - April 5	Yin Earth	Rabbit	Yin Wood	Snake	Mar	50	3: 01
April 5 - May 6	Yang Metal	Dragon	Yin Wood	Snake	April	21	8: 07
May 6 - June 6	Yin Metal	Snake	Yin Wood	Snake	May	51	1: 42
June 6 - July 7	Yang Water	Horse	Yin Wood	Snake	June	22	6: 02
July 7 - August 8	Yin Water	Sheep	Yin Wood	Snake	July	52	16: 22
August 8 - September 8	Yang Wood	Monkey	Yin Wood	Snake	Aug	23	2: 05
September 8 – October 8	Yin Wood	Cock	Yin Wood	Snake	Sep	54	4: 48
October 8 - November 7	Yang Fire	Dog	Yin Wood	Snake	Oct	24	20: 11
November 7 - December 7	Yin Fire	Pig	Yin Wood	Snake	Nov	55	23: 07
December 7 - January 5	Yang Earth	Rat	Yin Wood	Snake	Dec	25	15: 46

Branch	Pig	Rat	Ox	Tiger	Rabbit	Dragon	Snake	Horse	Sheep	Monkey	Cock	Dog
Main Element	Yang Water	Yin Water	Yin Earth	Yang Wood	Yin Wood	Yang Earth	Yang Fire	Yin Fire	Yin Earth	Yang Metal	Yin Metal	Yang Earth
Hidden Elements	Yang Wood		Yin Water	Yang Fire		Yin Wood	Yang Earth	Yin Earth	Yin Fire	Yang Earth		Yin Metal
			Yin Metal	Yang Earth		Yin Water	Yang Metal		Yin Wood	Yang Water		Yin Fire

1966

Find your Day Here	Month Stem	Branch	Year Stem	Branch	Day	Day	Time
January 5 – February 4	Yin Earth	Ox	Yin Wood	Snake	Jan	56	2:55
February 4 – 29, March 6	Yang Metal	Tiger	Yang Fire	Horse	Feb	27	14:38
March 6 – April 5	Yin Metal	Rabbit	Yang Fire	Horse	Mar	55	8:51
April 5 – May 6	Yang Water	Dragon	Yang Fire	Horse	April	26	13:57
May 6 – June 6	Yin Water	Snake	Yang Fire	Horse	May	56	7:31
June 6 – July 7	Yang Wood	Horse	Yang Fire	Horse	June	27	11:50
July 7 – August 8	Yin Wood	Sheep	Yang Fire	Horse	July	57	22:07
August 8 – September 8	Yang Fire	Monkey	Yang Fire	Horse	Aug	28	7:49
September 8 – October 9	Yin Fire	Cock	Yang Fire	Horse	Sep	59	10:32
October 9 – November 8	Yang Earth	Dog	Yang Fire	Horse	Oct	29	1:57
November 8 – December 7	Yin Earth	Pig	Yang Fire	Horse	Nov	60	4:56
December 7 – January 6	Yang Metal	Rat	Yang Fire	Horse	Dec	30	21:38

1967

Find your Day Here	Month Stem	Branch	Year Stem	Branch	Day	Day	Time
January 6 – February 4	Yin Metal	Ox	Yang Fire	Horse	Jan	1	8:48
February 4 - March 6	Yang Water	Tiger	Yin Fire	Sheep	Feb	32	20:31
March 6 - April 5	Yin Water	Rabbit	Yin Fire	Sheep	Mar	60	14:42
April 5 - May 6	Yang Wood	Dragon	Yin Fire	Sheep	April	31	19:45
May 6 – June 6	Yin Wood	Snake	Yin Fire	Sheep	May	1	13:18
June 6 - July 8	Yang Fire	Horse	Yin Fire	Sheep	June	32	17:36
July 8 - August 8	Yin Fire	Sheep	Yin Fire	Sheep	July	2	3:54
August 8 - September 8	Yang Earth	Monkey	Yin Fire	Sheep	Aug	33	13:35
September 8 – October 9	Yin Earth	Cock	Yin Fire	Sheep	Sep	4	16:18
October 9 - November 8	Yang Metal	Dog	Yin Fire	Sheep	Oct	34	7:42
November 8 - December 8	Yin Metal	Pig	Yin Fire	Sheep	Nov	5	10:38
December 8 - January 6	Yang Water	Rat	Yin Fire	Sheep	Dec	35	3:18

Branch	Pig	Rat	Ox	Tiger	Rabbit	Dragon	Snake	Horse	Sheep	Monkey	Cock	Dog
Main Element	Yang Water	Yin Water	Yin Earth	Yang Wood	Yin Wood	Yang Earth	Yang Fire	Yin Fire	Yin Earth	Yang Metal	Yin Metal	Yang Earth
Hidden Elements	Yang Wood		Yin Water	Yang Fire		Yin Wood	Yang Earth	Yin Earth	Yin Fire	Yang Earth		Yin Metal
			Yin Metal	Yang Earth		Yin Water	Yang Metal		Yin Wood	Yang Water		Yin Fire

1968

Find your Day Here	Month Stem	Branch	Year Stem	Branch	Day	Day	Time
January 6 – February 5	Yin Water	Ox	Yin Fire	Sheep	Jan	6	14: 26
February 5 – 29, - March 5	Yang Wood	Tiger	Yang Earth	Monkey	Feb	37	2: 08
March 5 - April 5	Yin Wood	Rabbit	Yang Earth	Monkey	Mar	6	20: 18
April 5 - May 5	Yang Fire	Dragon	Yang Earth	Monkey	April	37	1: 21
May 5 – June 5	Yin Fire	Snake	Yang Earth	Monkey	May	7	18: 56
June 5 - July 7	Yang Earth	Horse	Yang Earth	Monkey	June	38	23: 19
July 7 - August 7	Yin Earth	Sheep	Yang Earth	Monkey	July	8	9: 42
August 7 - September 7	Yang Metal	Monkey	Yang Earth	Monkey	Aug	39	19: 27
September 7 – October 8	Yin Metal	Cock	Yang Earth	Monkey	Sep	10	22: 12
October 8 - November 7	Yang Water	Dog	Yang Earth	Monkey	Oct	40	13: 35
November 7 - December 7	Yin Water	Pig	Yang Earth	Monkey	Nov	11	16: 29
December 7 - January 5	Yang Wood	Rat	Yang Earth	Monkey	Dec	41	9: 09

1969

Find your Day Here	Month Stem	Branch	Year Stem	Branch	Day	Day	Time
January 5 – February 4	Yin Wood	Ox	Yang Earth	Monkey	Jan	12	20: 17
February 4 - March 6	Yang Fire	Tiger	Yin Earth	Cock	Feb	43	7: 59
March 6 - April 5	Yin Fire	Rabbit	Yin Earth	Cock	Mar	11	2: 11
April 5 - May 6	Yang Earth	Dragon	Yin Earth	Cock	April	42	7: 15
May 6 – June 6	Yin Earth	Snake	Yin Earth	Cock	May	12	: 50
June 6 - July 7	Yang Metal	Horse	Yin Earth	Cock	June	43	5: 12
July 7 - August 8	Yin Metal	Sheep	Yin Earth	Cock	July	13	15: 32
August 8 - September 8	Yang Water	Monkey	Yin Earth	Cock	Aug	44	1: 14
September 8 – October 8	Yin Water	Cock	Yin Earth	Cock	Sep	15	3: 56
October 8 - November 7	Yang Wood	Dog	Yin Earth	Cock	Oct	45	19: 17
November 7 - December 7	Yin Wood	Pig	Yin Earth	Cock	Nov	16	22: 12
December 7 - January 6	Yang Fire	Rat	Yin Earth	Cock	Dec	46	14: 51

Branch	Pig	Rat	Ox	Tiger	Rabbit	Dragon	Snake	Horse	Sheep	Monkey	Cock	Dog
Main Element	Yang Water	Yin Water	Yin Earth	Yang Wood	Yin Wood	Yang Earth	Yang Fire	Yin Fire	Yin Earth	Yang Metal	Yin Metal	Yang Earth
Hidden Elements	Yang Wood		Yin Water	Yang Fire		Yin Wood	Yang Earth	Yin Earth	Yin Fire	Yang Earth		Yin Metal
			Yin Metal	Yang Earth		Yin Water	Yang Metal		Yin Wood	Yang Water		Yin Fire

1970

Find your Day Here	Month Stem	Branch	Year Stem	Branch	Day	Day	Time
January 6 – February 4	Yin Fire	Ox	Yin Earth	Cock	Jan	17	1:59
February 4 - March 6	Yang Earth	Tiger	Yang Metal	Dog	Feb	48	13:46
March 6 - April 5	Yin Earth	Rabbit	Yang Metal	Dog	Mar	16	7:51
April 5 - May 6	Yang Metal	Dragon	Yang Metal	Dog	April	47	12:54
May 6 – June 6	Yin Metal	Snake	Yang Metal	Dog	May	17	6:28
June 6 - July 7	Yang Water	Horse	Yang Metal	Dog	June	48	10:51
July 7 - August 8	Yin Water	Sheep	Yang Metal	Dog	July	18	21:14
August 8 - September 8	Yang Wood	Monkey	Yang Metal	Dog	Aug	49	6:58
September 8 – October 9	Yin Wood	Cock	Yang Metal	Dog	Sep	20	9:42
October 9 - November 8	Yang Fire	Dog	Yang Metal	Dog	Oct	50	1:06
November 8 - December 7	Yin Fire	Pig	Yang Metal	Dog	Nov	21	4:01
December 7 - January 6	Yang Earth	Rat	Yang Metal	Dog	Dec	51	21:41

1971

Find your Day Here	Month Stem	Branch	Year Stem	Branch	Day	Day	Time
January 6 – February 4	Yin Earth	Ox	Yang Metal	Dog	Jan	22	7: 45
February 4 – 29, March 6	Yang Metal	Tiger	Yin Metal	Pig	Feb	53	19 :26
March 6 – April 5	Yin Metal	Rabbit	Yin Metal	Pig	Mar	21	13: 35
April 5 – May 6	Yang Water	Dragon	Yin Metal	Pig	April	52	18: 36
May 6 – June 6	Yin Water	Snake	Yin Metal	Pig	May	22	12: 08
June 6 – July 8	Yang Wood	Horse	Yin Metal	Pig	June	53	16: 29
July 8 – August 8	Yin Wood	Sheep	Yin Metal	Pig	July	23	2:51
August 8– September 8	Yang Fire	Monkey	Yin Metal	Pig	Aug	54	12: 40
September 8 – October 9	Yin Fire	Cock	Yin Metal	Pig	Sep	25	17: 30
October 9 – November 8	Yang Earth	Dog	Yin Metal	Pig	Oct	55	6: 59
November 8 – December 8	Yin Earth	Pig	Yin Metal	Pig	Nov	26	9:57
December 8 – January 6	Yang Metal	Rat	Yin Metal	Pig	Dec	56	2:36

Branch	Pig	Rat	Ox	Tiger	Rabbit	Dragon	Snake	Horse	Sheep	Monkey	Cock	Dog
Main Element	Yang Water	Yin Water	Yin Earth	Yang Wood	Yin Wood	Yang Earth	Yang Fire	Yin Fire	Yin Earth	Yang Metal	Yin Metal	Yang Earth
Hidden Elements	Yang Wood		Yin Water	Yang Fire		Yin Wood	Yang Earth	Yin Earth	Yin Fire	Yang Earth		Yin Metal
			Yin Metal	Yang Earth		Yin Water	Yang Metal		Yin Wood	Yang Water		Yin Fire

1972

Find your Day Here	Month Stem	Branch	Year Stem	Branch	Day	Day	Time
January 6 – February 5	Yin Metal	Ox	Yin Metal	Pig	Jan	27	13:43
February 5 - 29, - March 5	Yang Water	Tiger	Yang Water	Rat	Feb	58	13:20
March 5 - April 5	Yin Water	Rabbit	Yang Water	Rat	Mar	27	19:28
April 5 - May 5	Yang Wood	Dragon	Yang Water	Rat	April	58	12:29
May 5 – June 5	Yin Wood	Snake	Yang Water	Rat	May	59	18:16
June 5 - July 7	Yang Fire	Horse	Yang Water	Rat	June	59	22:22
July 7 - August 7	Yin Fire	Sheep	Yang Water	Rat	July	29	8:43
August 7 - September 7	Yang Earth	Monkey	Yang Water	Rat	Aug	31	18:29
September 7 – October 8	Yin Earth	Cock	Yang Water	Rat	Sep	31	21:15
October 8 - November 7	Yang Metal	Dog	Yang Water	Rat	Oct	1	14:42
November 7 - December 7	Yin Metal	Pig	Yang Water	Rat	Nov	32	15:40
December 7 - January 5	Yang Water	Rat	Yang Water	Rat	Dec	2	8:19

1973

Find your Day Here	Month Stem	Branch	Year Stem	Branch	Day	Day	Time
January 5 – February 4	Yin Water	Ox	Yang Water	Rat	Jan	33	19:26
February 4 - March 6	Yang Wood	Tiger	Yin Water	Ox	Feb	4	7:04
March 6 - April 5	Yin Wood	Rabbit	Yin Water	Ox	Mar	32	1:13
April 5 - May 5	Yang Fire	Dragon	Yin Water	Ox	April	3	6:14
May 5 – June 6	Yin Fire	Snake	Yin Water	Ox	May	33	23:47
June 6 - July 7	Yang Earth	Horse	Yin Water	Ox	June	4	4:07
July 7 - August 8	Yin Earth	Sheep	Yin Water	Ox	July	34	14:28
August 8 - September 8	Yang Metal	Monkey	Yin Water	Ox	Aug	5	:13
September 8 – October 8	Yin Metal	Cock	Yin Water	Ox	Sep	36	3:00
October 8 - November 7	Yang Water	Dog	Yin Water	Ox	Oct	6	18:27
November 7 - December 7	Yin Water	Pig	Yin Water	Ox	Nov	37	21:28
December 7 – January 6	Yang Wood	Rat	Yin Water	Ox	Dec	7	14:11

Branch	Pig	Rat	Ox	Tiger	Rabbit	Dragon	Snake	Horse	Sheep	Monkey	Cock	Dog
Main Element	Yang Water	Yin Water	Yin Earth	Yang Wood	Yin Wood	Yang Earth	Yang Fire	Yin Fire	Yin Earth	Yang Metal	Yin Metal	Yang Earth
Hidden Elements	Yang Wood		Yin Water	Yang Fire		Yin Wood	Yin Earth	Yin Earth	Yin Fire	Yang Earth		Yin Metal
			Yin Metal	Yang Earth		Yin Water	Yang Metal		Yin Wood	Yang Water		Yin Fire

1974

Find your Day Here	Month Stem	Branch	Year Stem	Branch	Day	Day	Time
January 6 – February 4	Yin Wood	Ox	Yin Water	Ox	Jan	38	1: 20
February 4 - March 6	Yang Fire	Tiger	Yang Wood	Tiger	Feb	9	13: 00
March 6 - April 5	Yin Fire	Rabbit	Yang Wood	Tiger	Mar	37	7: 07
April 5 - May 6	Yang Earth	Dragon	Yang Wood	Tiger	April	8	12: 05
May 6 – June 6	Yin Earth	Snake	Yang Wood	Tiger	May	38	5: 34
June 6 - July 7	Yang Metal	Horse	Yang Wood	Tiger	June	9	9: 52
July 7 - August 8	Yin Metal	Sheep	Yang Wood	Tiger	July	39	20: 13
August 8 - September 8	Yang Water	Monkey	Yang Wood	Tiger	Aug	10	5: 57
September 8 – October 9	Yin Water	Cock	Yang Wood	Tiger	Sep	41	8:45
October 9 - November 8	Yang Wood	Dog	Yang Wood	Tiger	Oct	11	: 15
November 8 - December 7	Yin Wood	Pig	Yang Wood	Tiger	Nov	42	3: 18
December 7 – January 6	Yang Fire	Rat	Yang Wood	Tiger	Dec	12	20: 05

1975

Find your Day Here	Month Stem	Branch	Year Stem	Branch	Day	Day	Time
January 6 – February 4	Yin Fire	Ox	Yang Wood	Tiger	Jan	43	7:18
February 4 - March 6	Yang Earth	Tiger	Yin Wood	Rabbit	Feb	14	18: 59
March 6 – April 5	Yin Earth	Rabbit	Yin Wood	Rabbit	Mar	42	13: 06
April 5 – May 6	Yang Metal	Dragon	Yin Wood	Rabbit	April	13	18: 02
May 6 – June 6	Yin Metal	Snake	Yin Wood	Rabbit	May	43	11: 27
June 6 – July 8	Yang Water	Horse	Yin Wood	Rabbit	June	14	15: 42
July 8 – August 8	Yin Water	Sheep	Yin Wood	Rabbit	July	44	2: 00
August 8– September 8	Yang Wood	Monkey	Yin Wood	Rabbit	Aug	15	11: 45
September 8 – October 9	Yin Wood	Cock	Yin Wood	Rabbit	Sep	46	14:33
October 9 – November 8	Yang Fire	Dog	Yin Wood	Rabbit	Oct	16	6: 02
November 8 – December 8	Yin Fire	Pig	Yin Wood	Rabbit	Nov	47	9: 03
December 8 – January 6	Yang Earth	Rat	Yin Wood	Rabbit	Dec	17	1: 46

Branch	Pig	Rat	Ox	Tiger	Rabbit	Dragon	Snake	Horse	Sheep	Monkey	Cock	Dog
Main Element	Yang Water	Yin Water	Yin Earth	Yang Wood	Yin Wood	Yang Earth	Yang Fire	Yin Fire	Yin Earth	Yang Metal	Yin Metal	Yang Earth
Hidden Elements	Yang Wood		Yin Water	Yang Fire		Yin Wood	Yang Earth	Yin Earth	Yin Fire	Yang Earth		Yin Metal
			Yin Metal	Yang Earth		Yin Water	Yang Metal		Yin Wood	Yang Water		Yin Fire

1976

Find your Day Here	Month Stem	Branch	Year Stem	Branch	Day	Day	Time
January 6 – February 5	Yin Earth	Ox	Yin Wood	Rabbit	Jan	48	12: 58
February 5 - 29, - March 5	Yang Metal	Tiger	Yang Fire	Dragon	Feb	19	: 40
March 5 - April 4	Yin Metal	Rabbit	Yang Fire	Dragon	Mar	48	18: 48
April 4 - May 5	Yang Water	Dragon	Yang Fire	Dragon	April	19	23: 47
May 5 – June 5	Yin Water	Snake	Yang Fire	Dragon	May	49	17: 15
June 5 - July 7	Yang Wood	Horse	Yang Fire	Dragon	June	20	21: 31
July 7 - August 7	Yin Wood	Sheep	Yang Fire	Dragon	July	50	7: 51
August 7 - September 7	Yang Fire	Monkey	Yang Fire	Dragon	Aug	21	17: 39
September 7 – October 8	Yin Fire	Cock	Yang Fire	Dragon	Sep	52	20:28
October 8 - November 7	Yang Earth	Dog	Yang Fire	Dragon	Oct	22	11: 58
November 7 - December 7	Yin Earth	Pig	Yang Fire	Dragon	Nov	53	14: 59
December 7 - January 5	Yang Metal	Rat	Yang Fire	Dragon	Dec	23	7: 41

1977

Find your Day Here	Month Stem	Branch	Year Stem	Branch	Day	Day	Time
January 5 – February 4	Yin Metal	Ox	Yang Fire	Dragon	Jan	54	18: 51
February 4 - March 6	Yang Water	Tiger	Yin Fire	Snake	Feb	25	6: 34
March 6 - April 5	Yin Water	Rabbit	Yin Fire	Snake	Mar	53	: 44
April 5 - May 5	Yang Wood	Dragon	Yin Fire	Snake	April	24	5: 46
May 5 – June 6	Yin Wood	Snake	Yin Fire	Snake	May	54	23: 16
June 6 - July 7	Yang Fire	Horse	Yin Fire	Snake	June	25	3: 32
July 7 - August 7	Yin Fire	Sheep	Yin Fire	Snake	July	55	13: 48
August 7 - September 8	Yang Earth	Monkey	Yin Fire	Snake	Aug	26	23: 30
September 8 – October 8	Yin Earth	Cock	Yin Fire	Snake	Sep	57	2: 16
October 8 - November 7	Yang Metal	Dog	Yin Fire	Snake	Oct	27	17: 44
November 7 - December 7	Yin Metal	Pig	Yin Fire	Snake	Nov	58	20: 46
December 7 – January 6	Yang Water	Rat	Yin Fire	Snake	Dec	28	13: 31

Branch	Pig	Rat	Ox	Tiger	Rabbit	Dragon	Snake	Horse	Sheep	Monkey	Cock	Dog
Main Element	Yang Water	Yin Water	Yin Earth	Yang Wood	Yin Wood	Yang Earth	Yang Fire	Yin Fire	Yin Earth	Yang Metal	Yin Metal	Yang Earth
Hidden Elements	Yang Wood		Yin Water	Yang Fire		Yin Wood	Yang Earth	Yin Earth	Yin Fire	Yang Earth		Yin Metal
			Yin Metal	Yang Earth		Yin Water	Yang Metal		Yin Wood	Yang Water		Yin Fire

1978

Find your Day Here	Month Stem	Branch	Year Stem	Branch	Day	Day	Time
January 6 – February 4	Yin Water	Ox	Yin Fire	Snake	Jan	59	: 43
February 4 - March 6	Yang Wood	Tiger	Yang Earth	Horse	Feb	30	12: 27
March 6 - April 5	Yin Wood	Rabbit	Yang Earth	Horse	Mar	58	6: 38
April 5 - May 6	Yang Fire	Dragon	Yang Earth	Horse	April	29	11: 39
May 6 – June 6	Yin Fire	Snake	Yang Earth	Horse	May	59	5: 09
June 6 - July 7	Yang Earth	Horse	Yang Earth	Horse	June	30	9:23
July 7 - August 8	Yin Earth	Sheep	Yang Earth	Horse	July	60	19: 37
August 8 - September 8	Yang Metal	Monkey	Yang Earth	Horse	Aug	31	5: 18
September 8 – October 8	Yin Metal	Cock	Yang Earth	Horse	Sep	2	8: 03
October 8 - November 8	Yang Water	Dog	Yang Earth	Horse	Oct	32	23: 31
November 8 - December 7	Yin Water	Pig	Yang Earth	Horse	Nov	3	2: 34
December 7 – January 6	Yang Wood	Rat	Yang Earth	Horse	Dec	33	19: 20

1979

Find your Day Here	Month Stem	Branch	Year Stem	Branch	Day	Day	Time
January 6 – February 4	Yin Wood	Ox	Yang Earth	Horse	Jan	4	6: 32
February 4 - March 6	Yang Fire	Tiger	Yin Earth	Sheep	Feb	35	18: 13
March 6 - April 5	Yin Fire	Rabbit	Yin Earth	Sheep	Mar	3	12: 20
April 5 - May 6	Yang Earth	Dragon	Yin Earth	Sheep	April	34	17: 18
May 6 – June 6	Yin Earth	Snake	Yin Earth	Sheep	May	4	10: 47
June 6 - July 8	Yang Metal	Horse	Yin Earth	Sheep	June	35	15: 05
July 8 - August 8	Yin Metal	Sheep	Yin Earth	Sheep	July	5	1: 25
August 8 - September 8	Yang Water	Monkey	Yin Earth	Sheep	Aug	36	11: 11
September 8 – October 9	Yin Water	Cock	Yin Earth	Sheep	Sep	7	14: 00
October 9 - November 8	Yang Wood	Dog	Yin Earth	Sheep	Oct	37	5: 30
November 8 - December 8	Yin Wood	Pig	Yin Earth	Sheep	Nov	8	8: 33
December 8 – January 6	Yang Fire	Rat	Yin Earth	Sheep	Dec	38	1: 18

Branch	Pig	Rat	Ox	Tiger	Rabbit	Dragon	Snake	Horse	Sheep	Monkey	Cock	Dog
Main Element	Yang Water	Yin Water	Yin Earth	Yang Wood	Yin Wood	Yang Earth	Yang Fire	Yin Fire	Yin Earth	Yang Metal	Yin Metal	Yang Earth
Hidden Elements	Yang Wood		Yin Water	Yang Fire		Yin Wood	Yang Earth	Yin Earth	Yin Fire	Yang Earth		Yin Metal
			Yin Metal	Yang Earth		Yin Water	Yang Metal		Yin Wood	Yang Water		Yin Fire

1980

Find your Day Here	Month Stem	Branch	Year Stem	Branch	Day	Day	Time
January 6 – February 5	Yin Fire	Ox	Yin Earth	Sheep	Jan	9	12: 29
February 5 – 29, - March 5	Yang Earth	Tiger	Yang Metal	Monkey	Feb	40	: 10
March 5 – April 4	Yin Earth	Rabbit	Yang Metal	Monkey	Mar	9	18:17
April 4 – May 5	Yang Metal	Dragon	Yang Metal	Monkey	April	40	23:15
May 5 – June 5	Yin Metal	Snake	Yang Metal	Monkey	May	10	16:45
June 5 – July 7	Yang Water	Horse	Yang Metal	Monkey	June	41	21:04
July 7 – August 7	Yin Water	Sheep	Yang Metal	Monkey	July	11	7: 24
August 7– September 7	Yang Wood	Monkey	Yang Metal	Monkey	Aug	42	17:09
September 7 – October 8	Yin Wood	Cock	Yang Metal	Monkey	Sep	13	19:54
October 8 – November 7	Yang Fire	Dog	Yang Metal	Monkey	Oct	43	11:19
November 7 – December 7	Yin Fire	Pig	Yang Metal	Monkey	Nov	14	14:18
December 7 – January 5	Yang Earth	Rat	Yang Metal	Monkey	Dec	44	7: 02

1981

Find your Day Here	Month Stem	Branch	Year Stem	Branch	Day	Day	Time
January 5 – February 4	Yin Earth	Ox	Yang Metal	Monkey	Jan	15	18:13
February 4 - March 6	Yang Metal	Tiger	Yin Metal	Cock	Feb	46	5: 56
March 6 - April 5	Yin Metal	Rabbit	Yin Metal	Cock	Mar	14	: 05
April 5 - May 5	Yang Water	Dragon	Yin Metal	Cock	April	45	5: 05
May 5– June 6	Yin Water	Snake	Yin Metal	Cock	May	15	22:35
June 6 - July 7	Yang Wood	Horse	Yin Metal	Cock	June	46	2: 53
July 7 - August 7	Yin Wood	Sheep	Yin Metal	Cock	July	16	13:12
August 7 - September 8	Yang Fire	Monkey	Yin Metal	Cock	Aug	47	22:57
September 8 – October 8	Yin Fire	Cock	Yin Metal	Cock	Sep	18	1: 43
October 8 - November 7	Yang Earth	Dog	Yin Metal	Cock	Oct	48	17:10
November 7 - December 7	Yin Earth	Pig	Yin Metal	Cock	Nov	19	20:19
December 7 – January 6	Yang Metal	Rat	Yin Metal	Cock	Dec	49	12:51

	Pig	Rat	Ox	Tiger	Rabbit	Dragon	Snake	Horse	Sheep	Monkey	Cock	Dog
Main Element	Yang Water	Yin Water	Yin Earth	Yang Wood	Yin Wood	Yang Earth	Yang Fire	Yin Fire	Yin Earth	Yang Metal	Yin Metal	Yang Earth
Hidden Elements	Yang Wood		Yin Water	Yang Fire		Yin Wood	Yang Earth	Yin Earth	Yin Fire	Yang Earth		Yin Metal
			Yin Metal	Yang Earth		Yin Water	Yang Metal		Yin Wood	Yang Water		Yin Fire

1982

	Month		Year				
Find your Day Here	**Stem**	**Branch**	**Stem**	**Branch**	**Day**	**Day**	**Time**
January 6 – February 4	Yin Metal	Ox	Yin Metal	Cock	Jan	20	: 03
February 4 - March 6	Yang Water	Tiger	Yang Water	Dog	Feb	51	11: 46
March 6 - April 5	Yin Water	Rabbit	Yang Water	Dog	Mar	19	5: 55
April 5 - May 6	Yang Wood	Dragon	Yang Water	Dog	April	50	10: 53
May 6 – June 6	Yin Wood	Snake	Yang Water	Dog	May	20	4: 20
June 6 - July 7	Yang Fire	Horse	Yang Water	Dog	June	51	8: 36
July 7 - August 8	Yin Fire	Sheep	Yang Water	Dog	July	21	18: 55
August 8 - September 8	Yang Earth	Monkey	Yang Water	Dog	Aug	52	4: 42
September 8 – October 8	Yin Earth	Cock	Yang Water	Dog	Sep	23	7: 32
October 8 - November 8	Yang Metal	Dog	Yang Water	Dog	Oct	53	23: 02
November 8- December 7	Yin Metal	Pig	Yang Water	Dog	Nov	24	2: 04
December 7 – January 6	Yang Water	Rat	Yang Water	Dog	Dec	54	18: 48

1983

	Month		Year				
Find your Day Here	**Stem**	**Branch**	**Stem**	**Branch**	**Day**	**Day**	**Time**
January 6 – February 4	Yin Water	Ox	Yang Water	Dog	Jan	25	5: 59
February 4 - March 6	Yang Wood	Tiger	Yin Water	Pig	Feb	56	17: 40
March 6 - April 5	Yin Wood	Rabbit	Yin Water	Pig	Mar	24	11: 47
April 5 - May 6	Yang Fire	Dragon	Yin Water	Pig	April	55	16: 45
May 6 – June 6	Yin Fire	Snake	Yin Water	Pig	May	25	10: 11
June 6 - July 8	Yang Earth	Horse	Yin Water	Pig	June	56	14: 26
July 8 - August 8	Yin Earth	Sheep	Yin Water	Pig	July	26	: 43
August 8 - September 8	Yang Metal	Monkey	Yin Water	Pig	Aug	57	10: 30
September 8 – October 9	Yin Metal	Cock	Yin Water	Pig	Sep	28	13: 20
October 9 - November 8	Yang Water	Dog	Yin Water	Pig	Oct	58	4: 51
November 8 - December 8	Yin Water	Pig	Yin Water	Pig	Nov	29	7: 53
December 8 – January 6	Yang Wood	Rat	Yin Water	Pig	Dec	59	: 34

Branch	Pig	Rat	Ox	Tiger	Rabbit	Dragon	Snake	Horse	Sheep	Monkey	Cock	Dog
Main Element	Yang Water	Yin Water	Yin Earth	Yang Wood	Yin Wood	Yang Earth	Yang Fire	Yin Fire	Yin Earth	Yang Metal	Yin Metal	Yang Earth
Hidden Elements	Yang Wood		Yin Water	Yang Fire		Yin Wood	Yang Earth	Yin Earth	Yin Fire	Yang Earth		Yin Metal
			Yin Metal	Yang Earth		Yin Water	Yang Metal		Yin Wood	Yang Water		Yin Fire

1984

Find your Day Here	Month Stem	Month Branch	Year Stem	Year Branch	Day	Day	Time
January 6 – February 4	Yin Wood	Ox	Yin Water	Pig	Jan	30	11: 41
February 4 - 29, - March 5	Yang Fire	Tiger	Yang Wood	Rat	Feb	1	11: 19
March 5 – April 4	Yin Fire	Rabbit	Yang Wood	Rat	Mar	30	17: 25
April 4 – May 5	Yang Earth	Dragon	Yang Wood	Rat	April	1	22: 22
May 5 – June 5	Yin Earth	Snake	Yang Wood	Rat	May	31	15: 51
June 5 – July 7	Yang Metal	Horse	Yang Wood	Rat	June	2	20: 09
July 7 – August 7	Yin Metal	Sheep	Yang Wood	Rat	July	32	6: 29
August 7– September 7	Yang Water	Monkey	Yang Wood	Rat	Aug	3	16: 18
September 7 – October 8	Yin Water	Cock	Yang Wood	Rat	Sep	34	19: 10
October 8 – November 7	Yang Wood	Dog	Yang Wood	Rat	Oct	4	10: 43
November 7 – December 7	Yin Wood	Pig	Yang Wood	Rat	Nov	35	13: 45
December 7 – January 5	Yang Fire	Rat	Yang Wood	Rat	Dec	5	6: 28

1985

Find your Day Here	Month Stem	Month Branch	Year Stem	Year Branch	Day	Day	Time
January 5 – February 4	Yin Fire	Ox	Yang Wood	Rat	Jan	36	17: 35
February 4 - March 5	Yang Earth	Tiger	Yin Wood	Ox	Feb	7	5: 12
March 5 - April 5	Yin Earth	Rabbit	Yin Wood	Ox	Mar	35	23: 16
April 5 - May 5	Yang Metal	Dragon	Yin Wood	Ox	April	6	4: 14
May 5 – June 6	Yin Metal	Snake	Yin Wood	Ox	May	36	21: 43
June 6 - July 7	Yang Water	Horse	Yin Wood	Ox	June	7	2: 00
July 7 - August 7	Yin Water	Sheep	Yin Wood	Ox	July	37	12: 19
August 7 - September 7	Yang Wood	Monkey	Yin Wood	Ox	Aug	8	22: 04
September 8 – October 8	Yin Wood	Cock	Yin Wood	Ox	Sep	39	: 53
October 8 - November 7	Yang Fire	Dog	Yin Wood	Ox	Oct	9	16: 24
November 7 - December 7	Yin Fire	Pig	Yin Wood	Ox	Nov	40	19: 29
December 7 – January 5	Yang Earth	Rat	Yin Wood	Ox	Dec	10	12: 16

	Pig	Rat	Ox	Tiger	Rabbit	Dragon	Snake	Horse	Sheep	Monkey	Cock	Dog
Main Element	Yang Water	Yin Water	Yin Earth	Yang Wood	Yin Wood	Yang Earth	Yang Fire	Yin Fire	Yin Earth	Yang Metal	Yin Metal	Yang Earth
Hidden Elements	Yang Wood		Yin Water	Yang Fire		Yin Wood	Yang Earth	Yin Earth	Yin Fire	Yang Earth		Yin Metal
			Yin Metal	Yang Earth		Yin Water	Yang Metal		Yin Wood	Yang Water		Yin Fire

1986

		Month		Year				
Find your Day Here	Stem	Branch	Stem	Branch	Day	Day	Time
January 5 – February 4	Yin Earth	Ox	Yin Wood	Ox	Jan	41	23: 29
February 4 - March 6	Yang Metal	Tiger	Yang Fire	Tiger	Feb	12	11: 09
March 6 - April 5	Yin Metal	Rabbit	Yang Fire	Tiger	Mar	40	5: 11
April 5 - May 6	Yang Water	Dragon	Yang Fire	Tiger	April	11	10: 05
May 6– June 6	Yin Water	Snake	Yang Fire	Tiger	May	41	3: 30
June 6 - July 7	Yang Wood	Horse	Yang Fire	Tiger	June	12	7: 44
July 7 - August 8	Yin Wood	Sheep	Yang Fire	Tiger	July	42	18: 00
August 8 - September 8	Yang Fire	Monkey	Yang Fire	Tiger	Aug	13	3: 52
September 8 – October 8	Yin Fire	Cock	Yang Fire	Tiger	Sep	44	6:34
October 8 - November 8	Yang Earth	Dog	Yang Fire	Tiger	Oct	14	22: 08
November 8 - December 7	Yin Earth	Pig	Yang Fire	Tiger	Nov	45	1:1 2
December 7 – January 6	Yang Metal	Rat	Yang Fire	Tiger	Dec	15	18: 02

1987

		Month		Year				
Find your Day Here	Stem	Branch	Stem	Branch	Day	Day	Time
January 6 – February 4	Yin Metal	Ox	Yang Fire	Tiger	Jan	46	5: 13
February 4 - March 6	Yang Water	Tiger	Yin Fire	Rabbit	Feb	22	16: 52
March 6 - April 5	Yin Water	Rabbit	Yin Fire	Rabbit	Mar	45	10: 55
April 5 - May 6	Yang Wood	Dragon	Yin Fire	Rabbit	April	16	15: 44
May 6 – June 6	Yin Wood	Snake	Yin Fire	Rabbit	May	46	9: 07
June 6 - July 7	Yang Fire	Horse	Yin Fire	Rabbit	June	17	13: 20
July 7 - August 8	Yin Fire	Sheep	Yin Fire	Rabbit	July	47	23: 40
August 8 - September 8	Yang Earth	Monkey	Yin Fire	Rabbit	Aug	18	9: 30
September 8 – October 9	Yin Earth	Cock	Yin Fire	Rabbit	Sep	49	12: 25
October 9 - November 8	Yang Metal	Dog	Yin Fire	Rabbit	Oct	19	3: 59
November 8 - December7	Yin Metal	Pig	Yin Fire	Rabbit	Nov	50	7: 05
December 7 – January 6	Yang Water	Rat	Yin Fire	Rabbit	Dec	20	23: 51

Branch	Pig	Rat	Ox	Tiger	Rabbit	Dragon	Snake	Horse	Sheep	Monkey	Cock	Dog
Main Element	Yang Water	Yin Water	Yin Earth	Yang Wood	Yin Wood	Yang Earth	Yang Fire	Yin Fire	Yin Earth	Yang Metal	Yin Metal	Yang Earth
Hidden Elements	Yang Wood		Yin Water	Yang Fire		Yin Wood	Yang Earth	Yin Earth	Yin Fire	Yang Earth		Yin Metal
			Yin Metal	Yang Earth		Yin Water	Yang Metal		Yin Wood	Yang Water		Yin Fire

1988

Find your Day Here	Month Stem	Branch	Year Stem	Branch	Day	Day	Time
January 6 – February 4	Yin Water	Ox	Yin Fire	Rabbit	Jan	51	11: 04
February 4 – 29, - March 5	Yang Wood	Tiger	Yang Earth	Dragon	Feb	22	22: 43
March 5 - April 4	Yin Wood	Rabbit	Yang Earth	Dragon	Mar	51	16: 46
April 4 - May 5	Yang Fire	Dragon	Yang Earth	Dragon	April	22	21: 38
May 5 – June 5	Yin Fire	Snake	Yang Earth	Dragon	May	52	15: 02
June 5 - July 7	Yang Earth	Horse	Yang Earth	Dragon	June	23	19: 13
July 7 - August 7	Yin Earth	Sheep	Yang Earth	Dragon	July	53	5:33
August 7 - September 7	Yang Metal	Monkey	Yang Earth	Dragon	Aug	24	15: 19
September 7 – October 8	Yin Metal	Cock	Yang Earth	Dragon	Sep	55	18: 11
October 8 - November 7	Yang Water	Dog	Yang Earth	Dragon	Oct	25	9: 44
November 7 - December 7	Yin Water	Pig	Yang Earth	Dragon	Nov	56	12: 48
December 7 – January 5	Yang Wood	Rat	Yang Earth	Dragon	Dec	26	5: 34

1989

Find your Day Here	Month Stem	Branch	Year Stem	Branch	Day	Day	Time
January 5 – February 4	Yin Wood	Ox	Yang Earth	Dragon	Jan	57	16: 45
February 4 - March 5	Yang Fire	Tiger	Yin Earth	Snake	Feb	28	4: 27
March 5 - April 5	Yin Fire	Rabbit	Yin Earth	Snake	Mar	56	22: 34
April 5 - May 5	Yang Earth	Dragon	Yin Earth	Snake	April	27	3: 30
May 5 – June 6	Yin Earth	Snake	Yin Earth	Snake	May	57	20:54
June 6 - July 7	Yang Metal	Horse	Yin Earth	Snake	June	28	1:05
July 7 - August 7	Yin Metal	Sheep	Yin Earth	Snake	July	58	11:20
August 7 - September 8	Yang Water	Monkey	Yin Earth	Snake	Aug	29	21:05
September 8 – October 8	Yin Water	Cock	Yin Earth	Snake	Sep	60	23: 54
October 8 - November 7	Yang Wood	Dog	Yin Earth	Snake	Oct	30	15:28
November 7 - December 7	Yin Wood	Pig	Yin Earth	Snake	Nov	1	18: 34
December 7 – January 5	Yang Fire	Rat	Yin Earth	Snake	Dec	31	11: 21

Branch	Pig	Rat	Ox	Tiger	Rabbit	Dragon	Snake	Horse	Sheep	Monkey	Cock	Dog
Main Element	Yang Water	Yin Water	Yin Earth	Yang Wood	Yin Wood	Yang Earth	Yang Fire	Yin Fire	Yin Earth	Yang Metal	Yin Metal	Yang Earth
Hidden Elements	Yang Wood		Yin Water	Yang Fire		Yin Wood	Yang Earth	Yin Earth	Yin Fire	Yang Earth		Yin Metal
			Yin Metal	Yang Earth		Yin Water	Yang Metal		Yin Wood	Yang Water		Yin Fire

1990

Find your Day Here	Month Stem	Branch	Year Stem	Branch	Day	Day	Time
January 5 – February 4	Yin Fire	Ox	Yin Earth	Snake	Jan	2	22: 34
February 4 - March 6	Yang Earth	Tiger	Yang Metal	Horse	Feb	33	10: 15
March 6 - April 5	Yin Earth	Rabbit	Yang Metal	Horse	Mar	1	4: 21
April 5 - May 6	Yang Metal	Dragon	Yang Metal	Horse	April	32	9: 14
May 6– June 6	Yin Metal	Snake	Yang Metal	Horse	May	2	2: 34
June 6 - July 7	Yang Water	Horse	Yang Metal	Horse	June	33	6: 47
July 7 - August 8	Yin Water	Sheep	Yang Metal	Horse	July	3	17: 00
August 8 - September 8	Yang Wood	Monkey	Yang Metal	Horse	Aug	34	2: 46
September 8 – October 8	Yin Wood	Cock	Yang Metal	Horse	Sep	5	5: 38
October 8 - November 8	Yang Fire	Dog	Yang Metal	Horse	Oct	35	21: 13
November 8 - December 7	Yin Fire	Pig	Yang Metal	Horse	Nov	6	: 23
December 7 – January 6	Yang Earth	Rat	Yang Metal	Horse	Dec	36	17: 14

1991

Find your Day Here	Month Stem	Branch	Year Stem	Branch	Day	Day	Time
January 6 – February 4	Yin Earth	Ox	Yang Metal	Horse	Jan	7	4: 28
February 4 - March 6	Yang Metal	Tiger	Yin Metal	Sheep	Feb	38	16: 08
March 6 - April 5	Yin Metal	Rabbit	Yin Metal	Sheep	Mar	6	10: 13
April 5 - May 6	Yang Water	Dragon	Yin Metal	Sheep	April	37	15: 04
May 6 – June 6	Yin Water	Snake	Yin Metal	Sheep	May	7	8: 27
June 6 - July 7	Yang Wood	Horse	Yin Metal	Sheep	June	38	12: 37
July 7 - August 8	Yin Wood	Sheep	Yin Metal	Sheep	July	8	22: 52
August 8 - September 8	Yang Fire	Monkey	Yin Metal	Sheep	Aug	39	8: 36
September 8 – October 9	Yin Fire	Cock	Yin Metal	Sheep	Sep	10	11: 27
October 9 - November 8	Yang Earth	Dog	Yin Metal	Sheep	Oct	4	3: 01
November 8- December 7	Yin Earth	Pig	Yin Metal	Sheep	Nov	11	6: 08
December 7 – January 6	Yang Metal	Rat	Yin Metal	Sheep	Dec	41	22: 56

Branch	Pig	Rat	Ox	Tiger	Rabbit	Dragon	Snake	Horse	Sheep	Monkey	Cock	Dog
Main Element	Yang Water	Yin Water	Yin Earth	Yang Wood	Yin Wood	Yang Earth	Yang Fire	Yin Fire	Yin Earth	Yang Metal	Yin Metal	Yang Earth
Hidden Elements	Yang Wood		Yin Water	Yang Fire		Yin Wood	Yang Earth	Yin Earth	Yin Fire	Yang Earth		Yin Metal
			Yin Metal	Yang Earth		Yin Water	Yang Metal		Yin Wood	Yang Water		Yin Fire

1992

Find your Day Here	Month Stem	Month Branch	Year Stem	Year Branch	Day	Day	Time
January 6– February 4	Yin Metal	Ox	Yin Metal	Sheep	Jan	12	10: 09
February 4 – 29, - March 5	Yang Water	Tiger	Yang Water	Monkey	Feb	43	21: 48
March 5 - April 4	Yin Water	Rabbit	Yang Water	Monkey	Mar	12	15: 52
April 4 - May 5	Yang Wood	Dragon	Yang Water	Monkey	April	43	20: 45
May 5 – June 5	Yin Wood	Snake	Yang Water	Monkey	May	13	14: 09
June 5 - July 7	Yang Fire	Horse	Yang Water	Monkey	June	44	18: 24
July 7 - August 7	Yin Fire	Sheep	Yang Water	Monkey	July	14	4: 40
August 7 - September 7	Yang Earth	Monkey	Yang Water	Monkey	Aug	45	14: 28
September 7 – October 8	Yin Earth	Cock	Yang Water	Monkey	Sep	16	17: 19
October 8 - November 7	Yang Metal	Dog	Yang Water	Monkey	Oct	46	8: 52
November 7 - December 7	Yin Metal	Pig	Yang Water	Monkey	Nov	17	11: 57
December 7 – January 5	Yang Water	Rat	Yang Water	Monkey	Dec	47	4: 44

1993

Find your Day Here	Month Stem	Month Branch	Year Stem	Year Branch	Day	Day	Time
January 5 – February 4	Yin Water	Ox	Yang Water	Monkey	Jan	18	15: 57
February 4 - March 5	Yang Wood	Tiger	Yin Water	Cock	Feb	49	3: 38
March 5 – April 5	Yin Wood	Rabbit	Yin Water	Cock	Mar	17	21: 42
April 5 – May 5	Yang Fire	Dragon	Yin Water	Cock	April	48	2: 36
May 5 – June 6	Yin Fire	Snake	Yin Water	Cock	May	18	20: 02
June 6 – July 7	Yang Earth	Horse	Yin Water	Cock	June	49	: 15
July 7 – August 7	Yin Earth	Sheep	Yin Water	Cock	July	19	10: 31
August 7– September 7	Yang Metal	Monkey	Yin Water	Cock	Aug	50	20: 17
September 7 – October 8	Yin Metal	Cock	Yin Water	Cock	Sep	21	23: 07
October 8 – November 7	Yang Water	Dog	Yin Water	Cock	Oct	51	14: 41
November 7 – December 8	Yin Water	Pig	Yin Water	Cock	Nov	22	17: 46
December 7 – January 5	Yang Wood	Rat	Yin Water	Cock	Dec	52	10: 33

Branch	Pig	Rat	Ox	Tiger	Rabbit	Dragon	Snake	Horse	Sheep	Monkey	Cock	Dog
Main Element	Yang Water	Yin Water	Yin Earth	Yang Wood	Yin Wood	Yang Earth	Yang Fire	Yin Fire	Yin Earth	Yang Metal	Yin Metal	Yang Earth
Hidden Elements	Yang Wood		Yin Water	Yang Fire		Yin Wood	Yang Earth	Yin Earth	Yin Fire	Yang Earth		Yin Metal
			Yin Metal	Yang Earth		Yin Water	Yang Metal		Yin Wood	Yang Water		Yin Fire

1994

Find your Day Here	Month Stem	Branch	Year Stem	Branch	Day	Day	Time
January 5 – February 4	Yin Wood	Ox	Yin Water	Cock	Jan	23	21: 46
February 4 - March 6	Yang Fire	Tiger	Yang Wood	Dog	Feb	54	9: 31
March 6 - April 5	Yin Fire	Rabbit	Yang Wood	Dog	Mar	22	3: 37
April 5 - May 6	Yang Earth	Dragon	Yang Wood	Dog	April	53	8: 31
May 6 - June 6	Yin Earth	Snake	Yang Wood	Dog	May	23	1: 54
June 6 - July 7	Yang Metal	Horse	Yang Wood	Dog	June	54	6: 05
July 7 - August 8	Yin Metal	Sheep	Yang Wood	Dog	July	24	16: 19
August 8 - September 7	Yang Water	Monkey	Yang Wood	Dog	Aug	55	2: 05
September 8 – October 8	Yin Water	Cock	Yang Wood	Dog	Sep	26	4: 55
October 8 - November 7	Yang Wood	Dog	Yang Wood	Dog	Oct	56	20:30
November 7 - December 7	Yin Wood	Pig	Yang Wood	Dog	Nov	27	23: 36
December 7 – January 6	Yang Fire	Rat	Yang Wood	Dog	Dec	57	16: 24

1995

Find your Day Here	Month Stem	Branch	Year Stem	Branch	Day	Day	Time
January 6 – February 4	Yin Fire	Ox	Yang Wood	Dog	Jan	28	3: 34
February 4 - March 6	Yang Earth	Tiger	Yin Wood	Pig	Feb	59	15: 14
March 6 - April 6	Yin Earth	Rabbit	Yin Wood	Pig	Mar	27	9: 16
April 6 - May 6	Yang Metal	Dragon	Yin Wood	Pig	April	58	14: 09
May 6– June 7	Yin Metal	Snake	Yin Wood	Pig	May	28	7:31
June 7 - July 7	Yang Water	Horse	Yin Wood	Pig	June	59	11: 43
July 7 - August 8	Yin Water	Sheep	Yin Wood	Pig	July	29	22: 02
August 8 - September 8	Yang Wood	Monkey	Yin Wood	Pig	Aug	60	7: 53
September 8 – October 9	Yin Wood	Cock	Yin Wood	Pig	Sep	31	10: 49
October 9 - November 8	Yang Fire	Dog	Yin Wood	Pig	Oct	1	2: 27
November 8 - December 7	Yin Fire	Pig	Yin Wood	Pig	Nov	32	5: 35
December 7 – January 6	Yang Earth	Rat	Yin Wood	Pig	Dec	2	22: 22

Branch	Pig	Rat	Ox	Tiger	Rabbit	Dragon	Snake	Horse	Sheep	Monkey	Cock	Dog
Main Element	Yang Water	Yin Water	Yin Earth	Yang Wood	Yin Wood	Yang Earth	Yang Fire	Yin Fire	Yin Earth	Yang Metal	Yin Metal	Yang Earth
Hidden Elements	Yang Wood		Yin Water	Yang Fire		Yin Wood	Yang Earth	Yin Earth	Yin Fire	Yang Earth		Yin Metal
			Yin Metal	Yang Earth		Yin Water	Yang Metal		Yin Wood	Yang Water		Yin Fire

1996

Find your Day Here	Month		Year		Day	Day	Time
	Stem	Branch	Stem	Branch			
January 6 – February 4	Yin Earth	Ox	Yin Wood	Pig	Jan	33	9: 31
February 4 – 29, - March 5	Yang Metal	Tiger	Yang Fire	Rat	Feb	4	21 08
March 5- April 4	Yin Metal	Rabbit	Yang Fire	Rat	Mar	33	15:10
April 4 - May 5	Yang Water	Dragon	Yang Fire	Rat	April	4	20: 03
May 5 – June 5	Yin Water	Snake	Yang Fire	Rat	May	34	13: 26
June 5 - July 7	Yang Wood	Horse	Yang Fire	Rat	June	5	17:41
July 7 - August 7	Yin Wood	Sheep	Yang Fire	Rat	July	35	4:00
August 7 - September 7	Yang Fire	Monkey	Yang Fire	Rat	Aug	6	13:49
September 7 – October 8	Yin Fire	Cock	Yang Fire	Rat	Sep	37	16:41
October 8 - November 7	Yang Earth	Dog	Yang Fire	Rat	Oct	7	8:18
November 7 - December 7	Yin Earth	Pig	Yang Fire ·	Rat	Nov	38	11: 26
December 7 – January 5	Yang Metal	Rat	Yang Fire	Rat	Dec	8	4: 13

1997

Find your Day Here	Month		Year		Day	Day	Time
	Stem	Branch	Stem	Branch			
January 5 – February 4	Yin Metal	Ox	Yang Fire	Rat	Jan	39	15: 22
February 4 - March 5	Yang Water	Tiger	Yin Fire	Ox	Feb	10	3: 04
March 5 – April 5	Yin Water	Rabbit	Yin Fire	Ox	Mar	38	21: 14
April 5 – May 5	Yang Wood	Dragon	Yin Fire	Ox	April	9	2: 17
May 5 – June 5	Yin Wood	Snake	Yin Fire	Ox	May	39	19: 51
June 5 – July 7	Yang Fire	Horse	Yin Fire	Ox	June	10	: 13
July 7 – August 7	Yin Fire	Sheep	Yin Fire	Ox	July	40	10: 36
August 7– September 7	Yang Earth	Monkey	Yin Fire	Ox	Aug	11	20: 19
September 7 – October 8	Yin Earth	Cock	Yin Fire	Ox	Sep	42	23: 03
October 8 – November 7	Yang Metal	Dog	Yin Fire	Ox	Oct	12	14: 27
November 7 – December 7	Yin Metal	Pig	Yin Fire	Ox	Nov	43	17: 22
December 7 – January 5	Yang Water	Rat	Yin Fire	Ox	Dec	13	10: 02

Branch	Pig	Rat	Ox	Tiger	Rabbit	Dragon	Snake	Horse	Sheep	Monkey	Cock	Dog
Main Element	Yang Water	Yin Water	Yin Earth	Yang Wood	Yin Wood	Yang Earth	Yang Fire	Yin Fire	Yin Earth	Yang Metal	Yin Metal	Yang Earth
Hidden Elements	Yang Wood		Yin Water	Yang Fire		Yin Wood	Yang Earth	Yin Earth	Yin Fire	Yang Earth		Yin Metal
			Yin Metal	Yang Earth		Yin Water	Yang Metal		Yin Wood	Yang Water		Yin Fire

1998

Find your Day Here	Month Stem	Branch	Year Stem	Branch	Day	Day	Time
January 5 – February 4	Yin Water	Ox	Yin Fire	Ox	Jan	44	21:11
February 4 - March 6	Yang Wood	Tiger	Yang Earth	Tiger	Feb	15	8:53
March 6 - April 5	Yin Wood	Rabbit	Yang Earth	Tiger	Mar	43	3:03
April 5 - May 6	Yang Fire	Dragon	Yang Earth	Tiger	April	14	8:06
May 6– June 6	Yin Fire	Snake	Yang Earth	Tiger	May	44	1:40
June 6 - July 7	Yang Earth	Horse	Yang Earth	Tiger	June	15	6:02
July 7 - August 8	Yin Earth	Sheep	Yang Earth	Tiger	July	45	16:25
August 8 - September 8	Yang Metal	Monkey	Yang Earth	Tiger	Aug	16	2:08
September 8 – October 8	Yin Metal	Cock	Yang Earth	Tiger	Sep	47	4:52
October 8 - November 7	Yang Water	Dog	Yang Earth	Tiger	Oct	17	20:16
November 7 - December 7	Yin Water	Pig	Yang Earth	Tiger	Nov	48	23:11
December 7 – January 6	Yang Wood	Rat	Yang Earth	Tiger	Dec	18	15:51

1999

Find your Day Here	Month Stem	Branch	Year Stem	Branch	Day	Day	Time
January 6 – February 4	Yin Wood	Ox	Yang Earth	Tiger	Jan	49	3:00
February 4 - March 6	Yang Fire	Tiger	Yin Earth	Rabbit	Feb	20	14:42
March 6 - April 5	Yin Fire	Rabbit	Yin Earth	Rabbit	Mar	48	8:52
April 5 - May 6	Yang Earth	Dragon	Yin Earth	Rabbit	April	19	13:55
May 6 – June 6	Yin Earth	Snake	Yin Earth	Rabbit	May	49	7:29
June 6 - July 7	Yang Metal	Horse	Yin Earth	Rabbit	June	20	11:51
July 7 - August 8	Yin Metal	Sheep	Yin Earth	Rabbit	July	50	22:14
August 8 - September 8	Yang Water	Monkey	Yin Earth	Rabbit	Aug	21	7:57
September 8 – October 9	Yin Water	Cock	Yin Earth	Rabbit	Sep	52	10:41
October 9 - November 8	Yang Wood	Dog	Yin Earth	Rabbit	Oct	22	2:05
November 8 - December 7	Yin Wood	Pig	Yin Earth	Rabbit	Nov	53	5:01
December 7 – January 6	Yang Fire	Rat	Yin Earth	Rabbit	Dec	23	21:14

Branch	Pig	Rat	Ox	Tiger	Rabbit	Dragon	Snake	Horse	Sheep	Monkey	Cock	Dog
Main Element	Yang Water	Yin Water	Yin Earth	Yang Wood	Yin Wood	Yang Earth	Yang Fire	Yin Fire	Yin Earth	Yang Metal	Yin Metal	Yang Earth
Hidden Elements	Yang Wood		Yin Water	Yang Fire		Yin Wood	Yang Earth	Yin Earth	Yin Fire	Yang Earth		Yin Metal
			Yin Metal	Yang Earth		Yin Water	Yang Metal		Yin Wood	Yang Water		Yin Fire

2000

Find your Day Here	Month Stem	Branch	Year Stem	Branch	Day	Day	Time
January 6 – February 4	Yin Fire	Ox	Yin Earth	Rabbit	Jan	54	8: 50
February 4 – 29, - March 5	Yang Earth	Tiger	Yang Metal	Dragon	Feb	25	20: 32
March 5 - April 4	Yin Earth	Rabbit	Yang Metal	Dragon	Mar	54	14: 42
April 4 - May 5	Yang Metal	Dragon	Yang Metal	Dragon	April	25	19: 45
May 5 – June 5	Yin Metal	Snake	Yang Metal	Dragon	May	55	13: 19
June 5 - July 7	Yang Water	Horse	Yang Metal	Dragon	June	26	17: 41
July 7 - August 7	Yin Water	Sheep	Yang Metal	Dragon	July	56	4: 04
August 7 - September 7	Yang Wood	Monkey	Yang Metal	Dragon	Aug	27	13: 36
September 7 – October 8	Yin Wood	Cock	Yang Metal	Dragon	Sep	58	14: 33
October 8 - November 7	Yang Fire	Dog	Yang Metal	Dragon	Oct	28	7: 54
November 7 - December 7	Yin Fire	Pig	Yang Metal	Dragon	Nov	59	10:49
December 7 – January 5	Yang Earth	Rat	Yang Metal	Dragon	Dec	29	3: 29

2001

Find your Day Here	Month Stem	Branch	Year Stem	Branch	Day	Day	Time
January 5 – February 4	Yin Earth	Ox	Yang Metal	Dragon	Jan	60	14: 38
February 4 - March 5	Yang Metal	Tiger	Yin Metal	Snake	Feb	31	2: 20
March 5 – April 5	Yin Metal	Rabbit	Yin Metal	Snake	Mar	59	20: 30
April 5 – May 5	Yang Water	Dragon	Yin Metal	Snake	April	30	1: 33
May 5 – June 5	Yin Water	Snake	Yin Metal	Snake	May	60	19: 07
June 5 – July 7	Yang Wood	Horse	Yin Metal	Snake	June	31	23: 29
July 7 – August 7	Yin Wood	Sheep	Yin Metal	Snake	July	1	9: 52
August 7– September 7	Yang Fire	Monkey	Yin Metal	Snake	Aug	32	19: 34
September 7 – October 8	Yin Fire	Cock	Yin Metal	Snake	Sep	3	22: 18
October 8 – November 7	Yang Earth	Dog	Yin Metal	Snake	Oct	33	13: 42
November 7 – December 7	Yin Earth	Pig	Yin Metal	Snake	Nov	4	16: 37
December 7 – January 5	Yang Metal	Rat	Yin Metal	Snake	Dec	34	9: 17

Branch	Pig	Rat	Ox	Tiger	Rabbit	Dragon	Snake	Horse	Sheep	Monkey	Cock	Dog
Main Element	Yang Water	Yin Water	Yin Earth	Yang Wood	Yin Wood	Yang Earth	Yang Fire	Yin Fire	Yin Earth	Yang Metal	Yin Metal	Yang Earth
Hidden Elements	Yang Wood		Yin Water	Yang Fire		Yin Wood	Yang Earth	Yin Earth	Yin Fire	Yang Earth		Yin Metal
			Yin Metal	Yang Earth		Yin Water	Yang Metal		Yin Wood	Yang Water		Yin Fire

2002

Find your Day Here	Month Stem	Branch	Year Stem	Branch	Day	Day	Time
January 5 – February 4	Yin Metal	Ox	Yin Metal	Snake	Jan	5	20: 26
February 4 - March 6	Yang Water	Tiger	Yang Water	Horse	Feb	36	8: 08
March 6 - April 5	Yin Water	Rabbit	Yang Water	Horse	Mar	4	2: 18
April 5 - May 6	Yang Wood	Dragon	Yang Water	Horse	April	35	7: 21
May 6– June 6	Yin Wood	Snake	Yang Water	Horse	May	5	: 55
June 6 - July 7	Yang Fire	Horse	Yang Water	Horse	June	36	5: 17
July 7 - August 8	Yin Fire	Sheep	Yang Water	Horse	July	6	15: 40
August 8 - September 8	Yang Earth	Monkey	Yang Water	Horse	Aug	37	1: 23
September 8 – October 8	Yin Earth	Cock	Yang Water	Horse	Sep	8	4: 07
October 8 - November 7	Yang Metal	Dog	Yang Water	Horse	Oct	38	19: 31
November 7 - December 7	Yin Metal	Pig	Yang Water	Horse	Nov	9	22: 26
December 7 – January 6	Yang Water	Rat	Yang Water	Horse	Dec	39	15: 06

2003

Find your Day Here	Month Stem	Branch	Year Stem	Branch	Day	Day	Time
January 6 – February 4	Yin Water	Ox	Yang Water	Horse	Jan	10	2: 15
February 4 - March 6	Yang Wood	Tiger	Yin Water	Sheep	Feb	41	13: 57
March 6 - April 5	Yin Wood	Rabbit	Yin Water	Sheep	Mar	9	8: 07
April 5 - May 6	Yang Fire	Dragon	Yin Water	Sheep	April	40	13: 10
May 6 – June 6	Yin Fire	Snake	Yin Water	Sheep	May	10	6: 44
June 6 - July 7	Yang Earth	Horse	Yin Water	Sheep	June	41	11: 06
July 7 - August 8	Yin Earth	Sheep	Yin Water	Sheep	July	11	21: 29
August 8 - September 8	Yang Metal	Monkey	Yin Water	Sheep	Aug	42	7: 12
September 8 – October 9	Yin Metal	Cock	Yin Water	Sheep	Sep	13	9: 56
October 9 - November 8	Yang Water	Dog	Yin Water	Sheep	Oct	43	1: 20
November 8 - December 7	Yin Water	Pig	Yin Water	Sheep	Nov	14	4: 15
December 7 – January 6	Yang Wood	Rat	Yin Water	Sheep	Dec	44	20: 05

Branch	Pig	Rat	Ox	Tiger	Rabbit	Dragon	Snake	Horse	Sheep	Monkey	Cock	Dog
Main Element	Yang Water	Yin Water	Yin Earth	Yang Wood	Yin Wood	Yang Earth	Yang Fire	Yin Fire	Yin Earth	Yang Metal	Yin Metal	Yang Earth
Hidden Elements	Yang Wood		Yin Water	Yang Fire		Yin Wood	Yang Earth	Yin Earth	Yang Fire	Yang Earth		Yin Metal
			Yin Metal	Yang Earth		Yin Water	Yang Metal		Yin Wood	Yang Water		Yin Fire

2004

	Month		Year		Day	Day	Time
Find your Day Here	**Stem**	**Branch**	**Stem**	**Branch**			
January 6 – February 4	Yin Wood	Ox	Yin Water	Sheep	Jan	15	8:04
February 4-29 - March 5	Yang Fire	Tiger	Yang Wood	Monkey	Feb	46	19:58
March 5 - April 4	Yin Fire	Rabbit	Yang Wood	Monkey	Mar	15	13:57
April 4 - May 5	Yang Earth	Dragon	Yang Wood	Monkey	April	46	18:45
May 5 – June 5	Yin Earth	Snake	Yang Wood	Monkey	May	16	12:04
June 5 - July 7	Yang Metal	Horse	Yang Wood	Monkey	June	47	16:15
July 7 - August 7	Yin Metal	Sheep	Yang Wood	Monkey	July	17	2:33
August 7 - September 7	Yang Water	Monkey	Yang Wood	Monkey	Aug	48	12:21
September 7 – October 8	Yin Water	Cock	Yang Wood	Monkey	Sep	19	15:14
October 8 - November 7	Yang Wood	Dog	Yang Wood	Monkey	Oct	49	6:51
November 7 - December 7	Yin Wood	Pig	Yang Wood	Monkey	Nov	20	10:00
December 7 – January 5	Yang Fire	Rat	Yang Wood	Monkey	Dec	50	2:50

2005

	Month		Year		Day	Day	Time
Find your Day Here	**Stem**	**Branch**	**Stem**	**Branch**			
January 5 – February 4	Yin Fire	Ox	Yang Wood	Monkey	Jan	21	14:11
February 4 - March 5	Yang Earth	Tiger	Yin Wood	Cock	Feb	52	1:45
March 5 - April 5	Yin Earth	Rabbit	Yin Wood	Cock	Mar	20	19:59
April 5 - May 5	Yang Metal	Dragon	Yin Wood	Cock	April	51	:36
May 5– June 5	Yin Metal	Snake	Yin Wood	Cock	May	21	17:33
June 5 - July 7	Yang Water	Horse	Yin Wood	Cock	June	52	22:03
July 7 - August 7	Yin Water	Sheep	Yin Wood	Cock	July	22	8:18
August 7 - September 7	Yang Wood	Monkey	Yin Wood	Cock	Aug	53	18:05
September 7 – October 8	Yin Wood	Cock	Yin Wood	Cock	Sep	24	20:58
October 8 - November 7	Yang Fire	Dog	Yin Wood	Cock	Oct	54	12:35
November 7 - December 7	Yin Fire	Pig	Yin Wood	Cock	Nov	25	15:44
December 7 – January 5	Yang Earth	Rat	Yin Wood	Cock	Dec	55	8:34

Branch	Pig	Rat	Ox	Tiger	Rabbit	Dragon	Snake	Horse	Sheep	Monkey	Cock	Dog
Main Element	Yang Water	Yin Water	Yin Earth	Yang Wood	Yin Wood	Yang Earth	Yang Fire	Yin Fire	Yin Earth	Yang Metal	Yin Metal	Yang Earth
Hidden Elements	Yang Wood		Yin Water	Yang Fire		Yin Wood	Yang Earth	Yin Earth	Yin Fire	Yang Earth		Yin Metal
			Yin Metal	Yang Earth		Yin Water	Yang Metal		Yin Wood	Yang Water		Yin Fire

2006

Find your Day Here	Month Stem	Branch	Year Stem	Branch	Day	Day	Time
January 5 – February 4	Yin Earth	Ox	Yin Wood	Cock	Jan	26	19: 49
February 4 - March 6	Yang Metal	Tiger	Yang Fire	Dog	Feb	57	7: 29
March 6 - April 5	Yin Metal	Rabbit	Yang Fire	Dog	Mar	25	1: 30
April 5 - May 5	Yang Water	Dragon	Yang Fire	Dog	April	56	6: 17
May 5– June 6	Yin Water	Snake	Yang Fire	Dog	May	26	23: 32
June 6 - July 7	Yang Wood	Horse	Yang Fire	Dog	June	57	3: 38
July 7 - August 8	Yin Wood	Sheep	Yang Fire	Dog	July	27	13: 53
August 8 - September 8	Yang Fire	Monkey	Yang Fire	Dog	Aug	58	23: 42
September 8 – October 8	Yin Fire	Cock	Yang Fire	Dog	Sep	29	2: 40
October 8 - November 7	Yang Earth	Dog	Yang Fire	Dog	Oct	59	18: 23
November 7 - December 7	Yin Earth	Pig	Yang Fire	Dog	Nov	30	21: 36
December 7 – January 6	Yang Metal	Rat	Yang Fire	Dog	Dec	60	14: 28

2007

Find your Day Here	Month Stem	Branch	Year Stem	Branch	Day	Day	Time
January 6 – February 4	Yin Metal	Ox	Yang Fire	Dog	Jan	31	1: 42
February 4 - March 6	Yang Water	Tiger	Yin Fire	Pig	Feb	2	13: 20
March 6 - April 5	Yin Water	Rabbit	Yin Fire	Pig	Mar	30	7:19
April 5 - May 6	Yang Wood	Dragon	Yin Fire	Pig	April	1	12: 06
May 6– June 6	Yin Wood	Snake	Yin Fire	Pig	May	31	5:21
June 6 - July 7	Yang Fire	Horse	Yin Fire	Pig	June	2	9: 28
July 7 - August 8	Yin Fire	Sheep	Yin Fire	Pig	July	32	19: 43
August 8 - September 8	Yang Earth	Monkey	Yin Fire	Pig	Aug	3	5: 33
September 8 – October 9	Yin Earth	Cock	Yin Fire	Pig	Sep	34	8: 31
October 9 - November 8	Yang Metal	Dog	Yin Fire	Pig	Oct	4	: 13
November 8 - December 7	Yin Metal	Pig	Yin Fire	Pig	Nov	35	3: 25
December 7 – January 6	Yang Water	Rat	Yin Fire	Pig	Dec	5	20: 16

Branch	Pig	Rat	Ox	Tiger	Rabbit	Dragon	Snake	Horse	Sheep	Monkey	Cock	Dog
Main Element	Yang Water	Yin Water	Yin Earth	Yang Wood	Yin Wood	Yang Earth	Yang Fire	Yin Fire	Yin Earth	Yang Metal	Yin Metal	Yang Earth
Hidden Elements	Yang Wood		Yin Water	Yang Fire		Yin Wood	Yang Earth	Yin Earth	Yin Fire	Yang Earth		Yin Metal
			Yin Metal	Yang Earth		Yin Water	Yang Metal		Yin Wood	Yang Water		Yin Fire

2006

Find your Day Here	Month Stem	Branch	Year Stem	Branch	Day	Day	Time
January 5 – February 4	Yin Earth	Ox	Yin Wood	Cock	Jan	26	19: 49
February 4 - March 6	Yang Metal	Tiger	Yang Fire	Dog	Feb	57	7: 29
March 6 - April 5	Yin Metal	Rabbit	Yang Fire	Dog	Mar	25	1: 30
April 5 - May 5	Yang Water	Dragon	Yang Fire	Dog	April	56	6: 17
May 5– June 6	Yin Water	Snake	Yang Fire	Dog	May	26	23: 32
June 6 - July 7	Yang Wood	Horse	Yang Fire	Dog	June	57	3: 38
July 7 - August 8	Yin Wood	Sheep	Yang Fire	Dog	July	27	13: 53
August 8 - September 8	Yang Fire	Monkey	Yang Fire	Dog	Aug	58	23: 42
September 8 – October 8	Yin Fire	Cock	Yang Fire	Dog	Sep	29	2: 40
October 8 - November 7	Yang Earth	Dog	Yang Fire	Dog	Oct	59	18: 23
November 7 - December 7	Yin Earth	Pig	Yang Fire	Dog	Nov	30	21: 36
December 7 – January 6	Yang Metal	Rat	Yang Fire	Dog	Dec	60	14: 28

2007

Find your Day Here	Month Stem	Branch	Year Stem	Branch	Day	Day	Time
January 6 – February 4	Yin Metal	Ox	Yang Fire	Dog	Jan	31	1: 42
February 4 - March 6	Yang Water	Tiger	Yin Fire	Pig	Feb	2	13: 20
March 6 - April 5	Yin Water	Rabbit	Yin Fire	Pig	Mar	30	7:19
April 5 - May 6	Yang Wood	Dragon	Yin Fire	Pig	April	1	12: 06
May 6– June 6	Yin Wood	Snake	Yin Fire	Pig	May	31	5:21
June 6 - July 7	Yang Fire	Horse	Yin Fire	Pig	June	2	9: 28
July 7 - August 8	Yin Fire	Sheep	Yin Fire	Pig	July	32	19: 43
August 8 - September 8	Yang Earth	Monkey	Yin Fire	Pig	Aug	3	5: 33
September 8 – October 9	Yin Earth	Cock	Yin Fire	Pig	Sep	34	8: 31
October 9 - November 8	Yang Metal	Dog	Yin Fire	Pig	Oct	4	: 13
November 8 - December 7	Yin Metal	Pig	Yin Fire	Pig	Nov	35	3: 25
December 7 – January 6	Yang Water	Rat	Yin Fire	Pig	Dec	5	20: 16

Branch	Pig	Rat	Ox	Tiger	Rabbit	Dragon	Snake	Horse	Sheep	Monkey	Cock	Dog
Main Element	Yang Water	Yin Water	Yin Earth	Yang Wood	Yin Wood	Yang Earth	Yang Fire	Yin Fire	Yin Earth	Yang Metal	Yin Metal	Yang Earth
Hidden Elements	Yang Wood		Yin Water	Yang Fire		Yin Wood	Yang Earth	Yin Earth	Yin Fire	Yang Earth		Yin Metal
			Yin Metal	Yang Earth		Yin Water	Yang Metal		Yin Wood	Yang Water		Yin Fire

2008

Find your Day Here	Month Stem	Branch	Year Stem	Branch	Day	Day	Time
January 6 – February 4	Yin Water	Ox	Yin Fire	Pig	Jan	36	7: 26
February 4-29 - March 5	Yang Wood	Tiger	Yang Earth	Rat	Feb	7	19: 02
March 5 - April 4	Yin Wood	Rabbit	Yang Earth	Rat	Mar	36	13: 00
April 4 - May 5	Yang Fire	Dragon	Yang Earth	Rat	April	7	17: 47
May 5 – June 5	Yin Fire	Snake	Yang Earth	Rat	May	37	11: 05
June 5 - July 7	Yang Earth	Horse	Yang Earth	Rat	June	8	15: 13
July 7 - August 7	Yin Earth	Sheep	Yang Earth	Rat	July	38	1:29
August 7 - September 7	Yang Metal	Monkey	Yang Earth	Rat	Aug	9	11: 17
September 7 – October 8	Yin Metal	Cock	Yang Earth	Rat	Sep	40	14: 15
October 8 - November 7	Yang Water	Dog	Yang Earth	Rat	Oct	10	6: 02
November 7 - December 7	Yin Water	Pig	Yang Earth	Rat	Nov	41	9: 12
December 7 – January 5	Yang Wood	Rat	Yang Earth	Rat	Dec	11	1: 44

2009

Find your Day Here	Month Stem	Branch	Year Stem	Branch	Day	Day	Time
January 5 – February 4	Yin Wood	Ox	Yang Earth	Rat	Jan	42	13: 16
February 4 - March 5	Yang Fire	Tiger	Yin Earth	Ox	Feb	13	: 51
March 5 - April 4	Yin Fire	Rabbit	Yin Earth	Ox	Mar	41	18: 49
April 4 - May 5	Yang Earth	Dragon	Yin Earth	Ox	April	12	23: 35
May 5– June 5	Yin Earth	Snake	Yin Earth	Ox	May	42	16: 52
June 5 - July 7	Yang Metal	Horse	Yin Earth	Ox	June	13	21: 00
July 7 - August 7	Yin Metal	Sheep	Yin Earth	Ox	July	43	7: 15
August 7 - September 7	Yang Water	Monkey	Yin Earth	Ox	Aug	14	17: 02
September 7 – October 8	Yin Water	Cock	Yin Earth	Ox	Sep	45	19: 59
October 8 - November 7	Yang Wood	Dog	Yin Earth	Ox	Oct	15	11: 42
November 7 - December 7	Yin Wood	Pig	Yin Earth	Ox	Nov	46	14: 58
December 7 – January 5	Yang Fire	Rat	Yin Earth	Ox	Dec	16	7: 54

Branch	Pig	Rat	Ox	Tiger	Rabbit	Dragon	Snake	Horse	Sheep	Monkey	Cock	Dog
Main Element	Yang Water	Yin Water	Yin Earth	Yang Wood	Yin Wood	Yang Earth	Yang Fire	Yin Fire	Yin Earth	Yang Metal	Yin Metal	Yang Earth
Hidden Elements	Yang Wood		Yin Water	Yang Fire		Yin Wood	Yang Earth	Yin Earth	Yin Fire	Yang Earth		Yin Metal
			Yin Metal	Yang Earth		Yin Water	Yang Metal		Yin Wood	Yang Water		Yin Fire

2010

Find your Day Here	Month Stem	Branch	Year Stem	Branch	Day	Day	Time
January 5 – February 4	Yin Fire	Ox	Yin Earth	Ox	Jan	47	19: 10
February 4 - March 6	Yang Earth	Tiger	Yang Metal	Tiger	Feb	18	6: 49
March 6 - April 5	Yin Earth	Rabbit	Yang Metal	Tiger	Mar	46	1: 48
April 5 - May 5	Yang Metal	Dragon	Yang Metal	Tiger	April	17	5: 32
May 5– June 6	Yin Metal	Snake	Yang Metal	Tiger	May	47	22: 45
June 6 - July 7	Yang Water	Horse	Yang Metal	Tiger	June	18	2: 51
July 7 - August 7	Yin Water	Sheep	Yang Metal	Tiger	July	48	13: 04
August 7 - September 8	Yang Wood	Monkey	Yang Metal	Tiger	Aug	19	22: 50
September 8 – October 8	Yin Wood	Cock	Yang Metal	Tiger	Sep	50	1: 46
October 8 - November 7	Yang Fire	Dog	Yang Metal	Tiger	Oct	20	17: 28
November 7 - December 7	Yin Fire	Pig	Yang Metal	Tiger	Nov	51	20: 44
December 7 – January 6	Yang Earth	Rat	Yang Metal	Tiger	Dec	21	13: 40

Branch	Pig	Rat	Ox	Tiger	Rabbit	Dragon	Snake	Horse	Sheep	Monkey	Cock	Dog
Main Element	Yang Water	Yin Water	Yin Earth	Yang Wood	Yin Wood	Yang Earth	Yang Fire	Yin Fire	Yin Earth	Yang Metal	Yin Metal	Yang Earth
Hidden Elements	Yang Wood		Yin Water	Yang Fire		Yin Wood	Yang Earth	Yin Earth	Yin Fire	Yang Earth		Yin Metal
			Yin Metal	Yang Earth		Yin Water	Yang Metal		Yin Wood	Yang Water		Yin Fire

Flying Stars Feng Shui Charts

Flying Stars Feng Shui charts in this Appendix are organized with South at the top and North in the bottom. The following example illustrates the structure.

South East	South	South West
East		West
North East	North	North West

One reason charts are traditionally presented this way is in ancient times sunlight was of highest value. The North represents Yin, Water and darkness, the South Yang, Fire and light. The sun rises in the East and represents Spring, Wood and Sunlight and peaks in the South, which is the Fire element. Fire being Yang is positioned at the top, Yang ascends. North representing darkness is positioned at the bottom, Yin descends.

All of the following charts are organized by 20-Year Cycles and for each cycle there are 24 charts, representing every Mountain or Sitting positions. The sitting palace is high-lighted and shaded.

Flying Star chart: Cycle 1

Sitting: North 1

	S	
7 4 / 9	2 9 / 5	9 2 / 7
E 8 3 / 8	6 5 / 1	W 4 7 / 3
3 8 / 4	N 1 1 / 6	5 6 / 2

Sitting: North 2

	S	
5 6 / 9	1 1 / 5	3 8 / 7
E 4 7 / 8	6 5 / 1	W 8 3 / 3
9 2 / 4	N 2 9 / 6	7 4 / 2

Sitting: North 3

	S	
5 6 / 9	1 1 / 5	3 8 / 7
E 4 7 / 8	6 5 / 1	W 8 3 / 3
9 2 / 4	N 2 9 / 6	7 4 / 2

Sitting: North East 1

	S	
5 6 / 9	9 2 / 5	7 4 / 7
E 6 5 / 8	4 7 / 1	W 2 9 / 3
1 1 / 4	N 8 3 / 6	3 8 / 2

Sitting: North East 2

	S	
3 8 / 9	8 3 / 5	1 1 / 7
E 2 9 / 8	4 7 /	W 6 5 / 3
7 4 / 4	N 9 2 / 6	5 6 / 2

Sitting: North East 3

	S	
3 8 / 9	8 3 / 5	1 1 / 7
E 2 9 / 8	4 7 / 1	W 6 5 / 3
7 4 / 4	N 9 2 / 6	5 6 / 2

Sitting: East 1

	S	
9 2 / 9	4 7 / 5	2 9 / 7
E 1 1 / 8	8 3 / 1	W 6 5 / 3
5 6 / 4	N 3 8 / 6	7 4 / 2

Sitting: East 2

	S	
7 4 / 9	3 8 / 5	5 6 / 7
E 6 5 / 8	8 3 / 1	W 1 1 / 3
2 9 / 4	N 4 7 / 6	9 2 / 2

Sitting: East 3

	S	
7 4 / 9	3 8 / 5	5 6 / 7
E 6 5 / 8	8 3 / 1	W 1 1 / 3
2 9 / 4	N 4 7 / 6	9 2 / 2

Sitting: South East 1

	S	
8 3 / 9	4 7 / 5	6 5 / 7
E 7 4 / 8	9 2 / 1	W 2 9 / 3
3 8 / 4	N 5 6 / 6	1 1 / 2

Sitting: South East 2

	S	
1 1 / 9	5 6 / 5	3 8 / 7
E 2 9 / 8	9 2 / 1	W 7 4 / 3
6 5 / 4	N 4 7 / 6	8 3 / 2

Sitting: South East 3

	S	
1 1 / 9	5 6 / 5	3 8 / 7
E 2 9 / 8	9 2 / 1	W 7 4 / 3
6 5 / 4	N 4 7 / 6	8 3 / 2

Flying Star chart: Cycle 1

Sitting: South 1

	S	
4 7 / 9	9 2 / 5	2 9 / 7
E 3 8 / 8	5 6 / 1	W 7 4 / 3
8 3 / 4	N 1 1 / 6	6 5 / 2

Sitting: South 2

	S	
6 5 / 9	1 1 / 5	8 3 / 7
E 7 4 / 8	5 6 / 1	W 3 8 / 3
2 9 / 4	N 9 2 / 6	4 7 / 2

Sitting: South 3

	S	
6 5 / 9	1 1 / 5	8 3 / 7
E 7 4 / 8	5 6 / 1	W 3 8 / 3
2 9 / 4	N 9 2 / 6	4 7 / 2

Sitting: South West 1

	S	
6 5 / 9	2 9 / 5	4 7 / 7
E 5 6 / 8	7 4 / 1	W 9 2 / 3
1 1 / 4	N 3 8 / 6	8 3 / 2

Sitting: South West 2

	S	
8 3 / 9	3 8 / 5	1 1 / 7
E 9 2 / 8	7 4 / 1	W 5 6 / 3
4 7 / 4	N 2 9 / 6	6 5 / 2

Sitting: South West 3

	S	
8 3 / 9	3 8 / 5	1 1 / 7
E 9 2 / 8	7 4 / 1	W 5 6 / 3
4 7 / 4	N 2 9 / 6	6 5 / 2

Sitting: West 1

	S	
2 9 / 9	7 4 / 5	9 2 / 7
E 1 1 / 8	3 8 / 1	W 5 6 / 3
6 5 / 4	N 8 3 / 6	4 7 / 2

Sitting: West 2

	S	
4 7 / 9	8 3 / 5	6 5 / 7
E 5 6 / 8	3 8 / 1	W 1 1 / 3
9 2 / 4	N 7 4 / 6	2 9 / 2

Sitting: West 3

	S	
4 7 / 9	8 3 / 5	6 5 / 7
E 5 6 / 8	3 8 / 1	W 1 1 / 3
9 2 / 4	N 7 4 / 6	2 9 / 2

Sitting: North West 1

	S	
3 8 / 9	7 4 / 5	5 6 / 7
E 4 7 / 8	2 9 / 1	W 9 2 / 3
8 3 / 4	N 6 5 / 6	1 1 / 2

Sitting: North West 2

	S	
1 1 / 9	6 5 / 5	8 3 / 7
E 9 2 / 8	2 9 / 1	W 4 7 / 3
5 6 / 4	N 7 4 / 6	3 8 / 2

Sitting: North West 3

	S	
1 1 / 9	6 5 / 5	8 3 / 7
E 9 2 / 8	2 9 / 1	W 4 7 / 3
5 6 / 4	N 7 4 / 6	3 8 / 2

Flying Star chart: Cycle 2

Sitting: North 1

	S	
6 7 1	2 2 6	4 9 8
E 5 8 9	7 6 2	W 9 4 4
1 3 5	N 3 1 7	8 5 3

Sitting: North 2

	S	
8 5 1	3 1 6	1 3 8
E 9 4 9	7 6 2	W 5 8 4
4 9 5	N 2 2 7	6 7 3

Sitting: North 3

	S	
8 5 1	3 1 6	1 3 8
E 9 4 9	7 6 2	W 5 8 4
4 9 5	N 2 2 7	6 7 3

Sitting: North East 1

	S	
6 9 1	1 4 6	8 2 8
E 7 1 9	5 8 2	W 3 6 4
2 5 5	N 9 3 7	4 7 3

Sitting: North East 2

	S	
4 7 1	9 3 6	2 5 8
E 3 6 9	5 8 2	W 7 1 4
8 2 5	N 1 4 7	6 9 3

Sitting: North East 3

	S	
4 7 1	9 3 6	2 5 8
E 3 6 9	5 8 2	W 7 1 4
8 2 5	N 1 4 7	6 9 3

Sitting: East 1

	S	
8 5 1	4 9 6	6 7 8
E 7 6 9	9 4 2	W 2 2 4
3 1 5	N 5 8 7	1 3 3

Sitting: East 2

	S	
1 3 1	5 8 6	3 1 8
E 2 2 9	9 4 2	W 7 6 4
6 7 5	N 4 9 7	8 5 3

Sitting: East 3

	S	
1 3 1	5 8 6	3 1 8
E 2 2 9	9 4 2	W 7 6 4
6 7 5	N 4 9 7	8 5 3

Sitting: South East 1

	S	
9 2 1	5 7 6	7 9 8
E 8 1 9	1 3 2	W 3 5 4
4 6 5	N 6 8 7	2 4 3

Sitting: South East 2

	S	
2 4 1	6 8 6	4 6 8
E 3 5 9	1 3 2	W 8 1 4
7 9 5	N 5 7 7	9 2 3

Sitting: South East 3

	S	
2 4 1	6 8 6	4 6 8
E 3 5 9	1 3 2	W 8 1 4
7 9 5	N 5 7 7	9 2 3

Flying Star chart: Cycle 2

Sitting: South 1

	S	
7 6 / 1	2 2 / 6	9 4 / 8
E 8 5 / 9	6 7 / 2	W 4 9 / 4
3 1 / 5	N 1 3 / 7	5 8 / 3

Sitting: South 2

	S	
5 8 / 1	1 3 / 6	3 1 / 8
E 4 9 / 9	6 7 / 2	W 8 5 / 4
9 4 / 5	N 2 2 / 7	7 6 / 3

Sitting: South 3

	S	
5 8 / 1	1 3 / 6	3 1 / 8
E 4 9 / 9	6 7 / 2	W 8 5 / 4
9 4 / 5	N 2 2 / 7	7 6 / 3

Sitting: South West 1

	S	
9 6 / 1	4 1 / 6	2 8 / 8
E 1 7 / 9	8 5 / 2	W 6 3 / 4
5 2 / 5	N 3 9 / 7	7 4 / 3

Sitting: South West 2

	S	
7 4 / 1	3 9 / 6	5 2 / 8
E 6 3 / 9	8 5 / 2	W 1 7 / 4
2 8 / 5	N 4 1 / 7	9 6 / 3

Sitting: South West 3

	S	
7 4 / 1	3 9 / 6	5 2 / 8
E 6 3 / 9	8 5 / 2	W 1 7 / 4
2 8 / 5	N 4 1 / 7	9 6 / 3

Sitting: West 1

	S	
5 8 / 1	9 4 / 6	7 6 / 8
E 6 7 / 9	4 9 / 2	W 2 2 / 4
1 3 / 5	N 8 5 / 7	3 1 / 3

Sitting: West 2

	S	
3 1 / 1	8 5 / 6	1 3 / 8
E 2 2 / 9	4 9 / 2	W 6 7 / 4
7 6 / 5	N 9 4 / 7	5 8 / 3

Sitting: West 3

	S	
3 1 / 1	8 5 / 6	1 3 / 8
E 2 2 / 9	4 9 / 2	W 6 7 / 4
7 6 / 5	N 9 4 / 7	5 8 / 3

Sitting: North West 1

	S	
2 9 / 1	7 5 / 6	9 7 / 8
E 1 8 / 9	3 1 / 2	W 5 3 / 4
6 4 / 5	N 8 6 / 7	4 2 / 3

Sitting: North West 2

	S	
4 2 / 1	8 6 / 6	6 4 / 8
E 5 3 / 9	3 1 / 2	W 1 8 / 4
9 7 / 5	N 7 5 / 7	2 9 / 3

Sitting: North West 3

	S	
4 2 / 1	8 6 / 6	6 4 / 8
E 5 3 / 9	3 1 / 2	W 1 8 / 4
9 7 / 5	N 7 5 / 7	2 9 / 3

Flying Star chart: Cycle 3

Sitting: North 1

	S	
9 6 / 2	4 2 / 7	2 4 / 9
E 1 5 / 1	8 7 / 3	**W** 6 9 / 5
5 1 / 6	**N** 3 3 / 8	7 8 / 4

Sitting: North 2

	S	
7 8 / 2	3 3 / 7	5 1 / 9
E 6 9 / 1	8 7 / 3	**W** 1 5 / 5
2 4 / 6	**N** 4 2 / 8	9 6 / 4

Sitting: North 3

	S	
7 8 / 2	3 3 / 7	5 1 / 9
E 6 9 / 1	8 7 / 3	**W** 1 5 / 5
2 4 / 6	**N** 4 2 / 8	9 6 / 4

Sitting: North East 1

	S	
7 8 / 2	2 4 / 7	9 6 / 9
E 8 7 / 1	6 9 / 3	**W** 4 2 / 5
3 3 / 6	**N** 1 5 / 8	5 1 / 4

Sitting: North East 2

	S	
5 1 / 2	1 5 / 7	3 3 / 9
E 4 2 / 1	6 9 / 3	**W** 8 7 / 5
9 6 / 6	**N** 2 4 / 8	7 8 / 4

Sitting: North East 3

	S	
5 1 / 2	1 5 / 7	3 3 / 9
E 4 2 / 1	6 9 / 3	**W** 8 7 / 5
9 6 / 6	**N** 2 4 / 8	7 8 / 4

Sitting: East 1

	S	
9 4 / 2	5 9 / 7	7 2 / 9
E 8 3 / 1	1 5 / 3	**W** 3 7 / 5
4 8 / 6	**N** 6 1 / 8	2 6 / 4

Sitting: East 2

	S	
2 6 / 2	6 1 / 7	4 8 / 9
E 3 7 / 1	1 5 / 3	**W** 8 3 / 5
7 2 / 6	**N** 5 9 / 8	9 4 / 4

Sitting: East 3

	S	
2 6 / 2	6 1 / 7	4 8 / 9
E 3 7 / 1	1 5 / 3	**W** 8 3 / 5
7 2 / 6	**N** 5 9 / 8	9 4 / 4

Sitting: South East 1

	S	
3 5 / 2	7 9 / 7	5 7 / 9
E 4 6 / 1	2 4 / 3	**W** 9 2 / 5
8 1 / 6	**N** 6 8 / 8	1 3 / 4

Sitting: South East 2

	S	
1 3 / 2	6 8 / 7	8 1 / 9
E 9 2 / 1	2 4 / 3	**W** 4 6 / 5
5 7 / 6	**N** 7 9 / 8	3 5 / 4

Sitting: South East 3

	S	
1 3 / 2	6 8 / 7	8 1 / 9
E 9 2 / 1	2 4 / 3	**W** 4 6 / 5
5 7 / 6	**N** 7 9 / 8	3 5 / 4

Flying Star chart: Cycle 3

6 9 / 2	S 2 4 / 7	4 2 / 9
E 5 1 / 1	7 8 / 3	W 9 6 / 5
1 5 / 6	N 3 3 / 8	8 7 / 4

Sitting: South 1

8 7 / 2	S 3 3 / 7	1 5 / 9
E 9 6 / 1	7 8 / 3	W 5 1 / 5
4 2 / 6	N 2 4 / 8	6 9 / 4

Sitting: South 2

8 7 / 2	S 3 3 / 7	1 5 / 9
E 9 6 / 1	7 8 / 3	W 5 1 / 5
4 2 / 6	N 2 4 / 8	6 9 / 4

Sitting: South 3

8 7 / 2	S 4 2 / 7	6 9 / 9
E 7 8 / 1	9 6 / 3	W 2 4 / 5
3 3 / 6	N 5 1 / 8	1 5 / 4

Sitting: South West 1

1 5 / 2	S 5 1 / 7	3 3 / 9
E 2 4 / 1	9 6 / 3	W 7 8 / 5
6 9 / 6	N 4 2 / 8	8 7 / 4

Sitting: South West 2

1 5 / 2	S 5 1 / 7	3 3 / 9
E 2 4 / 1	9 6 / 3	W 7 8 / 5
6 9 / 6	N 4 2 / 8	8 7 / 4

Sitting: South West 3

4 9 / 2	S 9 5 / 7	2 7 / 9
E 3 8 / 1	5 1 / 3	W 7 3 / 5
8 4 / 6	N 1 6 / 8	6 2 / 4

Sitting: West 1

6 2 / 2	S 1 6 / 7	8 4 / 9
E 7 3 / 1	5 1 / 3	W 3 8 / 5
2 7 / 6	N 9 5 / 8	4 9 / 4

Sitting: West 2

6 2 / 2	S 1 6 / 7	8 4 / 9
E 7 3 / 1	5 1 / 3	W 3 8 / 5
2 7 / 6	N 9 5 / 8	4 9 / 4

Sitting: West 3

5 3 / 2	S 9 7 / 7	7 5 / 9
E 6 4 / 1	4 2 / 3	W 2 9 / 5
1 8 / 6	N 8 6 / 8	3 1 / 4

Sitting: North West 1

3 1 / 2	S 8 6 / 7	1 8 / 9
E 2 9 / 1	4 2 / 3	W 6 4 / 5
7 5 / 6	N 9 7 / 8	5 3 / 4

Sitting: North West 2

3 1 / 2	S 8 6 / 7	1 8 / 9
E 2 9 / 1	4 2 / 3	W 6 4 / 5
7 5 / 6	N 9 7 / 8	5 3 / 4

Sitting: North West 3

Flying Star chart: Cycle 4

Sitting: North 1

	S	
8 9 / 3	4 4 / 8	6 2 / 1
E 7 1 / 2	9 8 / 4	W 2 6 / 6
3 5 / 7	N 5 3 / 9	1 7 / 5

Sitting: North 2

	S	
1 7 / 3	5 3 / 8	3 5 / 1
E 2 6 / 2	9 8 / 4	W 7 1 / 6
6 2 / 7	N 4 4 / 9	8 9 / 5

Sitting: North 3

	S	
1 7 / 3	5 3 / 8	3 5 / 1
E 2 6 / 2	9 8 / 4	W 7 1 / 6
6 2 / 7	N 4 4 / 9	8 9 / 5

Sitting: North East 1

	S	
6 9 / 3	2 5 / 8	4 7 / 1
E 5 8 / 2	7 1 / 4	W 9 3 / 6
1 4 / 7	N 3 6 / 9	8 2 / 5

Sitting: North East 2

	S	
8 2 / 3	3 6 / 8	1 4 / 1
E 9 3 / 2	7 1 / 4	W 5 8 / 6
4 7 / 7	N 2 5 / 9	6 9 / 5

Sitting: North East 3

	S	
8 2 / 3	3 6 / 8	1 4 / 1
E 9 3 / 2	7 1 / 4	W 5 8 / 6
4 7 / 7	N 2 5 / 9	6 9 / 5

Sitting: East 1

	S	
3 7 / 3	7 2 / 8	5 9 / 1
E 4 8 / 2	2 6 / 4	W 9 4 / 6
8 3 / 7	N 6 1 / 9	1 5 / 5

Sitting: East 2

	S	
1 5 / 3	6 1 / 8	8 3 / 1
E 9 4 / 2	2 6 / 4	W 4 8 / 6
5 9 / 7	N 7 2 / 9	3 7 / 5

Sitting: East 3

	S	
1 5 / 3	6 1 / 8	8 3 / 1
E 9 4 / 2	2 6 / 4	W 4 8 / 6
5 9 / 7	N 7 2 / 9	3 7 / 5

Sitting: South East 1

	S	
2 6 / 3	7 1 / 8	9 8 / 1
E 1 7 / 2	3 5 / 4	W 5 3 / 6
6 2 / 7	N 8 9 / 9	4 4 / 5

Sitting: South East 2

	S	
4 4 / 3	8 9 / 8	6 2 / 1
E 5 3 / 2	3 5 / 4	W 1 7 / 6
9 8 / 7	N 7 1 / 9	2 6 / 5

Sitting: South East 3

	S	
4 4 / 3	8 9 / 8	6 2 / 1
E 5 3 / 2	3 5 / 4	W 1 7 / 6
9 8 / 7	N 7 1 / 9	2 6 / 5

Flying Star chart: Cycle 4

Sitting: South 1

	S	
9 8 / 3	4 4 / 8	2 6 / 1
E 1 7 / 2	8 9 / 4	W 6 2 / 6
5 3 / 7	N 3 5 / 9	7 1 / 5

Sitting: South 2

	S	
7 1 / 3	3 5 / 8	5 3 / 1
E 6 2 / 2	8 9 / 4	W 1 7 / 6
2 6 / 7	N 4 4 / 9	9 8 / 5

Sitting: South 3

	S	
7 1 / 3	3 5 / 8	5 3 / 1
E 6 2 / 2	8 9 / 4	W 1 7 / 6
2 6 / 7	N 4 4 / 9	9 8 / 5

Sitting: South West 1

	S	
9 6 / 3	5 2 / 8	7 4 / 1
E 8 5 / 2	1 7 / 4	W 3 9 / 6
4 1 / 7	N 6 3 / 9	2 8 / 5

Sitting: South West 2

	S	
2 8 / 3	6 3 / 8	4 1 / 1
E 3 9 / 2	1 7 / 4	W 8 5 / 6
7 4 / 7	N 5 2 / 9	9 6 / 5

Sitting: South West 3

	S	
2 8 / 3	6 3 / 8	4 1 / 1
E 3 9 / 2	1 7 / 4	W 8 5 / 6
7 4 / 7	N 5 2 / 9	9 6 / 5

Sitting: West 1

	S	
7 3 / 3	2 7 / 8	9 5 / 1
E 8 4 / 2	6 2 / 4	W 4 9 / 6
3 8 / 7	N 1 6 / 9	5 1 / 5

Sitting: West 2

	S	
5 1 / 3	1 6 / 8	3 8 / 1
E 4 9 / 2	6 2 / 4	W 8 4 / 6
9 5 / 7	N 2 7 / 9	7 3 / 5

Sitting: West 3

	S	
5 1 / 3	1 6 / 8	3 8 / 1
E 4 9 / 2	6 2 / 4	W 8 4 / 6
9 5 / 7	N 2 7 / 9	7 3 / 5

Sitting: North West 1

	S	
6 2 / 3	1 7 / 8	8 9 / 1
E 7 1 / 2	5 3 / 4	W 3 5 / 6
2 6 / 7	N 9 8 / 9	4 4 / 5

Sitting: North West 2

	S	
4 4 / 3	9 8 / 8	2 6 / 1
E 3 5 / 2	5 3 / 4	W 7 1 / 6
8 9 / 7	N 1 7 / 9	6 2 / 5

Sitting: North West 3

	S	
4 4 / 3	9 8 / 8	2 6 / 1
E 3 5 / 2	5 3 / 4	W 7 1 / 6
8 9 / 7	N 1 7 / 9	6 2 / 5

Flying Star chart: Cycle 5

Sitting: North 1

	S	
9 8 / 4	5 4 / 9	7 6 / 2
E 8 7 / 3	1 9 / 5	**W** 3 2 / 7
4 3 / 8	**N** 6 5 / 1	2 1 / 6

Sitting: North 2

	S	
2 1 / 4	6 5 / 9	4 3 / 2
E 3 2 / 3	1 9 / 5	**W** 8 7 / 7
7 6 / 8	**N** 5 4 / 1	9 8 / 6

Sitting: North 3

	S	
2 1 / 4	6 5 / 9	4 3 / 2
E 3 2 / 3	1 9 / 5	**W** 8 7 / 7
7 6 / 8	**N** 5 4 / 1	9 8 / 6

Sitting: North East 1

	S	
9 3 / 4	4 7 / 9	2 5 / 2
E 1 4 / 3	8 2 / 5	**W** 6 9 / 7
5 8 / 8	**N** 3 6 / 1	7 1 / 6

Sitting: North East 2

	S	
7 1 / 4	3 6 / 9	5 8 / 2
E 6 9 / 3	8 2 / 5	**W** 1 4 / 7
2 5 / 8	**N** 4 7 / 1	9 3 / 6

Sitting: North East 3

	S	
7 1 / 4	3 6 / 9	5 8 / 2
E 6 9 / 3	8 2 / 5	**W** 1 4 / 7
2 5 / 8	**N** 4 7 / 1	9 3 / 6

Sitting: East 1

	S	
2 6 / 4	7 2 / 9	9 4 / 2
E 1 5 / 3	3 7 / 5	**W** 5 9 / 7
6 1 / 8	**N** 8 3 / 1	4 8 / 6

Sitting: East 2

	S	
4 8 / 4	8 3 / 9	6 1 / 2
E 5 9 / 3	3 7 / 5	**W** 1 5 / 7
9 4 / 8	**N** 7 2 / 1	2 6 / 6

Sitting: East 3

	S	
4 8 / 4	8 3 / 9	6 1 / 2
E 5 9 / 3	3 7 / 5	**W** 1 5 / 7
9 4 / 8	**N** 7 2 / 1	2 6 / 6

Sitting: South East 1

	S	
5 7 / 4	9 2 / 9	7 9 / 2
E 6 8 / 3	4 6 / 5	**W** 2 4 / 7
1 3 / 8	**N** 8 1 / 1	3 5 / 6

Sitting: South East 2

	S	
3 5 / 4	8 1 / 9	1 3 / 2
E 2 4 / 3	4 6 / 5	**W** 6 8 / 7
7 9 / 8	**N** 9 2 / 1	5 7 / 6

Sitting: South East 3

	S	
3 5 / 4	8 1 / 9	1 3 / 2
E 2 4 / 3	4 6 / 5	**W** 6 8 / 7
7 9 / 8	**N** 9 2 / 1	5 7 / 6

Flying Star chart: Cycle 5

	S	
8 9 4	4 5 9	6 7 2
E 7 8 3	9 1 5	W 2 3 7
3 4 8	N 5 6 1	1 2 6

Sitting: South 1

	S	
1 2 4	5 6 9	3 4 2
E 2 3 3	9 1 5	W 7 8 7
6 7 8	N 4 5 1	8 9 6

Sitting: South 2

	S	
1 2 4	5 6 9	3 4 2
E 2 3 3	9 1 5	W 7 8 7
6 7 8	N 4 5 1	8 9 6

Sitting: South 3

	S	
3 9 4	7 4 9	5 2 2
E 4 1 3	2 8 5	W 9 6 7
8 5 8	N 6 3 1	1 7 6

Sitting: South West 1

	S	
1 7 4	6 3 9	8 5 2
E 9 6 3	2 8 5	W 4 1 7
5 2 8	N 7 4 1	3 9 6

Sitting: South West 2

	S	
1 7 4	6 3 9	8 5 2
E 9 6 3	2 8 5	W 4 1 7
5 2 8	N 7 4 1	3 9 6

Sitting: South West 3

	S	
6 2 4	2 7 9	4 9 2
E 5 1 3	7 3 5	W 9 5 7
1 6 8	N 3 8 1	8 4 6

Sitting: West 1

	S	
8 4 4	3 8 9	1 6 2
E 9 5 3	7 3 5	W 5 1 7
4 9 8	N 2 7 1	6 2 6

Sitting: West 2

	S	
8 4 4	3 8 9	1 6 2
E 9 5 3	7 3 5	W 5 1 7
4 9 8	N 2 7 1	6 2 6

Sitting: West 3

	S	
7 5 4	2 9 9	9 7 2
E 8 6 3	6 4 5	W 4 2 7
3 1 8	N 1 8 1	5 3 6

Sitting: North West 1

	S	
5 3 4	1 8 9	3 1 2
E 4 2 3	6 4 5	W 8 6 7
9 7 8	N 2 9 1	7 5 6

Sitting: North West 2

	S	
5 3 4	1 8 9	3 1 2
E 4 2 3	6 4 5	W 8 6 7
9 7 8	N 2 9 1	7 5 6

Sitting: North West 3

Flying Star chart: Cycle 6

Sitting: North 1

	S	
3 9 / 5	7 5 / 1	5 7 / 3
E 4 8 / 4	2 1 / 6	W 9 3 / 8
8 4 / 9	N 6 6 / 2	1 2 / 7

Sitting: North 2

	S	
1 2 / 5	6 6 / 1	8 4 / 3
E 9 3 / 4	2 1 / 6	W 7 8 / 8
5 7 / 9	N 7 5 / 2	3 9 / 7

Sitting: North 3

	S	
1 2 / 5	6 6 / 1	8 4 / 3
E 9 3 / 4	2 1 / 6	W 4 8 / 8
5 7 / 9	N 7 5 / 2	3 9 / 7

Sitting: North East 1

	S	
8 2 / 5	4 7 / 1	6 9 / 3
E 7 1 / 4	9 3 / 6	W 2 5 / 8
3 6 / 9	N 5 8 / 2	1 4 / 7

Sitting: North East 2

	S	
1 4 / 5	5 8 / 1	3 6 / 3
E 2 5 / 4	9 3 / 6	W 7 1 / 8
6 9 / 9	N 4 7 / 2	8 2 / 7

Sitting: North East 3

	S	
1 4 / 5	5 8 / 1	3 6 / 3
E 2 5 / 4	9 3 / 6	W 7 1 / 8
6 9 / 9	N 4 7 / 2	8 2 / 7

Sitting: East 1

	S	
5 9 / 5	9 4 / 1	7 2 / 3
E 6 1 / 4	4 8 / 6	W 2 6 / 8
1 5 / 9	N 8 3 / 2	3 7 / 7

Sitting: East 2

	S	
3 7 / 5	8 3 / 1	1 5 / 3
E 2 6 / 4	4 8 / 6	W 6 1 / 8
7 2 / 9	N 9 4 / 2	5 9 / 7

Sitting: East 3

	S	
3 7 / 5	8 3 / 1	1 5 / 3
E 2 6 / 4	4 8 / 6	W 6 1 / 8
7 2 / 9	N 9 4 / 2	5 9 / 7

Sitting: South East 1

	S	
6 6 / 5	1 2 / 1	8 4 / 3
E 7 5 / 4	5 7 / 6	W 3 9 / 8
2 1 / 9	N 9 3 / 2	4 8 / 7

Sitting: South East 2

	S	
4 8 / 5	9 3 / 1	2 1 / 3
E 3 9 / 4	5 7 / 6	W 7 5 / 8
8 4 / 9	N 1 2 / 2	6 6 / 7

Sitting: South East 3

	S	
4 8 / 5	9 3 / 1	2 1 / 3
E 3 9 / 4	5 7 / 6	W 7 5 / 8
8 4 / 9	N 1 2 / 2	6 6 / 7

352 / Treasures of Tao

Flying Star chart: Cycle 6

Sitting: South 1

	S	
9 3 / 5	5 7 / 1	7 5 / 3
E 8 4 / 4	1 2 / 6	W 3 9 / 8
4 8 / 9	N 6 6 / 2	2 1 / 7

Sitting: South 2

	S	
2 1 / 5	6 6 / 1	4 8 / 3
E 3 9 / 4	1 2 / 6	W 8 4 / 8
7 5 / 9	N 5 7 / 2	9 3 / 7

Sitting: South 3

	S	
2 1 / 5	6 6 / 1	4 8 / 3
E 3 9 / 4	1 2 / 6	W 8 4 / 8
7 5 / 9	N 5 7 / 2	9 3 / 7

Sitting: South West 1

	S	
2 8 / 5	7 4 / 1	9 6 / 3
E 1 7 / 4	3 9 / 6	W 5 2 / 8
6 3 / 9	N 8 5 / 2	4 1 / 7

Sitting: South West 2

	S	
4 1 / 5	8 5 / 1	6 3 / 3
E 5 2 / 4	3 9 / 6	W 1 7 / 8
9 6 / 9	N 7 4 / 2	2 8 / 7

Sitting: South West 3

	S	
4 1 / 5	8 5 / 1	6 3 / 3
E 5 2 / 4	3 9 / 6	W 1 7 / 8
9 6 / 9	N 7 4 / 2	2 8 / 7

Sitting: West 1

	S	
9 5 / 5	4 9 / 1	2 7 / 3
E 1 6 / 4	8 4 / 6	W 6 2 / 8
5 1 / 9	N 3 8 / 2	7 3 / 7

Sitting: West 2

	S	
7 3 / 5	3 8 / 1	5 1 / 3
E 6 2 / 4	8 4 / 6	W 1 6 / 8
2 7 / 9	N 4 9 / 2	9 5 / 7

Sitting: West 3

	S	
7 3 / 5	3 8 / 1	5 1 / 3
E 6 2 / 4	8 4 / 6	W 1 6 / 8
2 7 / 9	N 4 9 / 2	9 5 / 7

Sitting: North West 1

	S	
6 6 / 5	2 1 / 1	4 8 / 3
E 5 7 / 4	7 5 / 6	W 9 3 / 8
1 2 / 9	N 3 9 / 2	8 4 / 7

Sitting: North West 2

	S	
8 4 / 5	3 9 / 1	1 2 / 3
E 9 3 / 4	7 5 / 6	W 5 7 / 8
4 8 / 9	N 2 1 / 2	6 6 / 7

Sitting: North West 3

	S	
8 4 / 5	3 9 / 1	1 2 / 3
E 9 3 / 4	7 5 / 6	W 5 7 / 8
4 8 / 9	N 2 1 / 2	6 6 / 7

Flying Star chart: Cycle 7

	S	
2 3 6	7 7 2	9 5 4
E 1 4 5	3 2 7	W 5 9 9
6 8 1	N 8 6 3	4 1 8

Sitting: North 1

	S	
4 1 6	8 6 2	6 8 4
E 5 9 5	3 2 7	W 1 4 9
9 5 1	N 7 7 3	2 3 8

Sitting: North 2

	S	
4 1 6	8 6 2	6 8 4
E 5 9 5	3 2 7	W 1 4 9
9 5 1	N 7 7 3	2 3 8

Sitting: North 3

	S	
9 5 6	5 9 2	7 7 4
E 8 6 5	1 4 7	W 3 2 9
N 4 1 1	6 8 3	2 3 8

Sitting: North East 1

	S	
2 3 6	6 8 2	4 1 4
E 3 2 5	1 4 7	W 8 6 9
7 7 1	N 5 9 3	9 5 8

Sitting: North East 2

	S	
2 3 6	6 8 2	4 1 4
E 3 2 5	1 4 7	W 8 6 9
7 7 1	N 5 9 3	9 5 8

Sitting: North East 3

	S	
4 8 6	9 4 2	2 6 4
E 3 7 5	5 9 7	W 7 2 9
8 3 1	N 1 5 3	6 1 8

Sitting: East 1

	S	
6 1 6	1 5 2	8 3 4
E 7 2 5	5 9 7	W 3 7 9
2 6 1	N 9 4 3	4 8 8

Sitting: East 2

	S	
6 1 6	1 5 2	8 3 4
E 7 2 5	5 9 7	W 3 7 9
2 6 1	N 9 4 3	4 8 8

Sitting: East 3

	S	
7 9 6	2 4 2	9 2 4
E 8 1 5	6 8 7	W 4 6 9
3 5 1	N 1 3 3	5 7 8

Sitting: South East 1

	S	
5 7 6	1 3 2	3 5 4
E 4 6 5	6 8 7	W 8 1 9
9 2 1	N 2 4 3	7 9 8

Sitting: South East 2

	S	
5 7 6	1 3 2	3 5 4
E 4 6 5	6 8 7	W 8 1 9
9 2 1	N 2 4 3	7 9 8

Sitting: South East 3

Flying Star chart: Cycle 7

3 2 / 6	S 7 7 / 2	5 9 / 4
E 4 1 / 5	2 3 / 7	W 9 5 / 9
8 6 / 1	N 6 8 / 3	1 4 / 8

Sitting: South 1

1 4 / 6	S 6 8 / 2	8 6 / 4
E 9 5 / 5	2 3 / 7	W 4 1 / 9
5 9 / 1	N 7 7 / 3	3 2 / 8

Sitting: South 2

1 4 / 6	S 6 8 / 2	8 6 / 4
E 9 5 / 5	2 3 / 7	W 4 1 / 9
5 9 / 1	N 7 7 / 3	3 2 / 8

Sitting: South 3

5 9 / 6	S 9 5 / 2	7 7 / 4
E 6 8 / 5	4 1 / 7	W 2 3 / 9
1 4 / 1	N 8 6 / 3	3 2 / 8

Sitting: South West 1

3 2 / 6	S 8 6 / 2	1 4 / 4
E 2 3 / 5	4 1 / 7	W 6 8 / 9
7 7 / 1	N 9 5 / 3	5 9 / 8

Sitting: South West 2

3 2 / 6	S 8 6 / 2	1 4 / 4
E 2 3 / 5	4 1 / 7	W 6 8 / 9
7 7 / 1	N 9 5 / 3	5 9 / 8

Sitting: South West 3

8 4 / 6	S 4 9 / 2	6 2 / 4
E 7 3 / 5	9 5 / 7	W 2 7 / 9
3 8 / 1	N 5 1 / 3	1 6 / 8

Sitting: West 1

1 6 / 6	S 5 1 / 2	3 8 / 4
E 2 7 / 5	9 5 / 7	W 7 3 / 9
6 2 / 1	N 4 9 / 3	8 4 / 8

Sitting: West 2

1 6 / 6	S 5 1 / 2	3 8 / 4
E 2 7 / 5	9 5 / 7	W 7 3 / 9
6 2 / 1	N 4 9 / 3	8 4 / 8

Sitting: West 3

9 7 / 6	S 4 2 / 2	2 9 / 4
E 1 8 / 5	8 6 / 7	W 6 4 / 9
5 3 / 1	N 3 1 / 3	7 5 / 8

Sitting: North West 1

7 5 / 6	S 3 1 / 2	5 3 / 4
E 6 4 / 5	8 6 / 7	W 1 8 / 9
2 9 / 1	N 4 2 / 3	9 7 / 8

Sitting: North West 2

7 5 / 6	S 3 1 / 2	5 3 / 4
E 6 4 / 5	8 6 / 7	W 1 8 / 9
2 9 / 1	N 4 2 / 3	9 7 / 8

Sitting: North West 3

Flying Star chart: Cycle 8

Sitting: North 1

	S	
5 2 7	9 7 3	7 9 5
E 6 1 6	4 3 8	**W** 2 5 1
1 6 2	**N** 8 8 4	3 4 9

Sitting: North 2

	S	
3 4 7	8 8 3	1 6 5
E 2 5 6	4 3 8	**W** 6 1 1
7 9 2	**N** 9 7 4	5 2 9

Sitting: North 3

	S	
3 4 7	8 8 3	1 6 5
E 2 5 6	4 3 8	**W** 6 1 1
7 9 2	**N** 9 7 4	5 2 9

Sitting: North East 1

	S	
3 6 7	7 1 3	5 8 5
E 4 7 6	2 5 8	**W** 9 3 1
8 2 2	**N** 6 9 4	1 4 9

Sitting: North East 2

	S	
1 4 7	6 9 3	8 2 5
E 9 3 6	2 5 8	**W** 4 7 1
5 8 2	**N** 7 1 4	3 6 9

Sitting: North East 3

	S	
1 4 7	6 9 3	8 2 5
E 9 3 6	2 5 8	**W** 4 7 1
5 8 2	**N** 7 1 4	3 6 9

Sitting: East 1

	S	
7 9 7	2 5 3	9 7 5
E 8 8 6	6 1 8	**W** 4 3 1
3 4 2	**N** 1 6 4	5 2 9

Sitting: East 2

	S	
5 2 7	1 6 3	3 4 5
E 4 3 6	6 1 8	**W** 8 8 1
9 7 2	**N** 2 5 4	7 9 9

Sitting: East 3

	S	
5 2 7	1 6 3	3 4 5
E 4 3 6	6 1 8	**W** 8 8 1
9 7 2	**N** 2 5 4	7 9 9

Sitting: South East 1

	S	
6 8 7	2 4 3	4 6 5
E 5 7 6	7 9 8	**W** 9 2 1
1 3 2	**N** 3 5 4	8 1 9

Sitting: South East 2

	S	
8 1 7	3 5 3	1 3 5
E 9 2 6	7 9 8	**W** 5 7 1
4 6 2	**N** 2 4 4	6 8 9

Sitting: South East 3

	S	
8 1 7	3 5 3	1 3 5
E 9 2 6	7 9 8	**W** 5 7 1
4 6 2	**N** 2 4 4	6 8 9

Flying Star chart: Cycle 8

Sitting: South 1

	S	
2 5 / 7	7 9 / 3	9 7 / 5
E 1 6 / 6	3 4 / 8	**W** 5 2 / 1
6 1 / 2	**N** 8 8 / 4	4 3 / 9

Sitting: South 2

	S	
4 3 / 7	8 8 / 3	6 1 / 5
E 5 2 / 6	3 4 / 8	**W** 1 6 / 1
9 7 / 2	**N** 7 9 / 4	2 5 / 9

Sitting: South 3

	S	
4 3 / 7	8 8 / 3	6 1 / 5
E 5 2 / 6	3 4 / 8	**W** 1 6 / 1
9 7 / 2	**N** 7 9 / 4	2 5 / 9

Sitting: South West 1

	S	
6 3 / 7	1 7 / 3	8 5 / 5
E 7 4 / 6	5 2 / 8	**W** 3 9 / 1
2 8 / 2	**N** 9 6 / 4	4 1 / 9

Sitting: South West 2

	S	
4 1 / 7	9 6 / 3	2 8 / 5
E 3 9 / 6	5 2 / 8	**W** 7 4 / 1
8 5 / 2	**N** 1 7 / 4	6 3 / 9

Sitting: South West 3

	S	
4 1 / 7	9 6 / 3	2 8 / 5
E 3 9 / 6	5 2 / 8	**W** 7 4 / 1
8 5 / 2	**N** 1 7 / 4	6 3 / 9

Sitting: West 1

	S	
9 7 / 7	5 2 / 3	7 9 / 5
E 8 8 / 6	1 6 / 8	**W** 3 4 / 1
4 3 / 2	**N** 6 1 / 4	2 5 / 9

Sitting: West 2

	S	
2 5 / 7	6 1 / 3	4 3 / 5
E 3 4 / 6	1 6 / 8	**W** 8 8 / 1
7 9 / 2	**N** 5 2 / 4	9 7 / 9

Sitting: West 3

	S	
2 5 / 7	6 1 / 3	4 3 / 5
E 3 4 / 6	1 6 / 8	**W** 8 8 / 1
7 9 / 2	**N** 5 2 / 4	9 7 / 9

Sitting: North West 1

	S	
8 6 / 7	4 2 / 3	6 4 / 5
E 7 5 / 6	9 7 / 8	**W** 2 9 / 1
3 1 / 2	**N** 5 3 / 4	1 8 / 9

Sitting: North West 2

	S	
1 8 / 7	5 3 / 3	3 1 / 5
E 2 9 / 6	9 7 / 8	**W** 7 5 / 1
6 4 / 2	**N** 4 2 / 4	8 6 / 9

Sitting: North West 3

	S	
1 8 / 7	5 3 / 3	3 1 / 5
E 2 9 / 6	9 7 / 8	**W** 7 5 / 1
6 4 / 2	**N** 4 2 / 4	8 6 / 9

Flying Star chart: Cycle 9

Sitting: North 1

	S	
4 5 / 8	9 9 / 4	2 7 / 6
E 3 6 / 7	5 4 / 9	W 7 2 / 2
8 1 / 3	N 1 8 / 5	6 3 / 1

Sitting: North 2

	S	
6 3 / 8	1 8 / 4	8 1 / 6
E 7 2 / 7	5 4 / 9	W 3 6 / 2
2 7 / 3	N 9 9 / 5	4 5 / 1

Sitting: North 3

	S	
6 3 / 8	1 8 / 4	8 1 / 6
E 7 2 / 7	5 4 / 9	W 3 6 / 2
2 7 / 3	N 9 9 / 5	4 5 / 1

Sitting: North East 1

	S	
2 7 / 8	7 2 / 4	9 9 / 6
E 1 8 / 7	3 6 / 9	W 5 4 / 2
6 3 / 3	N 8 1 / 5	4 5 / 1

Sitting: North East 2

	S	
4 5 / 8	8 1 / 4	6 3 / 6
E 5 4 / 7	3 6 / 9	W 1 8 / 2
9 9 / 3	N 7 2 / 5	2 7 / 1

Sitting: North East 3

	S	
4 5 / 8	8 1 / 4	6 3 / 6
E 5 4 / 7	3 6 / 9	W 1 8 / 2
9 9 / 3	N 7 2 / 5	2 7 / 1

Sitting: East 1

	S	
6 3 / 8	2 7 / 4	4 5 / 6
E 5 4 / 7	7 2 / 9	W 9 9 / 2
1 8 / 3	N 3 6 / 5	8 1 / 1

Sitting: East 2

	S	
8 1 / 8	3 6 / 4	1 8 / 6
E 9 9 / 7	7 2 / 9	W 5 4 / 2
4 5 / 3	N 2 7 / 5	6 3 / 1

Sitting: East 3

	S	
8 1 / 8	3 6 / 4	1 8 / 6
E 9 9 / 7	7 2 / 9	W 5 4 / 2
4 5 / 3	N 2 7 / 5	6 3 / 1

Sitting: South East 1

	S	
9 9 / 8	4 5 / 4	2 7 / 6
E 1 8 / 7	8 1 / 9	W 6 3 / 2
5 4 / 3	N 3 6 / 5	7 2 / 1

Sitting: South East 2

	S	
7 2 / 8	3 6 / 4	5 4 / 6
E 6 3 / 7	8 1 / 9	W 1 8 / 2
2 7 / 3	N 4 5 / 5	9 9 / 1

Sitting: South East 3

	S	
7 2 / 8	3 6 / 4	5 4 / 6
E 6 3 / 7	8 1 / 9	W 1 8 / 2
2 7 / 3	N 4 5 / 5	9 9 / 1

Flying Star chart: Cycle 9

Sitting: South 1

	S	
5 4 / 8	9 9 / 4	7 2 / 6
E 6 3 / 7	4 5 / 9	W 2 7 / 2
1 8 / 3	N 8 1 / 5	3 6 / 1

Sitting: South 2

	S	
3 6 / 8	8 1 / 4	1 8 / 6
E 2 7 / 7	4 5 / 9	W 6 3 / 2
7 2 / 3	N 9 9 / 5	5 4 / 1

Sitting: South 3

	S	
3 6 / 8	8 1 / 4	1 8 / 6
E 2 7 / 7	4 5 / 9	W 6 3 / 2
7 2 / 3	N 9 9 / 5	5 4 / 1

Sitting: South West 1

	S	
7 2 / 8	2 7 / 4	9 9 / 6
E 8 1 / 7	6 3 / 9	W 4 5 / 2
3 6 / 3	N 1 8 / 5	5 4 / 1

Sitting: South West 2

	S	
5 4 / 8	1 8 / 4	3 6 / 6
E 4 5 / 7	6 3 / 9	W 8 1 / 2
9 9 / 3	N 2 7 / 5	7 2 / 1

Sitting: South West 3

	S	
5 4 / 8	1 8 / 4	3 6 / 6
E 4 5 / 7	6 3 / 9	W 8 1 / 2
9 9 / 3	N 2 7 / 5	7 2 / 1

Sitting: West 1

	S	
3 6 / 8	7 2 / 4	5 4 / 6
E 4 5 / 7	2 7 / 9	W 9 9 / 2
8 1 / 3	N 6 3 / 5	1 8 / 1

Sitting: West 2

	S	
1 8 / 8	6 3 / 4	8 1 / 6
E 9 9 / 7	2 7 / 9	W 4 5 / 2
5 4 / 3	N 7 2 / 5	3 6 / 1

Sitting: West 3

	S	
1 8 / 8	6 3 / 4	8 1 / 6
E 9 9 / 7	2 7 / 9	W 4 5 / 2
5 4 / 3	N 7 2 / 5	3 6 / 1

Sitting: North West 1

	S	
9 9 / 8	5 4 / 4	7 2 / 6
E 8 1 / 7	1 8 / 9	W 3 6 / 2
4 5 / 3	N 6 3 / 5	2 7 / 1

Sitting: North West 2

	S	
2 7 / 8	6 3 / 4	4 5 / 6
E 3 6 / 7	1 8 / 9	W 8 1 / 2
7 2 / 3	N 5 4 / 5	9 9 / 1

Sitting: North West 3

	S	
2 7 / 8	6 3 / 4	4 5 / 6
E 3 6 / 7	1 8 / 9	W 8 1 / 2
7 2 / 3	N 5 4 / 5	9 9 / 1

Replacement Stars

Ti Gua

Replacement Stars, Substitute Stars or Ti Gua are used when the facing and sitting directions are on or near the boundaries of one of the 24-Mountain positions, a common application is to use these stars when the orientation is within 3-degrees of a mountain position on the Lo Pan. In modern society there are many electrical and metal objects that can influence a compass, one should question the previous or current occupant(s) to determine which chart, the standard or replacement one, mostly accurately explains the life of the occupants.

The flowing tables provide the center palace mountain and water star for Replacement Charts, the formula for floating the stars is listed, just follow the standard method of floating stars.

Cycle	Sitting Position	Center Mountain Star	Center Water Star
1	N 1	6 descends	5 Ascends
	N 2, N 3	6 Ascends	5 Descends
	NE 1	6 Descends	9 Ascends
	NE 2, NE 3	6 Ascends	7 Descends
	E 1	7 Descends	1 Ascends
	E 2	7 Ascends	2 Descends
	E 3	9 Ascends	2 Descends
	SE 1	7 Ascends	2 Descends
	SE 2	9 Descends	2 Ascends
	SE 3	9 Descends	1 Ascends
	S 1	5 Ascends	6 Descends
	S 2, S 3	5 Descends	6 Ascends
	SW 1	9 Ascends	6 Descends
	SW 2, SW 3	7 Descends	6 Ascends
	W 1	1 Ascends	7 Descends
	W 2	2 Descends	7 Ascends
	W 3	2 Descends	9 Ascends
	NW 1	2 Descends	7 Ascends
	NW 2	2 Ascends	9 Descends
	NW 3	1 Ascends	9 Descends

Cycle	Sitting Position	Center Mountain Star	Center Water Star
2	N 1	9 Ascends	6 Descends
	N 2, N 3	7 Descends	6 Ascends
	NE 1	5 Descends	7 Descends
	NE 2	5 Ascends	7 Ascends
	NE 3	5 Ascends	9 Ascends
	E 1	7 Ascends	6 Descends
	E 2	9 Descends	6 Ascends
	E 3	9 Descends	6 Ascends
	SE 1	2 Ascends	1 Ascends
	SE 2	1 Descends	2 Descends
	SE 3	1 Descends	2 Descends
	S 1	6 Descends	9 Ascends
	S 2, S 3	6 Ascends	7 Descends
	SW 1	7 Descends	5 Descends
	SW 2	7 Ascends	5 Ascends
	SW 3	9 Ascends	5 Ascends
	W 1	6 Descends	7 Ascends
	W 2	6 Ascends	9 Descends
	W 3	6 Ascends	9 Descends
	NW 1	1 Ascends	2 Ascends
	NW 2	2 Descends	1 Descends
	NW 3	2 Descends	1 Descends

Cycle	Sitting Position	Center Mountain Star	Center Water Star
3	N1	7 Descends	9 Ascends
	N 2	7 Ascends	7 Descends
	N3	9 Ascends	7 Descends
	NE 1	6 Descends	7 Ascends
	NE 2, NE 3	6 Ascends	9 Descends
	E 1	2 Ascends	5 Ascends
	E 2	1 Descends	5 Descends
	E 3	1 Descends	5 Descends
	SE 1	2 Descends	6 Descends
	SE 2	2 Ascends	6 Ascends
	SE 3	1 Ascends	6 Ascends
	S 1	9 Ascends	7 Descends
	S2	7 Descends	7 Ascends
	S3	7 Descends	9 Ascends
	SW 1	7 Ascends	6 Descends
	SW 2, SW 3	9 Descends	6 Ascends
	W 1	5 Ascends	2 Ascends
	W 2	5 Descends	1 Descends
	W 3	5 Descends	1 Descends
	NW 1	6 Descends	2 Descends
	NW 2	6 Ascends	2 Ascends
	NW 3	6 Ascends	1 Ascends

Cycle	Sitting Position	Center Mountain Star	Center Water Star
4	N1	7 Ascends	7 Descends
	N 2	9 Descends	7 Ascends
	N3	9 Descends	9 Ascends
	NE 1	9 Ascends	2Ascends
	NE 2, NE 3	7 Descends	1 Descends
	E 1	2 Descends	6 Descends
	E 2	2 Ascends	6 Ascends
	E 3	1 Ascends	6 Ascends
	SE 1	1 Ascends	5 Descends
	SE 2	2 Descends	5 Ascends
	SE 3	2 Descends	5 Ascends
	S 1	7 Descends	7 Ascends
	S2	7 Ascends	9 Descends
	S3	9 Ascends	9 Descends
	SW 1	2 Descends	9 Ascends
	SW 2, SW 3	1 Descends	7 Descends
	W 1	6 Descends	2 Descends
	W 2	6 Ascends	2 Ascends
	W 3	6 Ascends	1 Ascends
	NW 1	5 Descends	1 Ascends
	NW 2	5 Ascends	2 Descends
	NW 3	5 Ascends	2 Descends

Cycle	Sitting Position	Center Mountain Star	Center Water Star
5	N1	2 Ascends	7 Ascends
	N 2, N 3	1 Descends	9 Descends
	NE 1	7 Descends	2 Descends
	NE 2	7 Ascends	2 Ascends
	NE 3	9 Descends	1 Ascends
	E 1	1 Ascends	9 Descends
	E 2	2 Descends	7 Descends
	E 3	2 Descends	7 Descends
	SE 1	6 Descends	6 Descends
	SE 2	6 Ascends	6 Ascends
	SE 3	6 Ascends	6 Ascends
	S 1	7 Ascends	2 Ascends
	S2, S3	9 Descends	1 Descends
	SW 1	2 Descends	7 Descends
	SW 2	2 Ascends	7 Ascends
	SW 3	1 Ascends	9 Ascends
	W 1	9 Ascends	1 Ascends
	W 2	7 Descends	2 Descends
	W 3	7 Descends	2 Descends
	NW 1	6 Descends	6 Descends
	NW 2	6 Ascends	6 Ascends
	NW 3	6 Ascends	6 Ascends

Cycle	Sitting Position	Center Mountain Star	Center Water Star
6	N1	2 Descends	2 Ascends
	N 2	2 Ascends	1 Descends
	N3	1 Ascends	1 Descends
	NE 1	7 Ascends	1 Ascends
	NE 2, NE 3	9 Descends	2 Descends
	E 1	6 Descends	7 Descends
	E 2	6 Ascends	7 Ascends
	E 3	6 Ascends	9 Ascends
	SE 1	5 Descends	9 Ascends
	SE 2	5 Ascends	7 Descends
	SE 3	5 Ascends	7 Descends
	S 1	2 Ascends	2 Descends
	S2	1 Descends	2 Ascends
	S3	1 Descends	1 Ascends
	SW 1	1 Ascends	7 Ascends
	SW 2	2 Descends	9 Descends
	SW 3	2 Descends	9 Descends
	W 1	7 Descends	6 Descends
	W 2	7 Ascends	6 Ascends
	W 3	9 Ascends	6 Ascends
	NW 1	9 Ascends	5 Descends
	NW 2	7 Descends	5 Ascends
	NW 3	7 Descends	5 Ascends

Cycle	Sitting Position	Center Mountain Star	Center Water Star
7	N1	1 Ascends	2 Descends
	N 2	2 Descends	2 Ascends
	N3	2 Descends	1 Ascends
	NE 1	2 Ascends	6 Descends
	NE 2, NE 3	1 Descends	6 Ascends
	E 1	5 Ascends	7 Ascends
	E 2	5 Descends	9 Descends
	E 3	5 Descends	9 Descends
	SE 1	6 Descends	7 Descends
	SE 2	6 Ascends	7 Ascends
	SE 3	6 Ascends	9 Ascends
	S 1	2 Descends	1 Ascends
	S2	2 Ascends	2 Descends
	S3	1 Ascends	2 Descends
	SW 1	6 Descends	2 Ascends
	SW 2, SW 3	6 Ascends	1 Descends
	W 1	7 Ascends	5 Ascends
	W 2	9 Descends	5 Descends
	W 3	9 Descends	5 Descends
	NW 1	7 Descends	6 Descends
	NW 2	7 Ascends	6 Ascends
	NW 3	9 Ascends	6 Ascends

Cycle	Sitting Position	Center Mountain Star	Center Water Star
8	N1	6 Descends	1 Ascends
	N 2, N 3	6 Ascends	2 Descends
	NE 1	2 Descends	5 Descends
	NE 2	2 Ascends	5 Ascends
	NE3	1 Ascends	5 Ascends
	E 1	6 Descends	2 Ascends
	E 2	6 Ascends	1 Descends
	E 3	6 Ascends	1 Descends
	SE 1	9 Ascends	7 Ascends
	SE 2	7 Descends	9 Descends
	SE 3	7 Descends	9 Descends
	S 1	1 Ascends	6 Descends
	S2, S3	2 Descends	6 Ascends
	SW 1	5 Descends	2 Descends
	SW 2	5 Ascends	2 Ascends
	SW 3	6 Ascends	1 Ascends
	W 1	2 Ascends	6 Descends
	W 2	1 Descends	6 Ascends
	W 3	1 Descends	6 Ascends
	NW 1	7 Ascends	9 Ascends
	NW 2	9 Descends	7 Descends
	NW 3	9 Descends	7 Descends

Cycle	Sitting Position	Center Mountain Star	Center Water Star
9	N1	5 Ascends	6 Descends
	N 2,N 3	5 Descends	6 Ascends
	NE 1	1 Ascends	6 Descends
	NE 2, NE 3	2 Descends	6 Ascends
	E 1	9 Ascends	2 Descends
	E 2	7 Descends	2 Ascends
	E 3	7 Descends	1 Ascends
	SE 1	7 Descends	2 Ascends
	SE 2	7 Ascends	1 Descends
	SE 3	9 Ascends	1 Descends
	S 1	6 Descends	5 Ascends
	S2, S3	6 Ascends	5 Descends
	SW 1	6 Descends	1 Ascends
	SW 2, SW 3	6 Ascends	2 Descends
	W 1	2 Descends	9 Ascends
	W 2	2 Ascends	7 Descends
	W 3	1 Ascends	7 Descends
	NW 1	2 Ascends	7 Descends
	NW 2	1 Descends	7 Ascends
	NW 3	1 Descends	9 Ascends

Printed in the United States
971400006BB